Underneath The Archers

BY THE SAME AUTHOR

The Killing of the Countryside
The Forgiveness of Nature
We Want Real Food
The Carbon Fields
Grass-Fed Nation

Underneath The Archers

Nature's secret agent on Britain's longest-running drama

Graham Harvey

First published in 2023

Unbound
c/o TC Group, 6th Floor King's House, 9-10 Haymarket,
London SW1Y 4BP
www.unbound.com

Text design by Jouve (UK), Milton Keynes

A CIP record for this book is available from the British Library

ISBN 978-1-80018-265-3 (hardback)
ISBN 978-1-80018-266-0 (ebook)

Printed in Great Britain by Clays Ltd, Elcograf S.p.A.

1 3 5 7 9 8 6 4 2

To Peter Henry Harvey

Contents

I

Radioland

IT'S THE AUTUMN OF 1984. The miners' strike is coming to an end. Stevie Wonder's topping the charts with 'I Just Called to Say I Love You'. And on the streets of the quiet market town of Borchester, a budding young entrepreneur called Nigel Pargetter is about to launch his new and soon-to-be glittering career (another one).

'Watch this, Lizzie. Watch and learn.'

The young woman gives him a sad and knowing smile. She doesn't hold out much hope for the new venture. Any more than she did for the last one, the ill-fated swimming pool business. To be honest, neither do I. We both know Nigel a little too well.

Bearing down on them is a stocky, middle-aged man dressed in faded denim. He's got a Dead Head tattoo on his forearm and carries a heavy-looking rucksack slung over one shoulder. Not a terribly promising candidate.

Nigel steps forward.

'One moment, sir. Have you ever considered how much easier life would be if one of your arms was a metre and a half long?'

'What are you on about?'

'All will be revealed, my friend. First, I must congratulate you. You're about to have a brush with destiny.'

'Just get out of my way, nutter.'

'With this handy, extendable cobweb brush, there's not a single remote crevice in your entire home that'll be out of reach to you.'

'Don't say I didn't warn you.'

'I say, have a care, old chap . . . what're you doing? Ouch . . . There's really no call for that sort of thing, you know.'

Nigel gets the rucksack shoved into his ribs, causing him to stumble off the kerb. His brush – trade name 'The Household Wonder', but we're not allowed to mention that – clatters to the pavement. Muttering profanities, the man strides on while the outraged Lizzie screams after him.

'Hey, what's your fucking problem? Dickhead.' This line gets cut from the recording.

Nigel rubs his bruised ribs, then stoops to pick up his brush. His expression is one of hurt bewilderment. Lizzie rests a comforting arm on his shoulder.

'Are you quite sure you're cut out for this sort of work?' she asks him gently.

'Listen, Lizzie. We Pargetters were selling wool to the dukes of Lombardy back in the fifteenth century. If I can't flog a few household gadgets in my local high street the family's in real trouble.'

End of scene. Cut to village shop.

Looking back, it was an odd thing to be doing. Who was I to be manipulating the lives of characters I had so little in common with? Nigel, for example. The guy was aristocracy, admittedly of the minor sort. He'd grown up on a large country estate, even if it was a bit run-down.

His early life had been all dogs, horses and deathwatch beetle. Except when he was away at school – Rugby School, that is, the one his father had gone to.

I, by contrast, had grown up in a three-bedroom semi on a council estate in Reading. My own education had been at the town's boys' grammar school, an institution, it must be admitted, that tried hard to pass itself off as a public school. That was the reason I disliked it so much. The posh school trappings were simply a device to make council-house kids like me feel uncomfortable, or so I believed.

To me, life on the Emmer Green estate was real life. While Nigel was out riding to hounds, I was happily speeding down Southdown Road on my mate John Elliott's soap-box cart, made by his dad out of pram wheels and bits of an old tea chest. What did I know about the manners and attitudes of the landed gentry?

In theory, Elizabeth Archer should have been more of an open book. She was, after all, the daughter of farmers. And farming was what I was supposed to know about. I'd studied it for several years at Bangor uni. Plus, I'd had ten years or so working as a journalist for *Farmers Weekly* and other bastions of the agricultural press.

Hardly *Newsnight* or the *Financial Times*, I give you that. Nevertheless, in the world of pig breeding and muck-spreading machines I was definitely at the top of my game.

Much of my working life until that moment in 1984 had been spent sitting in farmhouse kitchens listening to the everyday stories of farming folk, which is what had planted the thought in my head that maybe I could boost my freelance earnings by writing for the world's longest-running soap, set as it was in a farming community. Now

I'd been given a chance to prove myself, I'd surely have no trouble writing a farming character like Lizzie.

It proved more difficult than I had imagined. Her parents were *Archers* legends – Phil and Jill Archer, who'd been stars of the show since its early days in the 1950s. They lived in a large brick-and-timber farmhouse dating back to the sixteenth century, and owned not far short of 500 acres of prime farmland. As characters they were solidly middle class.

Elizabeth – their youngest child – had grown up in surroundings that provided security, space and freedom. It had been, as far as we know, an idyllic country childhood, in which (as with Nigel) horses had figured strongly. Her universe was definitely not my universe.

There was a further challenge: this seventeen-year-old hadn't spoken on the show for a number of years. She'd been played earlier as a young child, then joined the ranks of Ambridge's 'silent' characters. They're around, but they never get to utter a peep during the thirteen-and-a-half minutes each day when the microphones are live.

Now William Smethurst, *Archers* editor and puppet-master-in-chief, had decreed that the teenager should make her first appearance. It had to happen in my trial writing week, during episodes that would determine whether or not I'd be taken on as a regular scriptwriter. I needed to find a personality for this new character who'd been marked out for stardom by editor Smethurst.

The storyline for the week set out clearly how events were to unfold. First Nigel was to be dumped by his girlfriend, Elizabeth's older sister Shula. She'd had a fun time, but she couldn't see any long-term future with a man who was happiest doing drunken conga dances while wearing a gorilla suit. She decided to go back to her earlier love, the more sober-minded solicitor, Mark Hebden.

For a long-term job on the show, I had to find a way of bringing Nigel and Elizabeth together. I needed to invent a personality for this young woman whose comfortable, middle-class background still felt alien to me. Then inspiration handed me a freebie. Why not make her like Paula Brooks-Thomas?

I was sixteen when I encountered Paula. By then, we'd moved from my beloved estate at Emmer Green to what I judged enemy country: a posh (in parts) village near Henley-on-Thames. My parents had bought a detached country house with a big garden filled with fruit trees. To do so they'd taken on a large amount of debt. It was never going to enhance domestic harmony in a household already under strain.

We lived in a kind of icy wasteland where the cult of secrecy froze out all meaningful communication. The one thing you couldn't do at our place was speak honestly about your wants, desires, rages, disappointments, fears. We were living under a self-imposed rule of silence.

It created a permanent state of anxiety for all of us – my mum, my dad, my brother, me. Into this the fear of debt added another stress point. Sometimes the ice would crack and there'd be a full-blown row, though this seldom cleared the air.

We lived in a kind of inglorious isolation, with my mum and dad going to work each day, and me and my brother heading off to school eight miles away in Reading. Apart from that, we didn't really socialise with anyone. It was nearly a year before we had even talked to our neighbours.

*

I took a Saturday afternoon job delivering orders from the family greengrocer's shop in the village high street. They gave me one of those heavy trade bikes with the square metal frame at the front in which I would stack up the boxes containing the fruit-and-veg orders. When I arrived for work at one o'clock, the day's orders would be packed and ready for delivery. I'd check the names and addresses, then work out a series of routes for delivering them in the most efficient way. I got paid fifteen shillings for the afternoon, however late I worked.

The job took me to some of the poshest houses in the village. The biggest were mostly down by the River Loddon. When I knocked at the back door it was usually answered by the housekeeper or kitchen help.

Paula Brooks-Thomas didn't live in one of the really posh houses. Her family had one of a pair of large Edwardian villas on a road leading off the high street. The name on the order sheet was Mrs Bennett, and the first three times I called there it was Mrs Bennett herself who took in the order. She was a tall, middle-aged woman, with long grey hair and a friendly, open manner. She was invariably profuse in her thanks, more than could be said for a lot of the customers.

The fourth time I rang the bell at Whitstable House everything was different, and my life was to be in turmoil for months afterwards. This time a young woman of about my age opened the door. She had deep blue eyes and blond hair pulled back in a ponytail. Her dazzling smile robbed me of the power of speech.

'Oh hello,' she said brightly, 'what have you brought us this time? Anything nice?'

'Er . . .'

I handed over the box as I struggled to find words.

'Yippee, a pineapple. I hope it's ripe?'

'Er, yeah, it will be.'

'It had better be. Otherwise, I'll be down that shop of yours to complain.'

'It's not my shop.' Even as I said the words, I knew they were dumb. Of course she knew it wasn't my shop, but there was no way I could claw them back.

'Do you live in the village?' she asked. 'Only I haven't seen you around, I don't think . . .'

'You wouldn't have done. I go to school in Reading. Unfortunately.'

'Does that mean you're always at school? Evenings, weekends, holidays, Christmas Day?'

'No, course not.'

'Well anyway, I'll see you with the next order, OK?'

'Yeah, sure,' I said, at long last trying to sound cool. Then I went and undid it. 'I only work on Saturday afternoons. So, it has to be a Saturday order. You phone it in by twelve noon, then I deliver it before four. That's how it works.'

This information was clearly underwhelming. 'I'll make sure Mum knows, alright?'

'Er, yeah. Thanks.'

'See you next time, then.'

Then she was gone and I was staring at the front door. For a millisecond it flashed through my mind that I should ring again and ask her out to the new Cliff Richard film, which was showing in Henley at the time. The idea formed and I quashed it. There was as much chance of me ringing that doorbell a second time as there was of me going to the headmaster on Monday and telling him he could stuff his Saturday morning school. I was having my weekends off like everyone else.

The following week there was another order for Whitstable House. I could feel my heart pounding as I walked up the path and pressed the doorbell. Mrs Bennett answered and was her usual charming self. By then I'd worked out that, despite the name difference, she was Paula's mother. My response, sadly, was not as gracious as it would normally have been.

This was the pattern for the following three weeks. Each Saturday I delivered a veggie box to the friendly lady at Whitstable House. I thought about asking after her daughter but decided that would be presumptuous. I doubt she'd ever given me a thought after that first time.

Then the next week she was there, smiling that same devastating smile.

'Hello,' she said cheerfully, 'I was starting to wonder what had happened to you. Nice to see you again.' I passed over the box.

'I've been here every week,' I said curtly. It could have come over as a sulk but she didn't seem to notice. She put the box on a hall table, pushing the phone aside to make room for it.

'I meant to ask you,' she said. 'Do you play tennis?'

'Er, yes,' I mumbled, hurt pride instantly forgotten. 'Or rather I should say I *can* play tennis. Don't get a chance very often. They don't do tennis at my crappy school. Only rugby and cricket, and that's it. I mean, how backward is that? And they claim to be one of the top grammar schools in the country. Laughable.'

I thought about telling her I played outside-right for the village football team (third eleven) but decided this was risky. She might come along and watch. I didn't particularly want her to hear the name the other guys had for me. It encompassed my ability to move fast down the wing without necessarily taking the ball with me.

'You should come along to the tennis club,' she suggested. 'Meet a few people.'

'Yeah, I will. Definitely.'

'You know where it is?'

'Yeah, the rec. You a member?'

'Have been for three years. You should come one evening. I'll give you a game if you like.'

'Great.' I tried not to sound too excited.

'Make it Wednesday evening. Any time. It's open to non-members every Wednesday.'

'OK, I'll be there. Look forward to it.'

'Fine. Bye then.' Once again I was looking at the front door.

The following Wednesday I turned up at the tennis club. Paula was on one of the four courts playing a singles match against a tall, thickset guy with a Bobby Vee hairstyle. I guessed he wasn't a member as he was wearing jeans and a yellow T-shirt.

She gave me an extravagant wave and, between serves, ran across to greet me. All I could look at was her long brown legs perfectly set off by the short white skirt. I felt the now-familiar anguished, hollow feeling somewhere between my belly and my chest. Whatever was happening to me, it wasn't hurting any less.

'It's great you came,' she said, smiling at me through the steel netting. 'Pop in the clubhouse and give Terri your details. She's the club sec. I'll see you when I've finished off Joe.'

I was tempted to ask her what she meant by finishing him off, but she was gone.

Inside the clubhouse I gave Terri my details and she

organised three young guys to give me a game of doubles. They were all new to the game, she assured me, as I'd told her I was. In the men's changing room I pulled off my jeans. I had my white school gym shorts on underneath.

Out on the court I discovered that, far from being novices, the other three were potential junior champions. The one who'd drawn the short straw and was partnering me appeared to have some sort of speech disorder. He let out a series of clicking sounds and groans whenever I hit the ball.

It was a dire sort of match, not made any better as I watched Paula and Joe packing up their stuff and walking off across the park hand in hand. I wondered where they were going to finish things off. Suddenly remembering me, she turned and shouted across: 'Have a great game. See you Saturday.' Miserable though I felt, I couldn't suppress a twinge of pride as my tennis companions found a new respect for me.

'You know Paula?' one of them exclaimed with undisguised awe. 'Bloody hell.'

That was the way our relationship went over the next few months. If you could call it a relationship. Our lives would brush against each other at regular intervals without any deeper, more significant connections. While our lives touched, sadly our bodies didn't. Except for one momentous occasion on a youth club walk. But that's a story for another time.

As these thrilling yet unsatisfying events were being played out, I shared them with a couple of mates at school. Neither lived in my village so they didn't know Paula. Dave Baker was in no doubt the woman was bad news.

'She's playing you for a fool,' he commented. 'You

want to give her the bum's rush, that's what I'd do.' From that moment on, I knew he and I weren't going to be mates for much longer. My good friend Rich was more circumspect, which I'd expected.

'Listen, she's brought a bit of excitement to that dead-and-alive village of yours. You've stopped moaning about the place for the first time since you moved there. I'd stick with it if I were you. You never know how it's going to play out. You could end up with all your cherries in a row.'

This was basically the way I saw it. Maybe she was simply challenging me. Maybe at the start I'd been in with a chance. I simply hadn't responded, at least not in the way she wanted. Somewhere I knew she was out of my league. And she knew I knew it. The easiest thing for her would have been to tell me to shove off, to stop wasting her time.

But she never did. She carried on relating to me as if I mattered – as if I was important to her, even if the thing was going nowhere. At a lonely time in my life she made me feel good about myself. For that I'll always love her.

Now, twenty-five years on, Paula would become my Elizabeth Archer. The boss of the show had decreed the character should be silent no longer. She was to be given life, breath and personality, and it had fallen to me to give her these things.

I decided that she should appear in the final scene of my Friday episode. This is the hook scene, which is supposed to make it impossible for listeners not to tune in to the next episode, which would have been Monday in those days. I wasn't going to make this a hook of the conventional sort. This was going to be a promise of hilarious stories to come.

So here's the set-up. It's a sunny Friday afternoon. A gloomy Nigel is sitting in the orchard at Brookfield Farm, Shula's home, when a new, young voice rings out among the trees.

'Hello, Nigel. Why so glum?'

'Lizzie.'

'You've got a face like Dad's Hereford bull when the AI man drives in the yard.'

'It's your sister. She just dumped me.'

'What?'

'She's ended it. Waved ta-ta. Brought down the curtain on us. And shall I tell you the worst thing, Lizzie? The cruellest thing. She's chucked me for a solicitor. A solicitor, can you believe?'

'Mark.'

'It's devastating. After all the great times we've had together. Where've I gone wrong, Lizzie?'

'She doesn't deserve you. No need to despair though. As one door closes, another one opens and all that.'

'Does it?'

'Here's the good news, Nigel. You are now free and unencumbered. So you can jolly well go out with me, can't you? Well, don't look so shocked.'

'I'm not. I'm, er . . . I didn't expect it.'

'As it happens, I'm at a turning point in my life too. I'm out of school for good. I've decided. They're meant to be preparing us for life, but they're doing no such thing. Preparing us for half-lives, more like. For permanent greyness. Zombiehood.'

'Like being a solicitor.'

'Exactly. There's only one way to prepare for life – that's to live it. It's what I intend to do from now on. This is 1984, remember, and we don't actually have Big Brother or the Thought Police. We ought to be out there celebrating, right?'

Nigel is warming to the idea. 'Absolutely, Lizzie.'

'From here on in it's going to be full-on for me. I'm going to ride the big blue for as long as I can. Then when it crashes down on the beach, I'm going to head straight back out again and look for the next one. Are you with me, Nigel?'

'I'll say. I'm not exactly sure I know what you're talking about, but it's the best offer I've had all day. So yeah, I'm up for it. Just one question though? Have you told your dad yet?'

There was another page or so like this. Well, I had two minutes to fill, but this was the gist. At the end of my week, I sent my episodes off to William and waited for the verdict. It came in a phone call four days later.

'I have to tell you they weren't great,' he said. The words chilled like ice cubes down my back. 'It took me a full day's editing to make them fit to broadcast. Quite honestly I don't have the time for that sort of input on scripts.'

So that was it then. My one and only week of writing *The Archers*. Oh well, it would look good on my CV. Has written for the world's most famous radio drama. Once. But the voice on the phone hadn't finished yet.

'There was one scene I did like – your final scene on Friday. The one where you bring in Elizabeth. Very nicely done. Exactly the way I imagined her. So I've copied it round to the other writers. This is the way I want the character written from now on. So well done. See you at the script meeting.'

If a radio show can be said to have a beating heart, the monthly script meeting at the BBC's Pebble Mill centre in Birmingham was it. It was where the writers, editor and production team met around the boardroom table to plot new adventures for their characters. It was the closest we writers came to Ambridge. For me it was both exciting and terrifying in equal measure.

William gave great creative freedom to his writers, far more than any other editor I worked for on the programme; more than the writer of any TV soap would expect. He'd been a writer himself on the show before taking on the top job. *Archers*' writers, he said, had both freedom and power.

Reading some of his public pronouncements on the subject, you wouldn't necessarily know that. In a book called *The Archers*, published to mark the show's thirtieth anniversary, he set out the characteristics that made a good *Archers*' writer.

'Ideally he should live in Worcestershire or South Warwickshire, and be able to write with humour and understanding about the countryside and the people round about. He should be able to reflect rural society, from a pub darts match to a hunt ball, with perception and sympathy. If he's an officer in the Yeomanry, rides to hounds, and runs the tombola every year at the Conservative Garden Fete, then so much the better.'

If he'd stopped there, I'd never have gone near the show, but he went on to introduce some of his recent recruits to the writing team. They included Helen Leadbeater, a feminist lawyer's clerk from Islington who'd written a brilliant play for Radio 3; Mary Cutler, an Oxford-educated teacher from Birmingham who, like Helen, had appeared on *University Challenge* and written stories for *Jackie* while still at school; Susan Hill, the novelist and dramatist; Margaret Phelan, a trained midwife who worked in London as a solicitor's clerk; and Debbie Cook, a folk singer and composer of the hit song 'Day Trip to Bangor'.

For its first twenty years, *The Archers* had been written, produced and directed entirely by men. If they could have got away with it, they'd probably have found a male actor to play Doris Archer. However, the show I joined in the early 1980s had become a centre for powerful feminist writing, giving a new depth to the characters. The storylines sparkled; the dialogue had a new warmth and wit. The audience, which had slumped through the 1970s, was on the rise again.

Sitting at that boardroom table at Pebble Mill, I started to wonder what on earth I was doing there. Despite the mini-triumph of my Elizabeth character, I was clearly a fraud. The others at the table were proven writers. What had I done? A lot of stories about tractors and muck-spreaders, and that's about all. I was clearly there for the farming, and little else.

It made a kind of sense. At the time, the media were constantly complaining about *The Archers* having abandoned its farming roots. It was obvious William had recruited me to bring a breath of the farmyard to the show. I was the token farming writer recruited to get the media off his back. He wouldn't be looking to me for great dialogue. That's what the real writers were for.

I pushed these thoughts from my mind and joined in the discussions on new storylines. The general format of the meeting was that William would put out a few story ideas. The writers would then bat them around for a bit, while coming up with their own story ideas. Most of the time William would sit listening impassively, his arms folded. Every so often he would pick up his pen and start scribbling in his open notebook. This was the signal that a story was to go in the show.

I managed to chuck in a couple of stories. How about if twelve-year-old environmental activist Lucy Perks – daughter of Sid, the publican – suspects Phil Archer is injecting his cows with growth hormone, I suggested. It was a controversial subject at the time. What if she sneaks into the Brookfield Farm milking parlour one evening and pulls the drain plug from the bulk (storage) tank? Hundreds of pounds' worth of milk gets lost.

One of the other writers kindly supported my idea. 'It's the kind of thing Lucy would do in that moment. She's in that state of mind.' William's arms remained folded. As they did for my next idea.

'How about the Grundys' Hereford bull gets out,' I suggested. 'Let's have him go walkabout around the village. Say it's Sunday morning and he wanders into the churchyard during morning service. He's quite happy grazing around the gravestones. When the service ends, no one dares leave the church. Until Clarrie arrives and tells the bull to get home or else. And off he trots as quiet as a lamb.'

'Not really a story, is it,' said William, clearly unimpressed.

'It would be if he tossed Tom Forrest over the church hedge first,' said Mary with a chuckle. There was some animated chat about the consequences of having Ambridge's legendary gamekeeper gored by a Grundy bull. William was clearly amused, but he still didn't pick up his pen.

The meeting ended at four and we all started to pack away our notebooks.

'If you haven't got enough stories, you'll have to make up your own,' said William in a parting shot. 'Be sure to tell the next writer what you're doing. Happy writing.'

This was an extraordinary offer. No editor since has given writers such creative freedom. After William, editors started requiring writers to submit scene-by-scene synopses before they even started writing in earnest. There would then follow a couple of hours haggling on the phone about what should or shouldn't go into each scene.

William, by contrast, had no real idea what he was going to get each month until the scripts arrived in the post. As long as we each kept the writer following us informed of storyline changes, we were free to introduce tales of our own. It showed enormous trust and it produced results. In my view, the show has never been better written than in those days in the early 1980s. Which is why I thought my chances of a permanent place on the team weren't great.

Even so, I was determined to use that creative freedom for my second week's episodes. In addition to the agreed storylines, I would introduce a number of my own. In the village shop I'd have Martha Woodford scammed by a commercial rep. Jill Archer would tell Phil their marriage had become humdrum. On Jack Woolley's shoot, his chauffeur, the unspeaking Higgs, would be accidentally shot while beating. And I'd have the village pub broken into, with an end-of-episode hook that would make listeners fear for the safety of landlord Sid Perks and his daughter Lucy.

I sent off the finished scripts and awaited the verdict. When it came, it didn't exactly amount to a ringing endorsement.

'Well, you've certainly got plenty going on,' said William, in a tone that implied it wasn't a good thing. 'To be honest, I'm not convinced by the way you've told the stories. There's a way of handling the material for this show that you don't seem to have grasped, unfortunately.'

'I'm getting there, I really am.'

The anxiety must have registered in my voice because his tone softened. 'Alright, we'll give it another go. If that's what you want?'

'Yes, definitely. Thanks.'

Over the next two weeks I put the show under intense scrutiny. I listened to each episode two or three times over, carefully analysing the scene structure. I noted down the timings and recorded the points at which storylines dropped out and were later picked up again. Although I'd been listening to the show for years, on and off, I'd never examined it in such forensic detail.

As it happened, I was down to write the Christmas week's episodes. I made up my mind that if these were to be my last-ever scripts, I'd do my damnedest to make them memorable. I would enjoy the festive season in Ambridge in the company of my favourite characters. They would have to include the Grundys – Joe, Clarrie and Eddie, the downtrodden but ever-optimistic tenant farmers of Grange Farm, whose kitchen was already my favourite Ambridge location.

No one wanted complicated plot devices at Christmas, I decided. There was too much going on at home. What listeners wanted most were vignettes; brief glimpses of Ambridge life to show their favourite characters were having fun too. Or perhaps having their hearts broken. My job, it seemed, was to create scenes that would amuse and linger in the mind.

On Christmas Eve, we'd go to Grange Farm. It was going to be a very special year for the Grundys. There were two new members of the family – William, now almost two years old, and young Edward, just three months. The kitchen had always been a fairly chaotic place, shared at various times with dogs, Joe's ferrets, and the occasional orphaned lamb. This year there were going to be a couple of extra seasonal visitors.

I contrived a way of bringing two small piglets to live in the kitchen over Christmas.

'I've got no choice, Clarrie, love,' says Eddie as he reveals the wriggling animals under his coat. 'Their mum didn't survive and the heat lamp's on the blink. They'll have to stay in the warm until I can get the lamp working again.'

This plot device meant that each time we cut to a scene at Grange Farm, we heard the boys' shrieks mingling with the happy squeals of the piglets. A touch Dickensian, without a doubt, but somehow just right for the ramshackle Grundy household.

The Christmas Eve atmosphere in the staunchly middle-class home of Jill and Phil Archer couldn't have been more different. The couple are relaxing in the sitting room at Brookfield, Phil sipping sherry and enjoying *In Terra Pax*, a seasonal Christmas work by the English composer Gerald Finzi. The couple's daughters – Shula and Elizabeth – are out partying. Son David is soon to join them. For the middle-aged pair it's a moment of calm before the busy family Christmas begins.

Then Nigel turns up. He thought he had a date with Elizabeth but she seems to have forgotten. (I happen to know she stood him up, but Nigel always sees the best in people.) Kind Jill pours him a sherry and insists he stay for supper. Phil, who was very much enjoying his moment of calm, feels obliged to press home the invitation. That's the end of his Finzi. The rest of the evening is taken over by Nigel's explanation of why he's being packed off by his family to work on his uncle's farm in Zimbabwe.

'Pater thinks it'll make a man of me,' he says. 'Not that Lizzie's ever had any worries on that score. Oops, sorry, Mrs Archer. That didn't come out quite right.'

I was determined to include at least one scene featuring a couple of *Archers'* legends. There was no space on Christmas Day, but I managed to fit them into my Thursday episode. I chose an awesome duo – Dan Archer and Walter Gabriel, both characters from the show's trial run at Whitsun in 1950.

Dan Archer and his wife Doris had been the original occupants of Brookfield Farm. In the fifties, the couple were *Archers* royalty. Walter was meant to be the backward-looking small farmer, devised as a comic character to contrast the modern approach of the Archers. We may have dissed poor old Walter, but to listeners he became as big a star as Dan and Doris.

In my Christmas episode I put the two originals together over a gourmet meal. The plot device was that Walter's wayward son, wine-bar owner Nelson, had made a quick exit from the local town, Borchester, to escape his creditors. Though he wasn't able to join his dear old dad for Christmas, he sent along a Fortnum & Mason food hamper. The BBC didn't name the brand, obviously.

In my scene the two *Archers* originals are quaffing champagne and tucking into smoked salmon, to be followed by black cherries in kirsch, and fine blue cheese. As they eat, they reminisce about old times in Ambridge, even before the BBC began broadcasting its daily goings-on. Like the time Squire Lawson-Hope declared war on the local hunt.

I have Walter tell the story. 'There were a dozen of us working there that day. Lifting turnips. All on piece rates, of course. That's when the hunt came through at a gallop. The Squire was beside himself with rage. "Come on, chaps," he says, "let's give 'em a broadside." So we did. We pelted 'em with turnips, tops and all. There was a terrible fuss afterwards. He never apologised though, the old Squire. They don't make characters like that any more.'

I think I probably added Walter's famous catchline to his speech, 'me old pal, me old beauty'. I'd always wanted to write that line, but it didn't go out on air. William or someone must have cut it.

I ended my Christmas in Ambridge back where I started – with Nigel and Elizabeth. With a nod towards that classic sixties film *The Graduate*, I put them on the back seat of a bus. This was a particularly ancient one even for the time, the sort that were all grinding of gears and rattling metal seats. It was the last bus of the day from the village to Borchester. For all I knew it could have been the only bus of the day.

Nigel is explaining to Elizabeth why he needs to take his father's advice and have a spell working in Africa.

'Life's got too comfortable, Lizzie,' he says. 'Sometimes we need to get back to reality. The primeval struggle for survival.'

'That's why we go to parties.'

'You don't understand.'

'Yes I do. You've got a *Boys' Own* view of life under the stars. Most boys get over it when they leave the Cubs.'

'My life's had no real challenges. I need to test myself against elemental forces.'

'Listen, Nigel. The reality of your life has been selling swimming pools and loo brushes. That's a struggle for survival, too. The difference is the rules in Africa are a bit simpler. Here it's more complicated. It's a challenge just the same.'

'Are you saying you're going to miss me?'

'Of course I'm going to miss you, but if that's what you've got to do . . .'

'Why don't you come with me, Lizzie? You keep saying you're a free agent. So join my expedition. It's going to be an awfully great adventure.' SIG TUNE.

This time the verdict from *Archers* HQ was positive.

'You seem to be getting to know the village at last,' said William. 'There'll be a contract for you next year if you want it.'

I was ecstatic. I'd been accepted by the Ambridge community and it looked like I'd be staying around for a bit. What I never imagined was that I'd be there to see the Grundy boys grow up, to watch two generations of the Archer family take over at Brookfield Farm and have Elizabeth and Nigel finally tie the knot a decade after I'd brought them together. Nor that I'd play a part in the tragedy that ended their story.

Still less did I know that my time in that archetypal English village would help me work out a part of my own identity. Though I'd been born in a town and lived much of my early life on a housing estate, I learned about that part of me which belonged to the land. I don't simply mean that I loved the countryside, though I suppose I did. It's more a sense that I longed to be part of the unsung community which daily works the land for food: the farming community.

My guess is there are others in both town and country

who feel something like this. It may help to explain the enduring appeal of this radio drama. For generations it has provided a link, if a tenuous one, with our common heritage, which is the land that feeds us. I also have an idea that in the new, post-Covid, post-Brexit world it could help build even stronger connections, to the benefit of all of us.

None of this I knew when I joined the scriptwriting team in the mid-1980s. For the moment I'd landed myself a job on Britain's longest-running soap, and that was more than enough.

2

Escape to the Country

UNLIKELY AS IT SEEMS, the people I have to thank for my long residence in England's most famous village are the elected members of Reading Borough Council and their staff in the housing department. Not the present incumbents. We're talking here of the late 1940s, around the time BBC programmers were deciding whether or not to give the go-ahead to a new radio drama series set in the English countryside.

Down in Reading, our family was in trouble. There were seven of us living in my grandparents' semi-detached council house. Along with my grandparents, Tom and May, there was my mother Rhonda, my brother Tony and me. Mum's older brother, Uncle Alan, had a bedsit in what had been the front room. Finally, there was my dad, Peter, after he'd come back from the war, that is.

Things could get pretty crowded at times. We had no kitchen or bathroom. The toilet was a red-brick building at the end of the garden. To get washed you had to stand at the scullery sink or sit in a tin bath in front of the sitting room fire.

In the end, the council came up trumps and the four of us moved into a sparkling, new, three-bedroomed house.

Tony and I were awestruck. We'd never imagined there could be so much space. The idea that we might get rooms of our own hadn't occurred to us.

The council's gift turned out to be far bigger than simply putting a roof over our heads. Almost from the day we moved in, we felt part of a community. Our immediate neighbours we knew almost straight away. Within a few weeks we'd developed at least a nod-in-the-street relationship with pretty well everyone on the estate.

Everywhere there seemed to be open spaces. All the houses had large gardens, back and front. Out on the street there were wide pavements with well-trimmed green verges. Grassy play areas were plentiful. There was even a small wood with a stream running through, all within the boundaries of the estate. Best of all, at the end of our road the houses stopped, and you were into green fields with tall, rambling hedges; a mysterious, magical land that seemed to go on for ever.

Thanks to the council, my brother and I enjoyed something pretty close to a country childhood. However grim things became at home, we always felt we belonged to a close and kindly community. Looking back, it's hard to see how I could have been better prepared for life in Ambridge.

I'd been born one foggy November evening while the war still raged in Europe. My mum had temporarily moved next door to 'Auntie' Dorrie's house. Dorrie lived alone most of the time, her soldier husband being away with the army. With space at a premium in the family home, it was the only way Mum could be afforded some privacy.

It must have been a particularly stressful experience for

her. She'd had no communication with my dad for many weeks. He was away with the RAF, flying as an observer/navigator on bombing and photo-reconnaissance missions in a high-speed Mosquito fighter-bomber. It was dangerous work and the long silence from him had been unprecedented. She'd begun to fear he might have been killed and that the Air Ministry were withholding the news until after she'd given birth.

In fact, my dad was soon to be on his way to India, where a Japanese invasion was feared. As it turned out, none of us were to see him for the best part of three years.

I have few memories of those early years in my grandparents' council house. I can still see the laburnum tree that stood in the front garden, with its summer cascades of vivid yellow flowers. I remember it because my mum told me if I ate the pea-like pods I'd almost certainly die. I also recall standing on the front lawn as a cloud of brightly coloured butterflies drifted around me, as thick in the air as snowflakes in a winter storm.

My chief memory, however, is of the incredible garden at the back of the house. I read somewhere that only infants truly see nature as it is. As soon as we're able even to put names to birds or flowers, we're projecting our own constructs and ideas. Only the small child is able to gaze in wonder and so see things as they really are.

It's certainly true that even as a toddler I recognised our back garden as a place of extraordinary life and excitement. My granddad, Tom, had been a veteran of the Great War. Twice he'd been returned home with severe wounds, the first time in 1915 with his lungs scoured by chlorine gas, then again in 1917 with a fragment from a German shell lodged in his skull.

Though he'd never been able to work, he turned his

council-house garden into what must have been one of the most productive patches of land in the whole country. As well as supplying all our vegetables and a large quantity of soft fruit, he kept chickens for their eggs and rabbits for meat. I still recall the shock of finding out the meat in my bowl of stew was the sad-eyed animal I'd been feeding with dandelion leaves just a few days earlier.

Thanks to Granddad's garden, I'd been given a clear insight into the link between food and the earth. It's probably why I've never doubted that, given the sort of devotion he showed to the soil, there's no limit to what it'll give you in return.

I can see him now, sitting in his fireside armchair, endlessly leafing through copies of his favourite magazine, *The Great War . . . I Was There!* – if I showed even a scintilla of interest, he'd have me up on the chair arm and start pointing out the photos. Smiling men marching along dusty roads bounded by tall poplar trees, like those I could see from an upstairs window, beyond the houses and back gardens. Or men with despair written on their faces standing in a land of mud and shattered tree stumps. None of it made much sense, but it seemed to mean everything to him.

Though I always thought of him as a kindly man, he seemed to be treated with a certain wariness by my mum and my grandma. When I was older, Mum told me why. Though he'd mellowed in middle age, his personality had been volcanic throughout the years of her childhood. Frustration brought on by his disabilities and dashed hopes sometimes led to angry outbursts.

As usual the women – my mum and grandmother – bore the brunt. Though he never hit anyone, his rages could be intimidating in themselves. To minimise these storms, the women adopted a deferential manner in dealing with him. According to Mum, it became second nature to them. It must have put them under great strain.

They found some solace in the English countryside. As toddlers, Tony and I would usually be taken out on Sunday afternoons for a ramble. If we were lucky, it would start with a ride down the Shinfield Road in a big red Thames Valley bus. Sometimes the journey would be just a couple of stops. On other occasions, especially during the long days of summer, we'd get a corporation bus to the town centre, then catch another bus and head further afield. Even now the place names conjure up a timeless and beautiful England – Bucklebury Common, Burnham Beeches, Finchampstead Ridges, Christmas Common.

While relations in the house were strained at the best of times, they were about to get a good deal worse. When my brother was four and I was nearly three, my dad returned from his wartime service in India. He'd been traumatised by his experiences. Some sort of cataclysm was inevitable.

Mum and Dad had married in 1940 during one of his short-term leaves. The wedding, a small affair, had taken place in the registry office in Hastings, where he'd been posted soon after joining Bomber Command. Though they didn't know each other particularly well, as my mother later recalled, it was a time when couples couldn't be sure they'd even see each other again. Life seemed precarious and there'd been a mutual desire to make a commitment. Now, with the conflict over, what couples needed most was time together to renew and strengthen their relationships. There was little chance of that in our crowded house.

In cramped conditions and with young kids craving

attention, the opportunities for marriage-mending were virtually non-existent. Like so many after the war, my dad was in desperate need of support and counselling, but in those days neither were on offer. Like others, he looked for escape in alcohol and the dance hall life he'd enjoyed in pre-war years. He was a tall, good-looking man with more than a touch of arrogance about him.

Before the war, his image had been used in magazine ads for hair products. In small-town Reading he cut something of a dash as he drifted round the pubs and dance halls with his chum, Leslie, later to become my uncle when he married Dad's sister. When in 1938 the two of them signed on as 'weekend flyers' in the RAF Volunteer Reserve, they were soon in even greater demand.

Now faced with coolness at home – and haunted by his wartime experiences – he tried returning to his old life, spending long hours in town-centre pubs. Making friends, chatting up women. Sometimes getting drunk. Spending money the family couldn't spare. All this put yet more strain on the marriage. His attempt to return to his pre-war job of clerk to a local firm of solicitors lasted no more than a couple of months. Too much had happened for him to settle to an office routine.

While his rage was never far away, he could be good-humoured, jovial even, especially in company. Always the life and soul of the party was my dad. He could be kind, too, though sustained tenderness seemed beyond him. At any time, there was the risk of an angry outburst, way out of proportion with whatever had triggered it. We now had two ticking time-bombs in the house, both of them products of war.

In the end, the strain on the family became too great and my mother asked him to go. For a while he moved in with his widowed mother in her town-centre flat, vowing to sort out his life and become a good husband and father. Neither my brother nor I remembered these events. Years later my mum spoke of them and how the council's housing department came to our rescue. For us it was to be a turning point.

The estate at Emmer Green was the first social housing built in Reading following the post-war Labour victory. After the years of conflict, everyone now wanted to make the world a better place. Our little family were beneficiaries of this great ideal, though it nearly didn't happen.

I remember vividly my mum's outburst at the man from the council, probably because angry outbursts were not generally in her nature. That was Dad's department. Mum was usually a mild-mannered woman, timid, you could even say. This was the moment the worm turned. The unfortunate target of her rage was a visiting official from the housing department.

He'd come to inspect my grandparents' house to see if we'd make suitable tenants for the new estate. Only carefully chosen families were to be accepted, he told us. Then with a pained expression on his face, the man from the council informed us that we weren't likely to be among them. He'd found evidence of wilful vandalism in the room occupied by me and my brother. Someone had defaced a wall by scribbling on it in pencil. It looked like a child's impression of a cat.

I knew at that moment the man was an idiot. Anyone could see it wasn't a cat. It was Tiger Tim, copied from *Tiger Tim's Annual*, which, as it happens, my brother had been given for Christmas. It wasn't, however, the man's poor art appreciation that triggered the onslaught from my mum. It was his lack of common humanity.

Did he have the slightest inkling what families like ours had been through, she demanded to know. Wasn't it enough that my dad had been away serving King and Country? Did anyone in the housing department have the slightest idea what it was like bringing up two young boys when food was rationed and, in any case, there was scarcely enough money in the household to feed everyone?

The man muttered something about the council having its rules, then headed for the front gate. He wasn't quick enough, though. Mum sprinted across the lawn to cut him off. She resumed the attack by telling him how our garden had kept the neighbours supplied with eggs, soft fruit and rabbit meat throughout the war years. What had he been doing down at the council to protect the nation from the Nazi menace? The poor man finally made his escape. Shortly afterwards we learned that we were to get a three-bedroom semi-detached house on the new estate.

This was 1949, the year a producer of radio farming programmes in the BBC's Midland region was getting excited by his idea for a new daily soap. Though there hadn't been much enthusiasm from the Corporation's drama department, he'd set up a meeting with two drama writers to develop the idea further. The result was to be a daily serial that would take its radio audience to the very heart of the countryside.

As my brother and I set off for our new house we, too, were heading for an adventure in the English countryside. With my nan accompanying us, we took the corporation bus to the town centre. There we picked up another bus with the magical words 'Emmer Green' on its destination panel. With much gear grinding and engine whining it somehow hauled itself up Peppard Road. As the road levelled out in sunlit uplands, we caught our first glimpse of the estate.

It was a world more dazzling than we could have imagined. Dozens of bright new houses with colourful front doors, and streets wider than any we'd seen. We got off the bus at Evesham Road and walked down the hill, passing spindly new hedges and bare-earth garden plots. We crossed a little valley of stream and woodland that was to become our adventure playground, and up the hill on the other side.

By the time we got to number twenty-five with its smartly painted green gate, I felt almost sick with excitement. In our new kitchen, Mum was getting to grips with the electric cooker that had been delivered that morning. From upstairs came thumps, bangs and the occasional curse as Dad struggled to put together the two iron utility beds that my brother and I were to sleep on. We were together, the four of us, a family at last.

'I'm having the front bedroom,' Tony said. This was fine with me. Having a bedroom to myself was amazing enough. Who cared if it was at the front or back? From my new bedroom window I looked out over the collection of back gardens that seemed to go on for miles. Most of them were still bare earth. I tried to imagine what they'd be like when they had been planted up and stocked with chickens and rabbits like Granddad's garden. There'd be enough to feed the whole town.

Over the weeks, as I watched from the window, the gardens were sown and planted. There weren't any chickens or rabbits, but vegetables grew, flowers bloomed, the brown earth became green. I looked out often as the seasons passed and the skeletal hedges grew tall and muscular, creating a land of garden rooms, filled with colour and life.

Like the garden plants, we flourished, too, in that place of space and light. Tony and I went to the local primary school, appropriately called The Hill School, with views across Reading and the Thames Valley. Getting there involved a ten-minute walk and the crossing of the busy Buckingham Drive. It was worth it, though. The school, like our estate, was new, spacious and filled with light.

On the south side, the classroom walls were almost entirely glass. If you were bored, you could look out across the town to the far-distant land of Sunday rambles. This didn't happen often, though.

At home, the new surroundings produced only a temporary halt to hostilities. It wasn't long before rows between my parents kicked off again. There always seemed to be tension in the air and rows would flare up over very little. I remember one occasion when an angry exchange was sparked off by Mum's purchase of a five-shilling alarm clock from a door-to-door salesman.

The argument was ostensibly over her 'extravagance' at a time when money was tight. This was only the spark though. Truth was, as a couple, they seemed to live in a constant state of disappointment, each with the other.

There was another frequent trigger for domestic explosions – the Saturday night out, which happened about once a month. It followed a regular routine. My nan would come over on the bus to child-sit me and my brother, while Mum and Dad headed off to a dinner dance at their favourite venue, a hotel in nearby Caversham. Later we'd be woken in the early hours by Dad screaming obscenities. It was a frightening sound. I'd put the pillow over my head until it went away.

Though we barely understood it at the time, what seemed to happen was Dad would see a woman he found attractive, then flirt and joke with her as if my mum didn't exist. She'd feel hurt and humiliated, and when they got home the whole thing would blow up. Tony and I would wake up to a screaming row. It happened over and over again.

To me, it seemed weird behaviour on my dad's part. Looking back, I don't believe any of these random encounters with women led to further contacts, let alone affairs. It was like he had this need to constantly prove his appeal with women. Whatever the motivation, it seemed almost to take him over so he became a kind of automaton. Mum would be hurt and there'd be the inevitable bust-up later.

In one of my early scripts for William Smethurst, I had to write a breakfast scene at Home Farm, an everyday domestic encounter between Brian and Jennifer Aldridge. I wrote what I thought of as light-hearted banter between the two. Later, William asked me why I'd made the couple behave so unkindly toward each other. This came as a surprise. I thought I'd written a perfectly normal exchange between them.

My brother and I adopted very different survival mechanisms for dealing with the tensions at home. He invariably escaped into a book, while I got out of the house at every possible opportunity. It seemed easy to make friends on the estate. Most of the tenants were young families, so there were a lot of boys of my own age around.

I drifted quickly into friendships and sometimes quickly out of them. A lot of my free time would be spent in friends' houses, where the atmosphere was friendlier and more relaxed than in ours. For a while I was good mates with a builder's son called Joe Humphries. He and his brother Ed had, what seemed to me, a brilliant relationship with their parents, especially their dad. There were jokes and laughter all the time. It was unsettling but I loved being there.

Not many of my friends came round to us though. I didn't encourage it, mainly because of my dad's moods. If you caught him on a good day, he could be jokey and funny, at times way over the top. On a bad day, coming to our place was like walking into a fridge.

The other escape, one that slowly opened up as I got older, was the countryside. From our house, you didn't have to walk far to get deep into rural England. Three minutes would take you to the end of our road and St Barnabas Church, which marked the boundary of the estate. At that point the road surface turned from concrete to grey asphalt. You'd pass a few sedate old country houses; after that you were into fields and farmland. It was a world that drew me as if it had been pre-destined.

Our part of England was an unassuming sort of landscape, unspectacular and oddly comforting. The fields were small and mostly of pasture, with unkempt, rambling hedges. There were small woodlands, too, and here and there ponds and marshy areas. It was a gentle, small-scale landscape which in those days stretched away uninterrupted as far as the Chiltern Hills. I doubt it had changed much in centuries.

Joe and I, along with other friends, spent a lot of our time in that close-to-home yet far-off country. The places we returned to time and again were the pasture fields, of which there were several within a few minutes' biking distance of home. We'd spend hours there, especially in summer, re-enacting the Second World War or the shoot-out from the film *High Noon*. Or we'd just lie on our backs among the swaying seedheads, swapping jokes and banter and watching stories unfold in the drifting clouds.

Nowadays, grasslands are mostly quiet places, but not then. The moment you lay down and rested your head on the turf, it seemed as if all hell had been let loose. You were surrounded by sounds – a hissing, buzzing, clicking, scraping cacophony of noise. Small creatures would begin to land on you, scurry across you or fly close by you.

Some would be instantly recognisable: grasshoppers, large and small, brown, green and yellow. You'd see beetles, ladybirds, hoverflies, fast-running spiders and fluttering butterflies in a multitude of colours. There'd also be a host of nameless things – bugs and flying creatures with long legs and scary-looking mouthparts. Some would make you jump up in horror, brushing at your bare arms and legs, convinced you'd narrowly escaped a lethal bite from a venomous species your mum had failed to warn you about.

Down there at insect level all was noise, movement and conflict. In those days, the life of the grass field provided the summer soundtrack to our playtime. Today the fields are silent. Chemical fertilisers have seen off those fearsome friends of the turf.

In my Ambridge years, I tried many times to recreate those flower-filled pastures from childhood. It was one of my favourite locations for setting an outdoor scene. If I'd worked on the show in its early incarnation, it would have been enough to have written the words 'meadow sounds' at the top of the scene to suggest a sound effect. Some conscientious sound engineer would have headed out to the countryside of south Worcestershire to record those lost creatures of grass.

By the time I started writing for the programme, the pastures had already fallen silent. Whenever I set a scene in a pasture or meadows, I'd write the word 'skylarks' as a sound effect. Their song created its own magic without doubt, but it wasn't the special magic conjured up by that ancient insect chorus in the grass.

As it happens, *Archers*' creator Godfrey Baseley grew up in countryside not so different from the area I knew north of Reading. His home patch was an area stretching from Birmingham south to Evesham, and from the city of Worcester east to Stratford-upon-Avon. Like our part of Oxfordshire, it was a landscape of traditional mixed farms with the emphasis on grassland and grazing animals. He'd have known plenty of small pasture fields like the ones I'd discovered. He, too, would have heard the insect chorus.

The sounds of nature weren't the only childhood experience I was to take to Ambridge many years later. I'd also had an early taste of village life. The postal address showed Emmer Green to be part of Reading, but we who lived there had no doubt that it was a separate place entirely. When you sat on a corporation bus as it lumbered up Peppard Road, you felt you were leaving the town behind. Then as it rounded the brow and you saw the estate with its bright new houses and wide streets, you felt you were entering an entirely separate community, almost a village.

Though the idea of a 'New Jerusalem' is much disparaged, looking back, that's what it was. Perhaps we unwittingly Photoshop our memories as we age, but recalling that estate, I see only immaculately kept gardens and play areas totally free of litter. It was a community of working people who loved where they lived. Rather like the residents of Ambridge.

When *The Archers* began, the year after we moved to Emmer Green, it, too, was about a community of working people. The central couple, Dan and Doris Archer, were small farmers, as were most of Britain's farmers at the time. They didn't own their land, they rented it. To make a living they had to work long hours virtually every day of the year. Their grown-up son, Philip, had taken a job as farm manager of a large estate, and appeared to have middle-class aspirations.

Phil apart, it was essentially a drama about ordinary working people. I imagine this was why it attracted such a phenomenal audience, almost from the start. Working people saw it as a show for and about themselves.

By the time I joined as a scriptwriter in the 1980s, it had become unmistakeably middle class in its appeal. To be fair, this reflected changes that had taken place in the real countryside. Farms had got bigger through amalgamations, while the price of land had soared. For thirty years, farmers' incomes had been boosted by government subsidies, so many had adopted middle-class lifestyles.

In Ambridge, the central family, the Archers, now headed by Phil and Jill, had become distinctly middle class in their outlook. The Aldridges, Brian and Jennifer, even more so. No doubt because of my housing estate experience, I never felt particularly at home with these characters. I suppose you'd call it a kind of inverse snobbery, but I found the working-class characters easier and more enjoyable to write.

Take Susan Carter, for example. Now middle-aged, she's routinely portrayed as a social-climbing snob and number-one Ambridge gossip machine. It's true she's often tried to free herself from the dysfunctional Horrobin family she was born into. It's also true that if you wanted a nugget of information spread around the village in a hurry, you couldn't do better than pop in the village shop and tell Susan about it. Even so, to define the character in this way is to do her an injustice.

When I joined *The Archers*, she was twenty-one and newly married to pig herdsman Neil Carter. Like me, she'd grown up in a council house. Where mine was at the centre of a large housing estate, hers was one of just half a dozen, a small social-housing enclave in the middle of what had become a posh village. On our estate at Emmer Green everyone thought of themselves as equals. Class was seldom an issue since everyone was in similar circumstances.

From an early age, Susan would have been made aware that she and her family were not the equals of those around them. In rural England, home ownership is an unspoken token of class. Incomers to Ambridge would have understood that their comfortable cottages in leafy south Borsetshire gave them status in the community. Likewise, land-owning farmers would never for a moment have doubted their right to be there.

Susan would have grown up knowing that she was there not because of her family's own efforts but because they'd been helped by the state. No one would have mentioned it, of course. Everyone would have been far too polite. Even so, Susan would have understood that she and the family were not quite the social equals of their neighbours. She would have needed special reserves of courage and fortitude to get by in Ambridge.

Despite the social disadvantages, Susan made a good life for herself in the village. She and Neil built their own house – Ambridge View – and brought up two kids, Emma and Christopher, both popular and prominent in village life. Susan might easily have given up and walked away from the place and the various humiliations heaped on her by her family, especially her brother Clive, who succeeded in dragging her into his criminal lifestyle.

Writing off Susan simply as a gossip is to ignore her extraordinary courage. Likewise, her husband Neil, who came to the village as a farm apprentice in the early 1970s. He spent most of his working life with pigs that live outside in portable 'arks', as they're called, like little igloos. His particular gift is an instinctive understanding of animals – what used to be known in farming as 'stockmanship'.

As far as I know, Neil didn't grow up in a council house. There's nothing in the character's data file to tell you either way. My guess is one or other of his parents worked on a farm, perhaps milking dairy cows. If so, he'd have grown up in a 'tied cottage', as it was called, a house or cottage that went with the job. He's definitely the kind of character you'd have found on our estate, what I'd call an ordinary working guy. They both are, he and Susan.

If they had lived on our estate, I've no doubt they'd have been happy there. With farmland at the end of our road, Neil wouldn't have had far to travel to look after his pigs. He'd have gone off to work in his overalls, and after a day with the pigs, let's be honest, he'd have whiffed a bit when he came home. What I do know is, no one on our estate would have thought any less of him, which is more than you could say for Ambridge.

Most of the people I knew on our estate were happy there, certainly all my friends and their parents. The only person I knew who didn't like it there was my dad. He had a visceral dislike of anything that smacked of socialism, which, let's face it, was the reason the estate got built in the first place.

Dad hated the Labour party, its government and all it stood for. During one election, Reading's long-standing Labour MP Ian Mikardo came canvassing on our estate in a Vauxhall car. My dad swore blind that he'd parked his Roller in a side street in Caversham before driving up to Emmer Green.

Most of Dad's politics came direct from the *Daily Express*, in those days owned by Lord Beaverbrook and unapologetically for King and Empire. Dad was a Thatcherite before there was Margaret Thatcher. For him, to live in social housing was an admission of failure in life. He did his best to show that we weren't really council-house people and would be getting out as soon as we could. I can't imagine this endeared him particularly to our neighbours.

At around the time we moved to Emmer Green, he managed to land himself a job that suited his need for status and flamboyance. It was with an organisation known as the Thames Conservancy, whose job was to regulate and police navigation on the river. Dad started as assistant navigation officer and quickly rose to navigation inspector in charge of number two district, a stretch of the river extending from Wallingford to Windsor.

The job included a certain amount of office work, but much of his time was spent cruising up and down the river in a powerful patrol launch. To me, it seemed a brilliant way to earn a living, especially in winter, when there weren't many pleasure boats about. The clincher, from Dad's point of view, was that he got to wear an impressive naval-style uniform, complete with rings of gold braid on the lower sleeve and a cap badge that would have done justice to a rear admiral.

When Dad stepped off the corporation bus at the top of our road each evening, he might have come direct from a destroyer. His walk down Evesham Road stated loudly and clearly that he didn't belong here. This was a temporary berth forced on him by circumstances. He'd be on the move soon. Unfortunately for me, this turned out to be true.

Having made full inspector, he bought a car. We were among the first on the estate to get one. It was a black Ford Consul with a bench front seat and gear shift on the steering column. Registration plate UNO 869. Dad rented a lock-up garage a good twenty-minute walk away, but most of the time it sat in the road outside our house. Was this a further message to our neighbours that we'd soon be on our way?

In our first summer as car owners, we went on a week's holiday to Weymouth. The year before we'd had a week in Dawlish, travelling on the train from Reading. Apart from that, the only family breaks had been day trips on Smith's Coaches. In Weymouth we were booked into a bed-and-breakfast place near the seafront. In those days you had to leave the boarding house after breakfast and you weren't allowed back until supper time.

My chief memory of the holiday was walking up and down the seafront in the rain. The weather that August was wet and cold, and we simply didn't have the money to spend in cafés and restaurants. I couldn't wait to go home.

There was one exciting day, however. Tony and I had become friendly with the seventeen-year-old daughter of the landlady, a girl called Linda. She told us she was half-way through a course at the county's agricultural college, called, at that time, the Dorset Farm Institute. She wondered if we'd like to drive out and take a look at the place.

Desperate for an alternative to the rain-swept sea-front, we took up her offer with more enthusiasm than she could have expected. The next day we all piled into the Consul and drove for half an hour to the former stately home set in spacious parkland near Dorchester. Close to the old house was a cluster of new classrooms and farm buildings. Linda showed us around the tractors and farm machines, then we watched the cows being brought in for milking.

I found the whole place fascinating. It hadn't occurred to me that you could work on farms as a career choice. I assumed you had to be born a farmer. For me, it was the highlight of the holiday, though it must be admitted that apart from an hour at the Abbotsbury Swannery when it didn't actually rain, there hadn't been a lot of competition.

Back at home, my brother and I joined the church choir at St Barnabas. Dad had encouraged us to do this. He himself had a very fine tenor voice and often reminded us how he'd sung in the choir at St Laurence's, the big church in the centre of Reading, near the ruins of the abbey. The choir at Emmer Green was an all-male affair. There was nothing precious about us. We were ordinary estate boys who enjoyed getting together and singing a couple of times on a Sunday and one evening a week for practice.

As well as the boys, there were a few men in the choir, including a burly, rugby-playing policeman called Peter Wilkins. He had a powerful tenor voice, and with the help of a couple of basses we managed to make a pretty good sound.

The following Christmas, when I'd just turned eleven, I sang the first-verse solo of 'Once in Royal David's City' as we processed down the aisle for the candlelit carol service. As we reached our places in the choir stalls, I turned to look at Mum and Dad, who were sitting near the front. Mum was dabbing her eyes with a hankie. Dad gave me a thumbs-up. I felt very relieved.

The next year there was more good news for them. I managed to pass my eleven-plus exam. It came as a surprise because, talking to other kids on the way out, I realised I'd only read half the essay question. Instead of meeting travellers from another planet and telling them about our modern inventions, I'd gone back in time with them to the Dodge City of the Old West. Someone must have got the results mixed up because I still got a pass.

The day the letter arrived, I waited at our garden gate for Dad to step off the bus. And there he was, in his commodore's uniform and carrying his smart brown leather briefcase. I sprinted down the hill and up the other side in record time.

'I've passed,' I gasped breathlessly. 'I've passed to Reading School. Straight through. They don't even want me for an interview.'

My dad looked genuinely overjoyed. I'd seldom seen him react to any news with such obvious delight.

'Well done,' he said, 'very well done. That's terrific news.'

We walked down the road together, father and son. At that moment I believed he was proud of me. I couldn't remember ever feeling so happy.

As it happens, my brother and I were the only boys from the estate to get into the town's legendary grammar school. For my dad it meant we'd be getting the start in life he'd been denied by circumstances, his father having died young, leaving his mother struggling to make ends meet.

There'd also been the small matter of the Second World War. The traumas he suffered, whatever they were, had made it impossible for him to return to studying, as many returning service people had done. Dad felt he'd been robbed of a glittering future. Now there was a chance to live it through his sons.

For me, the grammar school experience wasn't a great one. I found myself surrounded by 'posh boys' from comfortable middle-class homes. Most had addresses in the upmarket districts of the town or in the villages round about. There were also a number of boarders, mostly sons of group captains or army majors stationed abroad.

From the very start, I felt them to be in some way 'other'. I've no idea where this prejudice arose from, but I'd clearly been inoculated with it by the time I was eleven. Though I did my best to make friends, the relationships rarely lasted beyond the first visit to their homes.

One brief friendship I remember was with a boy whose father had been a circuit judge. He invited me back for tea in one of the biggest houses on one of the smartest roads in Reading. On the day it was just him and me sitting at this huge dining table. We were served sandwiches and cake by the home help.

I felt awkward and for some strange reason angry. I made an excuse for leaving early and was glad to get out of there. My tea-time buddy was keen to carry on the friendship but I quickly froze him out. Even now, looking back, I feel shame at my attitude. It must have been hurtful. I'd somehow managed to make a class enemy at the age of twelve!

The only lasting friendships I established at school were with boys from backgrounds like mine. Of my three best friends, one was from a tough housing estate and another from a terrace house in a run-down part of the town. The third was a boarder, the son of an army officer. He was undoubtedly posh, but he was also a rebel and something of a social misfit, which made him alright in my book.

Looking back on those years, it was clearly an irrational prejudice. Even so, the feelings were real and continued to trouble me through much of my life. In my early days in Ambridge, it made life tricky as I found it hard to generate sympathy for the characters I considered to be privileged. Not a great attribute for a writer on a soap.

As it happens, it was at my grammar school that the village of Ambridge first entered my consciousness. It was at morning break-time and I'd thrown myself into the daily game of what we laughingly called football. It involved anywhere between ten and thirty first- and second-year boys chasing a tennis ball around the 'quadrangle' in the vague hope that you might actually see it and give it a kick.

Suddenly I had the ball at my feet but only because

everyone else had left the pitch. They were engaged in an animated discussion over by the milk crates. As I ran across to join them, I quickly gathered there'd been some sort of tragedy. Someone famous had died, it seemed. But who? Milk monitor Ade Howarth had the answers.

The victim, it turned out, had been someone called Grace Archer, the star of a radio show that was broadcast every night. It was called *The Archers*. I'd vaguely heard of it but never listened.

'It's a serial like *Dick Barton* used to be,' Ade explained. 'Only this one's about farming.'

'Doesn't sound a thrill a minute,' I said.

'Oh it doesn't?' said Ade in a tone combining contempt with abject pity. 'Well let me tell you, sunshine, half the nation were listening last night when she went back into that blazing barn.'

'Get fried, did she?'

'She died trying to save the horses. The papers are full of it this morning. They reckon the schools'll be shut for the funeral.'

'Good thing she snuffed it then. We'll get a day off.'

'Honestly, you fellers from the sticks. You need to get into the twentieth century. Don't they have the wireless out your way?'

When I got home, I asked my mum why we didn't listen to *The Archers*. I could have guessed the answer.

'Your father didn't think much of it. We did give it a try but he said it was ridiculous. Who wants to listen to a programme about cows?'

The fact is we were a television family. Just as we had one of the first cars on the estate, we also had one of the first TV sets, even before the Coronation. It's why half a dozen estate boys came round on Thursday afternoons to watch the cowboy serial. It was a pretty safe bet that Dad would be at work, but if he did happen to come home early, he was usually happy to find the locals admiring our TV. It had a full twelve-inch screen and smart mahogany doors, so no one would know it was a TV set when you weren't watching.

Life on the estate was never quite the same after I'd started at Reading School. It felt like an invisible barrier had come down, separating my brother and me from kids we'd been friendly with for years. Nothing was actually said, but there was an atmosphere. It felt as if we'd gone over to the enemy.

Off we went each morning wearing our school caps with the blue-and-white hoops, and grey flannel suits with short trousers. We seemed to be echoing what Dad had been saying with his naval uniform – we didn't much want to be there.

In the summer term it got even worse. Mum insisted we wear the official blue-and-white-striped blazers. It meant we had to walk to and from the bus stop at the top of Evesham Road looking like we'd come straight from Henley Regatta. We both drew the line at straw boaters. There was no way we were wearing those.

Soon after that, Mum and Dad started talking about the possibility of buying their own house. The conversation inevitably ended up in an argument over money. They needed to raise a deposit of £100, which Mum said was impossible. It seemed an unimaginable amount of money so I decided it was never going to happen.

It was not long before I made the astonishing discovery that was to haunt me for much of my life. I'd been rummaging around in a sitting-room cupboard looking for something to read. Buried under a pile of old *Gramophone* magazines (Dad was a classical music fan) I found a battered hardcover notebook in air-force blue. It had the words 'Observer's and Air Gunner's Flying Log Book' stencilled on the front. Below my dad's name and service number had been handwritten.

With mounting excitement, I opened the book and began flicking through the pages. At that time I knew next to nothing about his wartime career. He never talked about it. All I knew was the little my mum had told me – that he'd trained as a pilot before the war, and at the outbreak of hostilities had been called up to serve in Bomber Command. I'd always assumed he'd been a bomber pilot and made up stories about it to tell my friends.

The log book contained dozens of entries about training flights. A number of different aircraft were involved. The flying times, aircraft types and pilots were all noted. There was also a column for general remarks. The first entry was for November 1941.

By April 1943, the year I was born, Dad was flying as observer in the new, twin-engined de Havilland Mosquito. Entries for later that same year began to include remarks on bombing and reconnaissance operations over Germany and occupied Europe. There were low-level attacks on railway sheds near Brussels and Thionville in France.

Some of the ops were entered as 'PAMPA' flights. I didn't have a clue what this meant. The entries showed Dad took part in dozens of such flights over target areas which included Amsterdam, Essen and Hamburg. The last entry was for a flight over Dieppe on 24 August, the day after my brother's first birthday and a few weeks before I was born.

Excited and intrigued, I went out to the kitchen to ask Mum what it meant. When I showed her the book, she looked momentarily alarmed.

'Where on earth did you find that?' she demanded. The anxiety in her voice scared me.

'In the cupboard, under Dad's magazines.'

'Well, put it back where you found it. And please don't touch it again.'

'Why do the entries stop on the twenty-fourth of August in 1943? Did he go back to being a pilot?'

'Never you mind. It's not something he likes to talk about. So just you put it back and don't touch it again.'

I did, and it was never mentioned again. A few days later, when they were both out, I went to the cupboard to sneak another look. The log book had gone. Later I got into a conversation with a boy at school who was crazy about all things air force. I didn't know him particularly well, but someone said he was a walking encyclopaedia when it came to Bomber Command. I told him about the log book and how the entries had suddenly stopped in August.

'He wasn't one of those LMF cowards, was he?' The word 'coward' burned into me like hot coke in the kitchen boiler. It was a fear I had about myself, the way I avoided fights.

'What's LMF mean?'

'Lack of moral fibre. It used to get stamped on your passbook if you chickened out. In the RAF it was the biggest disgrace. Was your dad one of them?'

'No, it was nothing like that, I'm sure.' The truth was I wasn't sure about anything. Could it have been that? Might he have panicked when the flak was flying around? There was no indication that he was scared in the log-book entries, but then again, how could there have been?

I pushed the idea away, though it was to return big-time later in my life. For the moment I did what Mum appeared to have done – I buried it and got on with life.

The following year, we left the estate. Somehow Mum and Dad must have got their £100 together because they bought a house in a village near Henley. It could have been Ambridge except that the local river was the Thames rather than the Am.

Tony and I were taken to see it before the big move. We were going to a newish, red-brick, detached house with a big garden filled with apple and plum trees. I thought it looked alright and I got quite excited, but things didn't turn out well. I missed the estate and my friends. Rows at home multiplied, mainly over money.

Never again was I to experience that sense of safety and belonging I knew at Emmer Green, though years later I took the memory of it to Ambridge. This is a scene I wrote at Christmas 1995. Clarrie Grundy is sitting in St Stephen's Church a few minutes before the carol service begins. Phil Archer is playing the organ. There are whispered voices from other members of the congregation.

Clarrie is joined by her husband, Eddie. He's wearing his tatty working clothes, including his ancient wax jacket. Clarrie does not approve.

'You can't sit here in that,' she whispers. 'Take it off.'

'I can't, love.'

'It's filthy and it stinks. Now take it off.'

'I can't. Here, have a shufty.' Eddie unzips his jacket. 'What do you think of them?'

Clarrie does not approve.

'Eddie, you been out poaching again?'

'I had to. We're broke, ain't we? We've got to feed the kids this Christmas. Well, the Lord has provided. Two nice pheasants. The fruit of the earth.'

'And you've brought them into church. That's wicked.'

'No it ain't. I'm here to give thanks, aren't I?'

'Well, do your jacket up before someone sees 'em.'

'No one's going to see 'em. Anyway, they're turning the lights out. Why is that, Clarrie?'

'Shssh . . . It'll be our Edward.'

In the candlelight, a boy's treble voice rings clear in the darkened church.

'Once in Royal David's City,
Stood a lonely cattle shed,
Where a mother laid her baby,
In a manger for his bed.
Mary was that mother mild.
Jesus Christ her little child.'

(FADE UP CAROL. MIX INTO SIG TUNE)

3

Comedy's the Thing

FROM THE MOMENT I started writing for Britain's longest-running soap, I knew I'd have to play it for laughs. Humour hadn't really figured in the features I'd written for the farming mags. Their business was selling tractors, animal feeds and pesticides, that sort of stuff. They'd found this was best done with punchy, breathless prose containing some sort of implied business threat. How if you didn't buy the product your profits were likely to head south.

Irony and clever wordplay didn't generally do much for sales so they weren't encouraged. Except at Christmas, that is. For festive editions we were urged to write light-hearted pieces on subjects such as the efficient management of reindeer herds or 'my happy winter holiday harvesting chestnuts'. The point was to show readers we were human and not entirely business automatons. Besides, none of the big corporate advertisers were interested in taking space at Christmas, so there was nothing to be lost.

Writing for *The Archers* couldn't have been more different. It was, after all, the story of an English village, and the English seem incapable of holding a conversation on anything without spicing it up with jokes, jibes and general banter. It's a habit that seems to apply to all classes, genders and age groups.

Anthropologist Kate Fox took a close look at our attitudes to humour in her book *Watching the English*. She concludes that there's nothing particularly distinctive about this nation's sense of humour. There's no special form of wit or self-deprecation that can be called uniquely English. What's unusual is the intense pride that we as a nation appear to take in it. Apparently, we love the idea that humour is a key part of our national identity.

In other cultures there's usually 'a time and a place' for humour, Fox writes. It's a special, separate kind of talk, but not in England. In any conversation, there always has to be an undercurrent of humour. We can barely bring ourselves to say 'hello' or comment on the weather without somehow contriving to make a joke of it.

Archers' editor William Smethurst seems to have reached a similar conclusion during his years as a scriptwriter on the show. The audience had been on the slide for years, so much so that by the early 1970s the BBC were thinking of axing the programme. By the time Smethurst took over in 1978, he'd made up his mind to reinvent it as a social comedy.

According to Fox, the cardinal rule in any English conversation is to avoid at all costs being earnest. She goes as far as calling it the 'not being earnest rule'. There was clearly no such rule in the 1950s, at least not in Ambridge.

In the early days, earnestness was liable to break out anywhere without warning. You might be enjoying a scene of light-hearted banter in the village pub only to be thrust into a diatribe from Dan or Phil on the dangers of Newcastle disease in the henhouse. The programme regularly featured announcements that might have come straight from government press handouts. Often, they had.

Smethurst was determined to change all this and introduce more comic storylines. If he'd read the national mood right, the nation wanted a bit of light relief. At the time I arrived, the miners' strike – and the government's handling of it – had split the nation, leading to charges of police brutality. In October, the Provisional IRA had tried to assassinate Conservative party leaders in the Brighton hotel bombing.

What Britain needed now was a daily soap that gently sent up its characters. They'd be well-meaning and likeable, but with a propensity to lapse into the ridiculous from time to time. Rather like the rest of us. So out went outlandish storylines about kidnappings, train robberies and plane crashes. Out went the boring farming pronouncements.

Gone, too, were cardboard characters with bizarre and mysterious histories, secret service agents, mail-van robbers and hijackers. The show's new stars were, in Smethurst's words, the kind of people you might meet in any English village or pass in the high street of any market town.

Characters who'd previously played only minor roles in village life were now moving centre-stage. Among them were the sexually liberated teenager Shula Archer, a hunt-supporting member of the Young Conservatives, and Joe Grundy, the downtrodden but ever-irrepressible tenant of Grange Farm. Joe's son Eddie became co-conspirator in his many plots to put one over on the Archers.

I'd also have to include Nigel Pargetter in the new, all-star line-up, the fun-loving, warm-hearted offspring of minor gentry. In the 1980s you'd find at least one Nigel in the wine bars of just about every English market town.

In the hands of Smethurst's writing team, the dialogue became less shrill and the conflicts more nuanced. Sometimes established characters would go through changes of personality, as when farmer Pat Archer had a sort of political awakening and started an affair with a sociology lecturer called Roger. Without consulting her husband Tony, she switched Bridge Farm's daily newspaper from the *Express* to the *Guardian*, an action that would be guaranteed to cause ructions in the farming families I've known.

The show became characterised by gentle humour, warmth and wit, avoiding the former tendency to lapse into melodrama. Major storylines emerged from everyday domestic happenings such as Walter Gabriel losing his false teeth and Eddie Grundy being sick in the pub piano. Alright, being sick in a piano isn't so everyday, but you get my drift.

As an intermittent listener, I'd picked up on this as I drove around the English and Welsh countryside in search of stories for the farming press. I thought the changes were brilliant. So, it seems, did many others. Audience research showed a big increase over the previous five years, though it has to be admitted that some of this was the result of moving the weekly omnibus edition back to its popular Sunday morning spot after a disastrous experiment to run it in the evening.

What was beyond dispute was that the show was getting a lot more media attention, more than at any time since the 1950s.

Now I had a chance to help write this iconic British soap, and I couldn't have been happier. To be honest, I didn't expect to be there long. What I knew about story arcs and dramatic tension you could have written on the back of my return train ticket to Birmingham for the monthly script meeting.

My trial episodes had produced a far from enthusiastic response from editor Smethurst, who questioned my ability to use 'the material'. I hadn't been exactly sure what he meant by 'the material' but hadn't wanted to reveal my ignorance by asking.

To say I felt a fraud would be classic English understatement. Even so, I'd somehow got myself on the regular writing team. Perhaps Smethurst believed I was just a slow learner.

Under the system he'd developed, each writer was hired for six months, during which time he or she would write one week's episodes a month. At that time the programme was going out daily from Monday to Friday, which meant you'd write thirty episodes over your six-month stint. At the end of it you'd be chucked off the show for the next half-year.

You might hope to be called back for a further stint, but until then you were free to go trekking in the Himalayas or kayaking up the Orinoco for all anyone in Ambridge cared. Or in my case, chasing after scoops for the farming mags. Still, barring some unforeseen catastrophe, it looked like I'd be writing for *The Archers* at least until the New Year.

I consoled myself with the thought that if that were the end of it, I would at least be able to say I'd been a scriptwriter on the world's most famous radio drama. Maybe *Farmers Weekly* would offer me my own column with my photo at the top.

Realistically, the chances of getting taken on long term

didn't look great. My main asset seemed to be that I could write convincing dialogue for the farming characters. Not surprisingly, I'd absorbed the appropriate vocabulary and speech patterns during the hundreds of hours I'd spent sitting in farmhouse kitchens listening to tales of triumph and woe.

Unfortunately, only about 0.5 per cent of the *Archers* audience were likely to recognise authentic farming dialogue when they heard it. This wasn't the case with police or medical dramas, where long exposure in popular drama had given most people a fair idea what the real thing sounded like. For farming, no one apart from those in the job would know the difference.

To have any hope of lasting on the show I'd need a degree of competence in writing all the characters, not just the farmers. I'd have to feel as comfortable in the company of what I still thought of as posh people like Shula Archer and Caroline Bone as I was with the Grundys in their chaotic farmhouse kitchen. I had serious doubts that I'd ever reach this happy state. But I was determined to give it a go.

As it happens, the programme had just run a story centred on a very posh person, about as posh as you could get – the late Queen's sister, Princess Margaret.

The Princess was president of children's charity the NSPCC, and that summer they were launching a major fundraising campaign. The Duke of Westminster would be attending dinners and receptions across England. The society wrote to the BBC to ask if the villagers of Ambridge might host a dinner and be heard raising money for the cause. It was the sort of publicity request the programme is well used to.

Most get turned down, but the astute editor Smethurst

realised this one might make a great story for two of his favourite characters, Jack Woolley and Caroline Bone (later to become Caroline Sterling). Businessman Jack, owner of Ambridge's Grey Gables Country House Hotel, was fiercely proud of his origins in the working-class district of Stirchley in Birmingham. His ownership of a smart, country hotel was a mark of how far he'd come in life. Welcoming the Duke would give him a real thrill.

Caroline, his PA, was from a different mould. An aristocrat through and through, she was part of the ancient Bohun family of Darrington Manor and a distant relative of Lord Netherbourne. Sensing a PR opportunity, Smethurst wondered if she might also have been a relative of the Duke of Westminster. Extraordinarily enough, this turned out to be the case. The story idea was put to the Duke and he agreed. One of the fundraising events would be set at Ambridge's own Grey Gables.

What nobody had anticipated was that the NSPCC president might want to take a role in the drama – playing herself! So, in May a BBC party – which included actors Sara Coward (Caroline) and Arnold Peters (Jack), two sound engineers and editor Smethurst – set off secretly to Kensington Palace to record the Princess's part in the scene. She played it well, even sounding slightly bored, though no one was sure whether this was great acting or for real.

In the short scene – written by Joanna Toye – Jack was heard being obsequious to Princess Margaret and over-familiar with the Duke of Westminster. Posh Caroline came over as natural and relaxed throughout. As I listened to the scene on-air I felt a touch uncomfortable. I had a nagging suspicion that in those same circumstances I'd have behaved like Jack. To tell the truth, I'd probably have been obsequious with both of them.

Ever since university, I'd thought of myself as some way left of centre in politics. I believed, for example, that there ought to be a tax on land so it would get managed in the public interest and not just for the benefit of landowners. Unfortunately, whenever I found myself in the company of someone with a few thousand acres and a title, my radicalism would vanish like winter snow.

An instinct for deference would take over. I'd be metaphorically tugging my forelock, even as I despised myself for doing it. Where this came from I have no idea, but it's a characteristic I clearly shared with Jack. It seems we both wanted a sprinkling of the magic dust that seems to come with a title and an Eton education.

Returning from university one Christmas, I remember declaring at a family party that I was now a revolutionary socialist. 'Poppycock,' piped up Auntie Rita, my dad's sister. 'You're an inverted snob, that's what you are.' Looking back, I can see she had a point.

Later that autumn, the storyline required me to write a couple of scenes with the same two characters, Woolley and Bone. At the time they were among the most popular characters on the show, and putting them together had been a stroke of genius on Smethurst's part.

Woolley was the archetypal working-class lad made good. He'd grown up in a tough area of Birmingham and left school with few qualifications. He seems to have done well through an innate business ability. Though no one's sure how he made his money, my guess is he ran some sort of metal-bashing factory in the Black Country, bathroom fittings or something like that.

His fortune made, he moved to Ambridge in the early 1960s, buying Grey Gables Country Club. Over the years he turned it into a luxurious hotel, adding an eighteen-hole golf course, a swimming pool and a health club. With characteristic shrewdness, he took on Caroline Bone as his personal assistant. She would bring a touch of class and refinement to the place, something the working-class lad from Stirchley wanted in his new business.

Though I understood Jack well enough, I wasn't so sure about Caroline. What I knew was that after boarding school, she'd completed a course in cookery and hotel management at Lausanne and Paris. For a while she ran a wine bar in Bristol, then returned to Ambridge, where she introduced cordon bleu cooking to the village pub. At Grey Gables Hotel, she had established a special rapport with the hotel's temperamental French chef, Jean-Paul.

With their contrasting backgrounds, Woolley and Bone made a great comic pairing, though I didn't quite get it at first. Then as I wrote them, I started seeing them in the line of celebrated English comedy duos, up there with the Steptoes, father and son; Del Boy and Rodney in *Only Fools and Horses*; Captain Mainwaring and Sergeant Wilson in *Dad's Army*.

The difference was that their exchanges were gentler and less abrasive than between the iconic TV characters. Whereas the TV duos were generally locked in some sort of power struggle, Caroline and Jack's relationship was basically one of mutual affection and respect. The jokes were usually against the working-class Jack, so I suppose I should have taken his side more often. To be honest, the kind Caroline invariably sent him up so gently and affectionately that I was happy to join in the fun.

Here's one of my early encounters with them. The date is 31 October. Halloween. Location: the Gothic-style

Grey Gables Hotel. We're in the hotel ballroom, now decked out as a witch's grotto. In the background the band is warming up, the band being the Tommy Croker Quartet, featuring Tommy on alto sax and vocals. Woolley has been hiring the band for his winter dinner dances for as long as anyone can remember. Their repertoire is mostly from the dance-band era of the 1940s and 50s.

As far as Jack is concerned, Tommy Croker is the best thing that's happened in popular music since Mantovani. The cultured Caroline doesn't share his opinion, though she's careful not to be too brutal in her criticism. She once commented to her friend Shula that the band's greatest talent was their ability to remain a half-beat behind Tommy whenever he launched into a vocal break.

'If they ever caught him up they'd probably all get fired,' the chortling Shula had replied.

Today marks the first of Grey Gables' winter season of dinner dances, and as usual Jack is a touch apprehensive.

WOOLLEY	(IMPRESSED) You've made the place look absolutely wonderful. I think we're in for a night to remember.
BONE	I hope not. That was the *Titanic* film.
WOOLLEY	Oh was it? Why are you smiling?
BONE	I suddenly had this image of Tommy and the band doing their big number, 'In the Mood', just as the ship slips beneath the waves. (BEAT) Sorry, Mr Woolley.
WOOLLEY	Now is everything under control in the kitchen?

BONE	Perfectly. Jean-Paul's walking around with a serene smile on his face.
WOOLLEY	If he's been on the brandy already, he's fired.
BONE	Not that sort of smile. More the smile of a general who knows he's going to win the day.
WOOLLEY	That's what Napoleon thought.
BONE	It'll be fine, don't worry.
WOOLLEY	If you say so, Caroline. Do you know, I haven't had butterflies like this since our visit from royalty.
BONE	Are you happy with the agency waiters?
WOOLLEY	They seem alright. Except for the tall chap with the moustache.
BONE	Oh yes?
WOOLLEY	I'm glad he's not one of our regulars. I get the feeling that it wouldn't be long before he was sitting at my desk and I was waiting on tables.
BONE	Nonsense. He may be something of a showman, but you've got far more natural authority about you. Only you choose to run things with a light touch. So much more clever.
WOOLLEY	Do you think so, Caroline? A light touch, eh? I rather like that.
BONE	Believe me, it's far more effective. No question.

```
WOOLLEY  I suppose it is. Thank you,
         Caroline. Where on earth would
         I be without you?
```

As I listened to this scene on-air a couple of months after I'd written it, I felt a great relief. You never know how a scene's going to work until you hear it played by professionals. I knew the actors would make a decent job of it, but in this scene they had done more. They'd given it great charm by bringing out the characters' real affection for each other. I began to see what Smethurst meant about handling 'the material'.

Dad's Army made a running joke of the tensions between bank manager Mainwaring and the aristocratic Wilson when the army turned the social order on its head. In *Steptoe*, the familial ties that bound father and son together sometimes led to emotional blackmail and the frustration of thwarted ambition. In *The Archers*, characters would often laugh at each other's foibles without the all-too-common put-down. I began to enjoy the gentle style of Ambridge humour.

As it happens, in that same week I had to write scenes with another of Smethurst's comic creations, Nelson Gabriel, played by actor Jack May. Nelson had been around Ambridge for ever. He was the son of Walter Gabriel, the rascally small farmer who was one of the show's original characters. Over the years Nelson's career path took some strange twists and turns, not at all unusual for the early *Archers*.

In the 1950s he joined the RAF and disappeared from Ambridge for a few years. He turned up again in the 1960s and started going out with the young Jennifer Archer. When later she announced she was pregnant, he became the number-one suspect. Not instigated by me, I have to say.

In 1967, he was supposed to have been killed in a plane crash over France. It later transpired that he'd faked his own death. The following year he was put on trial for armed robbery, but to the great relief of his father, he got off. This might all sound a bit far-fetched, but it was a perfectly normal storyline for the old-style *Archers*.

Actor Jack May played Nelson as a suave charmer, running a wine bar and an antique shop. None of us could quite figure out how the son of Walter, the ramshackle old countryman, managed to sound so cultured. We all loved the character, though. He had an air of mystery about him, which gave rise to a good deal of myth-building by the writers.

Two stories I remember in particular. The first was that in his flat over the wine bar, he slept between black silk sheets. This allegation led to some wild speculation at script meetings. The other myth about the character was that he owned a half share in a Borchester massage parlour. I've no way of verifying either of these stories, but knowing Nelson's history, I wouldn't rule them out.

While still a new writer on the show, I got to meet actor Jack May at the BBC's Pebble Mill Studios. Writers were encouraged to sit in on recording sessions from time to time. It was a good way to learn what works in radio drama and what doesn't. You picked up on phrases and word constructions the actors found tricky. Since I was on notice that my time in Ambridge was likely to be short, I thought I'd make the most of the opportunity.

In the green room I met a number of actors who'd gathered for the read-through before moving into the studio for the recording. The only one I remember from the day was Jack. After the most cursory of greetings, he waved his script at me and asked in a tone that I took as a mild rebuke: 'What's the meaning of this word *haulm*?' He uttered the word with such stentorian tones everyone in the room fell silent.

I could feel my cheeks burning. Why the hell had I used the word? Nelson, the character, was neither a farmer nor a gardener, so there's no reason he'd know it. We'd been running a storyline in which Nelson was taking care of his elderly dad's garden, though. Maybe he'd picked it up from his dad. I honestly couldn't remember.

'Sorry,' I said. The way May had asked the question seemed to require an apology. 'It's the stem of a crop. Or a stalk probably. Could be peas or potatoes. Or it could be beans.' I was floundering. 'Anything like that.'

'The stem, you say?'

'Er, yeah. Not just one though. A lot of them. I mean collectively. For the whole crop.' He seemed satisfied with this and put his script down. There was a parting shot though.

'Perhaps we ought to ask the BBC to send us the *Farmers Weekly* with our scripts so we can make some sense of them.'

I was often nervous around actors. They exuded something I'd always been rather short of – confidence. They also had the power to turn words on a page into living, breathing people. Jack May I was particularly nervous around. I knew his face from numerous TV serials along with many films. He'd also played dozens of leading roles in the West End theatre.

Over the years I got to know him better and found him to be kind and an amusing raconteur as well as a great talent. In most of the scenes I wrote for him I put him in his natural setting, the wine bar. The place was fashionably down-at-heel and there was always something cool on the sound system, like Dave Brubeck.

This scene's at a tough time for Nelson. His businesses are struggling. He's decided to risk everything for one last big show. He's giving the wine bar a makeover, ready for the mystery singing star he plans to put on there in a couple of weeks' time.

She'll be a sensation, he tells everyone, bringing in the Borchester socialites in their droves. His dad, Walter, believes the mystery singer is going to be Petula Clark, but Nelson's not letting on, not even to Caroline when she pops in to inspect the refurbishment work.

CAROLINE You've spread those potted palms too thinly. They'd have more impact if you put them together in clumps.

NELSON And where do you suggest I place these thickets?

CAROLINE You could try the side of the stage. Give your artiste a more dramatic entrance.

NELSON I don't want her stepping out of a rainforest. She's not here to advertise antiperspirants.

CAROLINE Palms aren't from rainforests. They're arid plants. What are you planning on doing with the lighting?

NELSON You don't like my wall lights?

CAROLINE They'd be alright in an airport motel. I'd get some of those glass snowdrop things. You know, the ones with the brass stems.

NELSON There's about as much chance of getting a set of those as a chandelier off the *Titanic*.

CAROLINE This place is going to take some filling, Nelson. You must have a lot of confidence in this woman.

NELSON She's got the ageless appeal of all great performers. When she sings, every man feels like he's Errol Flynn.

CAROLINE What about the women?

NELSON They look misty-eyed across the table and see the man they've always dreamed of.

CAROLINE And how are you going to afford this superstar?

NELSON I'm not exactly sure. I only know I have to. I saw her at a Ritz tea dance. She brought the whole thing to a halt with her rendition of 'Singsong Girl of Old Shanghai'.

CAROLINE Gosh, you are smitten. Will she work the same magic in this place though?

NELSON I'm counting on it, Caroline. If she doesn't, it's the end of me in this town.

The singer in question turned out to be a real-life performer whom Smethurst had seen performing at the Ritz.

I'm not sure it was a brilliant career move for her, from the Ritz to Nelson's struggling wine bar in Borchester. She certainly didn't solve Nelson's mounting debt problems. Soon afterwards, he disappeared again, this time to London. We all knew he was far too popular a character to be allowed to stay away for long.

When it came to humour, the show had its own built-in catalyst that we writers could fire up whenever we chose: the Grundy family, comic characters whose purpose was to be sent up. The programme had been designed originally to make the Archer family look good as farmers. They were to be the rural nobility, representing all that's best in English farming. They had to be upright, caring and rock-solid reliable.

The Grundys were there to be none of those things. They were to be greedy, stupid and rubbish farmers, although they could be allowed to have hearts of gold. In fact, it was vital they were loveable. They might be permanently on the make, sometimes bending the rules, but the listeners were to be in no doubt of their fundamental goodness.

It was a formula that had been successful in the show's earliest days. Since this was a drama about a farming community, there had to be a struggling small farmer (or family) who would stand against progress. This was the argument put forward by *Archers* creator Godfrey Baseley, to explain an earlier comic creation, Walter Gabriel.

As well as humour, we English are supposed to love an underdog, especially one who remains spirited and optimistic in the face of impossible odds. It's the bulldog spirit, the oratory of Winston Churchill in the war years. It's Stan Laurel and Captain Mainwaring. In early Ambridge it was also Walter Gabriel – catchphrase 'me old pal, me old beauty'. In his time he was an audience favourite, but by the mid-1980s his comic potential had probably been exhausted. The Grundys – Joe and Eddie – were brought in as the new official underdogs, doubling as jesters in the court of King Phil Archer.

When I moved to Ambridge, Joe had already been knocking around for a few years. It was Smethurst who raised his status to that of comic-in-chief. From the moment I joined the show, I felt I knew him. I'd met so many small farmers struggling to stay in business now the European farm subsidy system had effectively handed over the countryside to the big operators. I had the germ of an idea.

Autumn was the time for farming conferences. Why not have the two biggest wheat growers in the village – Brian Aldridge and Phil Archer – go to a conference on growing premium wheat for the milling trade? At that time the agrochemical companies were making serious money from the cereals boom. They were keen to sponsor these technical events, sometimes providing lavish hospitality as an inducement to big-spending farmers. It was like drug companies putting on flashy events for doctors.

Brian and Phil were certain to get invitations to an event like this. Joe Grundy, with his measly ten acres of wheat, certainly wouldn't. Which set me thinking. What if he was to blag a ticket from somewhere? A knock-off version, perhaps, from one of his mates down at the cattle market. What if he turned up, an uninvited guest? The ramshackle tenant farmer gate-crashing the party for the grain kings, the new masters of the countryside?

I loved it and so would the audience. It was a story to warm the hearts of all but the most hard-hearted. The downtrodden peasant striking a blow against an unfair system.

I set my conference scene during the lunchtime break. Over drinks, Brian is pointing out some of the faces he recognises among the other attendees. They include a couple of Borsetshire's biggest landowners. I was determined to play Joe Grundy's surprise appearance for laughs, which meant highlighting its sheer incongruity.

Looking back at the scene, I definitely missed a trick in not including some mention of Joe's attire. My guess is he was dressed in his old Fair Isle jumper, patched at the elbows (thanks to Clarrie) and with a faint whiff of cow manure. No doubt he'd have had on his well-worn brown corduroys, perhaps for once not held up with baler twine, the plastic cord that's used to tie up hay bales. For this occasion he'd have probably worn a leather belt.

```
JOE     Well, if it ain't the two Ambridge
        corn kings.
BRIAN   (SURPRISED) Joe, this is a surprise!
JOE     (BELLIGERENT) Why, it's a farmer's
        conference, ain't it? I'm a farmer
        too, you know.
PHIL    How are you, Joe?
JOE     As well as can be expected.
        (COUGHING FIT) What with me farmer's
        lung, that is.
BRIAN   So what brings you here, Joe?
JOE     Same as you, I shouldn't wonder.
        Professional development, ain't that
        what they call it?
BRIAN   Well, yes . . .
```

JOE It ain't just for you big fellas, you know. Trousering all them subsidies. When you've only got a small farm like me and Eddie, you've got to keep up to date to stay in business.

PHIL Let me get you a drink, Joe. What is it, a pint?

JOE No, no, I'll get 'em in. I owes you one from a while back.

PHIL It's a free bar.

JOE Oh is it? Who'd have thought it? I'll get 'em in anyway. Can't have you saying we Grundys don't stand our round, can we?

When I wrote this scene I remember wondering if the editor would let it through. It's all about that great English preoccupation, class, a constant source of comedy in *The Archers*. In this case, though, the joke was set in the world of farmers and farming. Would the verbal tussle between the working-class tenant farmer Joe and the two big land-owning farmers be a little too subtle for our non-farming boss?

I needn't have worried. The scene went through unchanged. I had no doubt our regular listeners would get it: the Grundys – Joe, Eddie and Clarrie – could always be relied on to add humour to an episode. They were a sort of comic default mechanism, playing on the English enthusiasm for seeing the pompous and the self-important brought down. You could always rely on a Grundy story to brighten up an episode.

*

When I joined the show almost every scene had to be written with a comic touch. Humour had become deeply embedded in the whole drama, which accounted for its new rise in popularity.

As Kate Fox says, humour is the default mode of the English. It's like breathing: we can't function without it.

I must have grasped this when I wrote an early scene with the two Archers sisters, Shula and Elizabeth, their father Phil, and the vet, Martin Lambert, who'd just finished taking blood samples from the cows. At the time Shula's lawyer boyfriend, Mark, was away working in Hong Kong, leading to speculation from her mischief-making sister that she'd got her eye on Martin.

Earlier they'd learned that Martin had helped out a woman who'd unexpectedly gone into labour. This was enough comic inspiration to set Elizabeth off.

ELIZABETH	You vets still get out on farms, then? You're not too busy helping out the NHS?
SHULA	Ignore my sister. She's going through a difficult phase.
ELIZABETH	Have you looked at Graham Collard's leg? He fell off his motorbike, did he tell you?
PHIL	Give Martin some peace to drink his coffee.
MARTIN	It's OK, I'm used to it.
ELIZABETH	Think of the cash the NHS would save if they sent their appendicitis patients to the vet.
SHULA	She can't help it, poor thing.

MARTIN Actually it's not such a daft idea. Most vets do far more surgery than the average doctor.

ELIZABETH (MOCK SURGEON) How many on the list today, sister? Let's see . . . Two torn udders and a tractor driver with a hernia.

MARTIN All in a day's work. Humans are just one more species.

It was a great time to be writing for *The Archers*. Smethurst's idea of reimagining the show as a social comedy was giving it a new lease of life. There seemed to be a growing audience for a soap in which the dialogue was liberally spiced with humour. Kate Fox thinks that the English obsession with humour arises from the awkwardness many of us feel in our dealings with other people. She calls it 'the English social disease'.

I'm not sure I go along with that. I like to think of humour as a way of defusing conflict. If we can smile at each other's foibles, we don't have to get into fights over them. What I can say is I loved writing the Ambridge characters in this gentle and affectionate way. To me it was far more appealing than the aggressive, in-your-face writing style I'd got used to as a farming journo.

I had other ambitions for my time on the programme, even if, as I thought then, my stint in Ambridge was destined to be short. Somehow, I'd acquired a passable knack for writing comedy. Now it was time to play my ace card. Humour would continue as the default mood of my episodes, but I'd sprinkle them with even more stories from the world I knew best. It would be playing to my strength. It's what had got me onto the show in the first place, apart from my invention of the Elizabeth character.

If asked, the production team would always insist that farming was at the heart of the programme. But I knew from the script meetings that it wasn't a subject of great interest. A token farming storyline every couple of months was thought to be enough.

Not for me. I had this theory that even in urban societies like ours, there's a deep-down desire in many of us to reconnect to the land which has sustained us throughout our human story. After all, not many of us are more than a few generations away from working the land, wherever our families are from. If I was right, the audience would respond to storylines that took them deep inside the world I knew, from my journalist days, to be full of drama.

That's what had made *The Archers* a massive hit show within months of its launch back in the 1950s. For as long as I remained on the programme, I would do my best to take it back to its roots. In my episodes at least, farming would once more move centre stage.

4

The Eternal Round

ON A WARM SUMMER evening, a tractor tows a laden farm trailer along a quiet country lane. Whoever built the load has done an expert job. There are nearly 200 hay bales of the small, rectangular sort stacked on the low-slung trailer, making a heap nearly five metres high. Though it looks solid enough, no one's taking any chances. It's been lashed down with ropes so no sudden lurch will bring the whole lot tumbling down.

If that were to happen it wouldn't be too healthy for the two young people riding on the top. Elizabeth Archer and Nigel Pargetter lie stretched out on the hay, gazing up through the twilight foliage into a darkening sky. All afternoon and evening they've been labouring on the Brookfield hay harvest. Now they're riding the last load home.

EXT. LANE NEAR BROOKFIELD.
TUESDAY 9.45PM. (TRACTOR ENGINE)

ELIZABETH	What's the bright star up there? To the left of the moon.
NIGEL	That'll be Jupiter.

ELIZABETH (SURPRISED) Really? You know that?

NIGEL Quite soon we should see Antares. It's a red supergiant in Scorpius constellation.

ELIZABETH Wow! That's impressive.

NIGEL I used to be into all that sort of stuff. Mummy bought me a telescope one Christmas. She thought I was spending too much time reading *Viz*. She wanted me to set my eyes on more heavenly things.

ELIZABETH And did you?

NIGEL For a bit. Unfortunately, I took it back to school with me. My chums wanted to use it to spy on couples in the park. The thing got confiscated in the end.

ELIZABETH You got it back?

NIGEL Eventually. It's up in the attic somewhere.

ELIZABETH And here's me thinking you were all gorilla suits and point-to-points. You're quite a Renaissance man on the quiet.

NIGEL Keep it to yourself, eh, Lizzie? My reputation would be shot down the polo club.

ELIZABETH Well anyway, I'm really grateful. Helping us out with the hay-making. Dad gets a bit wound up at this time of the

	year. 'Specially when the forecast's iffy.
NIGEL	Glad to be of service.
ELIZABETH	We had quite a crowd in the end. What with Eddie and Joe.
NIGEL	To be honest, I enjoyed it. Getting the bales stacked. Everyone mucking in. Joe's cider went down pretty well too.
ELIZABETH	Yeah, I noticed.
NIGEL	Can't let the old traditions die, can we? Cider for the hay-makers. Like that other old custom your dad was telling me about. Midsummer in the hay meadow.
ELIZABETH	Oh yeah, Granddad used to talk about it.
NIGEL	Apparently if you had your eye on someone . . . a young woman. That's when you'd let her know you were interested. You'd give her . . .
ELIZABETH	. . . a bunch of wild thyme. Yes, I remember him saying. <u>(TUFT OF HAY PULLED FROM BALE)</u>
NIGEL	How about a bunch of fresh hay? Think that might do the trick?
ELIZABETH	(SOFTLY) I don't know. It might do . . . possibly. (THEY KISS)

Riding the last load home got to be a habit with me on the farm where I worked in the 1960s. It was near the Thames-side village my parents had moved to around the time I was at university in North Wales. Most vacations, I'd join the regular staff as a casual worker. This coincided with busy times like the hay-making. After a day heaving bales about, I'd climb up on top of the load for the ride back to the barn. The regulars thought I was nuts.

Though no one worried about the safety implications in those days, Tim, the foreman, was suspicious. He assumed I'd be sitting up there rolling joints. Once I'd assured him the day's harvest wouldn't be going up in smoke, he withdrew his objection. With a look of amused bewilderment, he watched as I clambered up the back of the load, grasping for hand holds between the bales.

There was something magical about being up there on the sweet-smelling hay, fusion of earth and summer sunshine, looking up at the lights going on in a wide universe.

After many hours of hard physical work – sometimes in blazing sunshine – I always felt pleasantly fatigued. At the same time, my senses seemed alive to a heightened degree. There was a satisfaction in knowing I'd been part of a process that had engaged human beings for about five thousand years, probably since the first farmers herded their cattle across the open grasslands at the start of Britain's pastoral story.

It was the kind of timeless experience that work on the land sometimes provides. It's as if, in those moments, you stand outside the everyday flow of events. You become part of something everlasting. Some of those moments remain vivid in my memory.

Feeding hay to cattle or sheep on a cold, clear winter

morning is one of them. For some inexplicable reason, the sight of animals contentedly munching – their breath hanging in white clouds on the frosty air – is both calming and reassuring. All's well with the world.

Then there's the pleasure of leading cows to spring pasture for the first time after they've spent the winter months inside. If you've never watched an elderly dairy cow dance for the sheer joy of sunshine, grass and freedom, I'd definitely recommend it for the bucket list.

Ploughing isn't approved of these days. It's considered to be damaging to soil life. But in my view, it still has its place. Few jobs on the farm are more satisfying than watching the furrows turn as lapwings dive in to feast on the subterranean harvest.

Perhaps more than any of these, I'd recommend a night in the lambing shed. In our relationship with animals, there's surely no better way to experience the wonder and the sadness of the journey we're all on together.

I wanted to work moments like these into my scripts and storylines. I'm not sure my writer colleagues agreed. They took the view that the audience wanted drama rather than 'atmosphere'. Soaps are meant to be story-driven, they reminded me. Every scene should move the narrative on.

I didn't see *The Archers* quite like that. Rather than constantly rushing to get somewhere else, our listeners might sometimes want to linger in the lane, looking at the hedgerow flowers or smelling the wild honeysuckle. Maybe even to reflect on the bigger drama we're all part of. After all, the programme was about people whose day-to-day business dealings were with endless cycles of death and decay, renewal and growth.

The first *Archers* audiences were certainly interested in such matters. The experience of war had raised them in the national consciousness. The countryside and its communities were among the things we were supposed to have been fighting for. They were common themes for many writers, artists and songwriters.

The surprise bestselling book of 1944 was the story of a small farm on the edge of the Cotswold Hills. Called *The Farming Ladder*, it sold over 100,000 copies and ran to thirteen editions. Many of those who bought the book were young servicemen and women who dreamed of getting their own farms and smallholdings after the war. Author George Henderson and his brother Frank had done just that after the First World War. George's book explaining how they'd done it proved inspirational to a later generation. I was one of them.

It was only a few years later that the BBC launched its ground-breaking new soap. Here was a drama in which farmers were the heroes. Listeners were invited to eavesdrop on the daily lives of people whose worries and concerns extended to their land, their crops and their animals, as well as to family and friends.

In those days no one questioned the farming scenes. In the wake of the turmoil and upheaval of war, people wanted the reassurance of a world where things went on in much the same way as they'd always done. *The Archers* had unwittingly occupied this space. Its creators had set out to entertain and provide information to farmers, but they'd tapped into something far deeper, an unspoken national desire to connect with the eternal.

For me, springtime scenes in the lambing sheds became as much a seasonal regular as the summer flower and produce show and Christmas carols in St Stephen's Church. When David and Ruth Archer took their cows out to pasture at the end of the winter, they'd invariably lean on the field gate for a few moments and enjoy the sight of mature cows running around like young calves in an ecstasy of freedom.

While go-ahead farmers like Adam Macy were experimenting with new ways of getting seeds into the ground without ploughing – the no-till drill, for example – I'd have retired farmworker Bert Fry indulging his lifelong love of ploughing (and mine) by entering the Borchester and district ploughing competition. It was a timeless symbol of renewal that I believed should still be in the show.

It's why I never missed the chance to bring in haymaking and the last load home. Here's part of an exchange between David Archer and incomer Lynda Snell when they meet on a bridleway at Brookfield Farm. David explains that until he and Ruth created the new farm tracks across the fields, the bridleway provided their main access to Midsummer Meadow, which was sometimes cut for hay.

'Now then, there should be a ditch in here somewhere . . .' says David. 'Yeah, there it is, a bit overgrown. This is where it happened.'

'Where what happened?' Lynda wants to know.

'I'll never forget it. It was the last load of the day, and I was riding up on top. As usual. I suppose I must have been about twelve or thirteen.'

'Rather dangerous I'd have thought?'

'Oh yeah. Totally against health and safety. We hadn't roped it down particularly well either. You know what it's like at the end of a long day.'

'You must have been exhausted.'

'Jethro Larkin was on the tractor. He took the bend a little bit too tight. Managed to drop the two right-hand wheels in the ditch, and down came the top three layers with me in the middle.'

'You survived, obviously.'

'Yeah, a few bruises, that's all. Jethro pulled me out. White as a sheet, he was. Poor chap.'

'Well, I hope you learned the lesson?'

'Do you know, Lynda, I'm not sure I did. I was back riding on the top the very next day, if I remember.'

'Oh, David.' Lynda finds David's actions incomprehensible. 'But why?'

'This is going to sound crazy, but I felt I had to. A way of saying thanks, I suppose. For the hay crop. It's funny, I've never really thought of myself as particularly religious.'

'It's rather touching.'

'There's something else about hay. Sometimes when you're feeding it in the middle of winter, you can be knee-deep in snow, feeding it to a bunch of ewes, and as soon as you break open the bale and get that smell of summer sunshine, it's like you're back there on top of the load. Now you will think I'm crazy.'

'Not at all. I think you're a bit of a poet on the quiet.'

'Really? Don't tell Pip. She'll think I'm ready for a retirement home.'

I hoped moments like this might bring to mind an older story of farming. I also made sure the modern developments were in the mix too, especially when they offered new locations for scene-setting. Here's one during the cereals' harvest at Home Farm:

INT. HOME FARM. COMBINE HARVESTER.
WEDNESDAY 4.30PM.
(COMBINE CUTTING WHEAT)

IAN You must feel like Captain Kirk sitting up here. Surrounded by all this technology.

ADAM (DRIVING) No warp drive, unfortunately. It's got pretty much everything else though.

IAN What's on the screen?

ADAM That one? Crop yield. Moisture content. Plus the running field total. All linked to satellite tracking.

IAN Amazing.

ADAM At the end of the day I can download all the data onto my laptop.

IAN What about *Match of the Day*? Can you get that?

ADAM No, unfortunately. Not a bad little workstation though, is it?

IAN It's great. Countryside views. Music on demand. A cool box for your sarnies. Five-star luxury, I'd say.

To be honest, I was never particularly keen on dialogue like this. It's the kind of wide-eyed enthusiasm you sometimes get in TV documentaries on agriculture. It takes me back to my years writing for the farming press, where you're constantly trying to enthral readers with some gadget that'll make their lives easier or provide them with more profit. It often turns out differently.

I eventually came to the conclusion that most new technologies were for the benefit of suppliers rather than their customers, the farmers. To me, they were a distraction from the real business of agriculture, which was about making the best use of resources given freely by nature – sunlight, rain and soil. No smart technology was going to make a farm successful if these fundamentals were wrong.

At the same time, I realised new technologies needed to be in the show every so often. Sending Pip Archer off to look at robotic milking machines or having Adam Macy use drones to inspect his wheat crop were stories we needed to carry. Besides, I was protecting my back. The last thing I wanted was for one of the producers to hear of some new development on *Farming Today* or *Countryfile* and wonder why it hadn't been on *The Archers*.

I didn't overdo the techie stories though. I preferred to concentrate on that bigger tale, our engagement with the natural world. To me, it was endlessly fascinating, the proper business of a rural drama. Those things that don't change from age to age. The eternal round, never better summarised than in those lines of Thomas Hardy:

Only a man harrowing clods
In a slow silent walk
With an old horse that stumbles and nods
Half asleep as they stalk.

Only thin smoke without flame
From the heaps of couch-grass;
Yet this will go onward the same
Though Dynasties pass.

It was Hardy's writings which, in a roundabout way, led me to Ambridge. I started reading his novels as an agricultural student, though it was a film that first got me into it, John Schlesinger's 1967 version of *Far from the Madding Crowd*. I went with a couple of other agri-students to see it at Bangor's City Cinema. I wasn't the only one to fall instantly in love with Julie Christie.

We felt we had a special connection with Bathsheba, a woman trying to make her way in a countryside that was overwhelmingly male-dominated. We all recognised that place. Socially, nothing much had changed since Hardy's time. Farming was still overwhelmingly male and white.

Schlesinger's film, with its sumptuous portrayal of the Dorset countryside, made me realise that the landscape itself could become a character in a drama. I'd never thought about it before, but in the film it was clear. By setting the lives and loves of your characters in scenery of such beauty and grandeur, you transform a plain tale into an epic.

Inspired by the film, I started reading Hardy's novels. The landscape was there in all of them – *Tess*, *The Mayor of Casterbridge*, *The Return of the Native*, even *Jude the Obscure*. It helped that at the time I had an English student as a girlfriend. We didn't have many conversations about farming, but I do remember a heated discussion over the symbolism of Egdon Heath.

By this time, I was working as a postgraduate on a research project at Bangor University farm. It was a grassland study that involved a number of experimental sites, some of them in the mountains of Snowdonia. Clad in my all-weather gear, I'd spend many hours gathering growth data among the rocky crags while buffeted by winds off the Irish Sea. I started to see myself as the star of my own Hardy-esque epic.

Sadly, I also had to spend many hours in the computer lab trying to make sense of the data, for me a rather less appealing pastime. After the freedom of data-gathering, my life became one long frustration of punch cards and error messages. It took me weeks to process material that Adam Macy would one day be analysing on his phone in seconds.

I decided I'd had enough of academic life. It was time to immerse myself in the real world of farming, particularly the traditional kind – that's if any remnant of it still remained. I slammed off a letter to the secretary of the Dorset branch of the National Farmers' Union asking if any of their members might be brave enough to take me on.

I had some theoretical knowledge, I explained, but not a great deal of practical experience. To a working farmer it was hardly an irresistible offer. Fine if they'd wanted to get to grips with the comparative photosynthetic efficiency of Italian ryegrass, but I'd yet to meet a farmer who was remotely interested. It came as something of a surprise to get a call from a farmer willing to take me on. Even more amazing, he was prepared to pay me!

The farm was close to a village about halfway between Dorchester and Blandford Forum. The very heart of Hardy's Wessex. It was mostly on stony, chalk soils, which in earlier times would have been known as 'hungry', meaning they were not particularly fertile. In pre-chemical days they'd have relied on sheep grazing to keep them productive.

I loved the place from the day I started. Though the fields were large, there were plenty of hedgerows. There were also extensive beech woods close to the farmhouse and the cottage where I lived. The owner, Bill, was a third-generation farmer on a farm of around a thousand acres, which was big for the early 1970s. His grandfather, a butcher, had bought the place in the 1920s when land was cheap following the price collapse after the First World War.

Bill farmed it in much the same way as his grandfather, and probably in much the same way as it had been farmed in Hardy's time. The main objective was to retain and recycle nutrients so the thin, stony soils would remain fertile without the need for too many expensive chemicals. The technology had changed, of course. Tractors had replaced draught horses and a combine harvester had done away with the need for the steam-powered threshing machine.

Even so, the principle of retaining fertility in the soil was the same as it had been for centuries. It was never an easy way to farm. You needed grasslands and grazing animals along with your arable fields growing wheat and barley. The benefits included being largely self-sufficient, so you didn't fall for the blandishments of fertiliser companies or feed reps.

This was Bill's philosophy. He was skilled at his job and fiercely independent. At that moment in farming history, he needed to be. All around him the world was changing fast. Governments had led the way with their farm subsidies. Sensing a killing to be made, an army of business consultants, banks and chemical reps swooped in like gulls following the plough.

There was a lot of hype about the new chemical methods doing away with the need for traditional rotations. Advisers who'd never grown so much as a carrot in their entire lives stood up at conferences and told farmers they had to be more business-minded. Farming was no longer a way of life, they informed their audiences.

The old ways were no longer fit for the modern age. The tried-and-tested systems had to be abandoned. The nation needed farms to specialise and become efficient and competitive. This basically meant reinventing themselves as large animal factories or prairie-style crop farms, both of which required heavy investment in buildings, machinery and chemicals. Bill recognised it for what it was: marketing hype. He also knew he was up against powerful forces.

The UK was soon to enter the European Common Market, as it was then called. There would be guaranteed prices for farmers, so land prices were predicted to rise. Pension funds and insurance companies became interested in farms for their investment portfolios. Some of Bill's neighbours were already thinking of selling, but he was having none of it. He would go on farming his land in the way nature decreed for as long as he was able.

I worked on that farm for the best part of a year and I'm still grateful to the unknown NFU secretary who passed on my details. Had he or she known of my interest in Hardy? I hadn't mentioned it in my letter. Now I worked in a setting where you almost expected to see Bathsheba Everdene in her sprung-cart coming to check on your work.

I'd been taken on to look after the beef cattle and most days I knew what needed to be done. Even so, I was expected to appear in the yard at seven-thirty each morning along with tractor driver George, a Dorset native in his mid-fifties. In the time-honoured routine, the boss would come down and give us our daily orders.

George himself might have stepped straight out of a

Hardy novel. He usually turned up wearing gaiters, the lower-leg covering you see in sepia photographs of harvest workers in the early 1900s. He spoke in staccato sentences like bursts from an automatic rifle. They made every utterance sound like an admonishment. But I soon found this impression was wrong. He was a kind and gentle man, generous in sharing his considerable knowledge.

Though he was as sharp as a tack, highly skilled in many farm trades, I discovered he could neither read nor write. He lived in a farm cottage with his elderly mother, whose accent was so thick I had trouble understanding her. George had a fund of stories about the sort of characters you never read about in the glossy country magazines: country men and women who pulled pints, pumped out septic tanks, trapped moles and travelled round the villages treating corns and bunions.

The stories seemed to tumble out of him, liberally laced with irony and expletives, but invariably delivered with humour. Many of his tales, at least the cleaned-up versions, were destined to get an airing years later in lines spoken by Jethro Larkin, Bill Insley, Bert Fry and Joe Grundy. I owe much to that kind and talented man. His stories were the life-blood of his rural community.

How long he was able to stay on that farm I never knew. Farming was changing fast and for all his talents he'd never have found employment among the technocrats of the new-style agribusiness farms.

The other full-time worker on the farm was Dick, the shepherd. He was one of the last of a legendary group known as the 'downland shepherds'. They made up a sort of aristocracy among farm staff, managing the sheep flocks that kept the thin chalk soils fertile and productive before the age of chemicals. Dick wasn't expected to wait in the yard for his orders each day. He was left alone to get on with caring for what the boss thought of as the farm's main asset, its flock of pedigree Dorset Down sheep.

Shepherds like Dick could trace their craft back to the Neolithic livestock herders, the first farmers to manage the downlands. He mostly worked on his own, though George and I were sometimes asked to give him a hand at busy times such as lambing. It was a humbling experience to watch him at work in his calm, methodical way, always showing care and kindness in the way he handled the animals in his charge.

Thinking back, I can see his influence in many of the scenes I wrote around the handling of farm animals. When farmer Ruth Archer trimmed the feet of a lame cow or vet Alistair Lloyd dealt with a difficult calving, the patience and care they showed was due in part to the Dorset shepherd I'd known many years earlier.

Running the whole glorious enterprise was Farmer Bill, who, it's fair to say, represented the old style of land managers. He didn't have much time for what you'd call the scientific approach to farming, the sort I'd been preoccupied with during my five years at uni. It wasn't that he rejected science. He simply believed it had been taken over by commercial interests with products to sell. I was inclined to agree with him.

To Bill, scientific agriculture usually meant having to buy stuff – new machines, imported animal feeds, chemical fertilisers, and pesticides. You'd probably be required to put up fancy buildings and spread acres of concrete. There'd be business consultants and advisers to pay, and the chances were you'd end up with a far bigger debt with the bank.

He was convinced that if you ran a balanced farming

system with grazing animals as well as crops, you didn't need any of these things to make a decent profit. If you took care of your soil, nature would provide: that was his philosophy.

I worked on his farm for a little under a year. In that time I learned more about real farming than in my five years at uni. I learned, for example, that proper farming didn't mean the obliteration of wildlife. Like the farms around our council estate back in the 1950s, this Dorset farm was teeming with life.

In spring, the hedgerows were alive with songbirds, small mammals and grey partridges. In the fields, hares were a common sight, and the only time I've been up close and personal with a barn owl was on that farm. I'd climbed to the top of the hay store to throw down a few winter bales for the cattle. That's when we came face to face, the owl and I. I'm not sure which of us was the more surprised.

That farm became the yardstick against which I judged the many I would visit as a working journalist. Though Bill would have been horrified at the thought, he'd set the bar for British farming as far as I was concerned. More than a decade later, he was to become my model for Ambridge's leading farmer, Phil Archer of Brookfield. Later, when Phil's son David took over at Brookfield, he too became a version of Farmer Bill.

In the summer of 1972, I left the seemingly unchanging world of that Dorset farm to join the forces gathering to put it out of business. Not that I realised it at the time. I thought by working on the country's top farming publication I'd get to see and write about a lot more farms like Bill's. The bitter truth was that I'd soon be helping to bring about their downfall.

Farmers Weekly was part of a business empire located in Fleet Street, still the heart of the newspaper industry in those days. Though we farming journos liked to think of ourselves as fearless chasers after truth, in reality our job was to sell products for our biggest-spending advertisers who, at the time, were fertiliser companies, tractor manufacturers, animal feed compounders and the fast-growing pesticide industry.

Our advertisers were about to enjoy their greatest bonanza in years, which would mean boom times for magazines like ours. To collect the generous new European grants and subsidies, farmers had to go flat out for maximum production. Talk over the farm gate switched from food to 'yields per acre' or, for dairy farmers, 'yields per cow'. From now on it was quantity not quality that mattered. Dairy farmers began expanding their herds and breeding high-yield 'super cows'. Arable farmers enlarged their fields, bought bigger machines and spread more chemical fertilisers.

The countryside was under attack, with hedges pulled out, wetlands drained, orchards grubbed up and woodlands felled. To farmers like Bill, my old boss, who believed there was a right way to take care of the land, it must have seemed as if the very laws of the universe were being overturned.

In *The Archers*, a new character was introduced to represent the new breed of agribusiness farmers, his name Brian Aldridge. I can't say I took to him, particularly when I found out his backstory. It seems he'd inherited the family farm in Hertfordshire on the death of his parents, then promptly sold it, using the cash to buy Home Farm in Ambridge, about 1,500 acres.

He was twenty-eight years old, with no mortgage to pay, and he'd become the biggest landowner in the village. He set about transforming the place into what he saw as an efficient farm. The village archives show that no farmer in Ambridge ripped out more hedges, felled more trees or filled in more ponds than Brian Aldridge. Like many of his generation, he had something of a change of heart in later life. He attempted to make some sort of amends by planting new woods and hedges, but none of it made up for what had been lost.

In his own way, Brian was a likeable enough character, a charming family man as well as a serial philanderer. My main interest was in the way he looked after his land. Knowing his history, I tried, where possible, to highlight the rapacious side of his character despite his mellowing in later life.

I couldn't escape the feeling he ought somehow to be made to pay for the damage he caused. Thirty years later I came up with a storyline inspired by Hardy. Like Michael Henchard, the Mayor of Casterbridge, a long-forgotten 'indiscretion' from the past would come back to haunt him.

For now, he was wreaking havoc in the Ambridge countryside, even as something similar was happening across the real British countryside. I'd seen first-hand how good farming could create a landscape of intense beauty; a treasury of natural riches. Now I was reporting on the destruction of age-old landscapes and an ancient English culture. As a farming journalist I was supposed to spin it as a great national enterprise, something the whole country could be proud about.

I tried writing articles on organic farming, but the features editor told me advertisers found them annoying. The *Weekly*, he informed me, believed in scientific agriculture, not 'muck and mystery'. I told him that the science he had in mind was paid for by the agro-chemical corporations. The comment didn't go down well.

I went to interview a pioneer organic farmer called Barry Wookey on his farm in Wiltshire. He told me of a particularly good wheat crop he'd grown a couple of years earlier. He'd been so proud of it that he'd stuck a hand-painted sign in the middle, easily visible to passing traffic. It declared no chemicals had been used to grow the crop. A fertiliser company rep who happened to pass by was so incensed that he called at the farm to remonstrate with the farmer. 'You've no right to make a claim like that,' he raged, 'it's obviously false.'

I knew it wasn't false. I'd worked for a farmer who knew perfectly well how to grow a decent crop without chemicals. It was the gift of a fertile soil, as farmers down the ages had known. Now many were buying into the myth that the earth unaided couldn't support us. I realised it was time to say goodbye to *Farmers Weekly* and my company Ford Cortina.

In the mid-1970s I moved from London to a small rented cottage in a village, half-hidden in the folds of the Wiltshire downs, near Stonehenge. I would still report what was happening in the English countryside, but to a broader audience. This time I would write the whole, shocking truth.

On my portable Olivetti typewriter, I banged off a series of features for *New Scientist* magazine. I alerted the science world to how European farm subsidies were fuelling a rush into high-input wheat growing at the expense of valuable wildlife habitats. Next, I blew the whistle on the use of growth hormones in beef production. Then, in a feature called 'Poor Cow', I warned the British public that cereal grains fed to dairy cows were making them sick and lame.

The British public didn't seem that interested. The global animal feed industry was, though. The chief executive of one of the biggest companies in the business cornered me at a press event and proceeded to tear me off a strip. Though he didn't contest my facts, he told me my article had 'let the industry down'.

I told him his products were causing cows to go lame; that's what had let the industry down. I wasn't bothered by the exchange. I'd been standing up for proper farms like Bill's in Dorset. I was starting to wonder, though, if I'd ever make a living writing this politically loaded stuff. This was the moment fate took a hand in the shape of an unlikely country-and-western singer called Eddie Grundy.

For farming journos like me, the high point in the seasonal calendar was the annual Royal Show, which took place each summer in Warwickshire. For the best part of a week, a stretch of quiet parkland was transformed into a city of marquees, wooden villas and trade stands. Almost every company in the business of selling stuff to farmers had a presence there, together with linked organisations like the Ministry of Agriculture and the farmers' unions.

Sunday was press preview day before the show opened to the public on Monday morning. The year was 1983 and I'd had a hectic day hunting down science stories. In the evening I turned up for the annual bash put on for the media. The format didn't change much – a buffet supper, a steel band and an endless supply of free booze. This year there was an added attraction – a twenty-minute comic turn from someone I'd never seen but recognised instantly.

He had long hair, a cheeky grin and a wide-brimmed hat with a couple of goats' horns sticking out of the top. It was a form of headgear made legendary by my comic-book hero from boyhood, Desperate Dan. There was only one person I knew to be wearing anything like this today.

In Ambridge, Eddie Grundy – or to give him his real name, actor Trevor Harrison – had once sung 'The Cowboy's Farewell to his Horse' at the vicar's Songs of Praise in St Stephen's Church. Now he had a record to plug and the press party at Britain's number-one farming show seemed like an appropriate place to launch it.

I'm not sure if he'd been warned, but there was a fair chance he'd get a frosty reception. We farming hacks could be a cynical bunch. We were used to mainstream journalists looking down their noses at what they thought of as the 'trade press'. There was every possibility my colleagues would view this promotion by a BBC radio soap star as patronising.

In the event, Eddie went down a storm. This may have been related to the fact that many of us had poured a fair bit of alcohol down our necks, but it was also due to the sheer warmth of his personality. He told a couple of passable jokes, delivering them with a gusto that was disarming.

He grinned a lot and declared his undying love for Clarrie, his Ambridge wife. She was the true reason for his appearance at the Royal, he explained. She'd been disappointed not to be there with him, but she'd had to stay at home to look after the kids and ferrets.

He told us how she'd been the inspiration behind his latest record release, which he was there to plug. We were all given a copy – 'Poor Pig' coupled with 'Clarrie'. The latter included the immortal line: 'She's my Venus de Milo; and what's more, she's got arms.'

I wasn't sure if 'Clarrie' or 'Poor Pig' was the 'A' side,

but it didn't really matter. We were told the record had gone straight into the chart at number one. We're talking here about the local chart in fictional Borchester. This was mostly governed by sales through the music section of Underwoods department store. There's no evidence the disc charted anywhere else in the UK.

At the end of his turn, I got Eddie to sign the record sleeve. I told him I thought the hat with horns was a great touch, if somewhat wasted on the radio.

'It was William's idea,' said Eddie, 'William Smethurst. The editor. The man's a genius.'

I told him how much I enjoyed the Grundy characters, Eddie, Clarrie and Joe. 'It's great to hear rebel voices on Radio Four,' I said, 'even if they don't really exist.'

'You're right,' he replied. 'It's them Archers. Taken over the world, they have. We hate 'em, me and Dad. We've got to stop 'em, eh?'

We both laughed and he turned away to talk to other fans. I felt elated and more than a touch star-struck. It was a year before I was to write my trial episodes for the programme, a possibility that hadn't yet entered my head. But I'd had a chance to meet a leading character from my favourite radio show. Given the choice, it was the character I'd have most wanted to meet.

In their comic way, the Grundys spoke for that forgotten English archetype, the peasant. Small tenant farmers like Joe and Eddie were, for me, direct descendants of the English peasantry. Over the past five centuries we (I liked to think of myself as one of them) had lost our land rights, or rather, we'd had them taken away, making us what we are today: basically the landless working class.

You might say the Grundys spoke for us council-house kids and our legitimate interests in the countryside. Our rights to good food and an unpolluted, wildlife-rich environment. As I headed back to my B&B in a residential block at nearby Warwick University, the idea grew on me. Here was the real reason Eddie and Joe had it in for the Archers. They'd been victims of the great ruling-class land grab.

Though I couldn't know it at the time, a few years later I'd have a chance to pick up this radical theme and develop it within one of Britain's most popular cultural institutions, very subtly of course. The Grundys would have to go on playing it for laughs, but I'd make sure there was a bitter edge to their mirth.

Basically, I'd be returning *The Archers* to what its original fans wanted it to be – the story of ordinary working people in village England. And leading the charge would be my new friend, Eddie Grundy.

5

Cows, Conflict and Fruitcake

IT WAS NEW YEAR'S DAY 2016, the sixty-fifth anniversary of the world's longest-running radio drama. Fans and critics alike were expecting a new and dramatic storyline. Soaps were in the habit of marking milestone episodes with sensational events like plane crashes or gas explosions.

Even if some catastrophe wasn't being planned for Ambridge, there'd surely be a major twist in one of the ongoing storylines. Would there be an explosion of a different sort as Helen Titchener finally broke free from the coercive control of her sinister husband, Rob? Would Ruth Archer, back from her extended visit to New Zealand, tell husband David their marriage was over?

Editor Sean O'Connor did nothing to dampen the speculation. In an interview he told the *Radio Times* he was 'ruling nothing in and ruling nothing out'. As an afterthought, he added that it would be 'completely different from any show's anniversary episode ever, and a defining one for *The Archers*'.

When the episode finally aired, everyone got a big surprise. There was no doom or destruction. Instead, most of the episode was devoted to a discussion on dairy farming.

When Sean had asked me to write it, he'd laid down a few basics. He wanted the entire episode set at Brookfield, the drama's central farm. It was also to feature all three generations of the family: Jill, the matriarch, her son David and his wife Ruth, plus their daughter Pip, representing the new generation.

Equally important, the theme of the episode was to be linked to farming. In a real sense we'd be taking *The Archers* back to its roots. In 1950, when the BBC began its trial run of the series, the first conversation took place in a cowshed and involved farmer Dan Archer and farmworker Simon Cooper.

To the sound of a mooing cow, Dan asks: 'Well, Simon, what do you think?'

'Ah well –'er might and 'er mightn't,' is Simon's reply. The first ever eavesdroppers in Ambridge were to be left in suspense about how long dairy cow Daffodil's labour would last.

On New Year's Day the following year, when the show went nationwide, the first scene was also set at Brookfield Farm. It, too, featured generations of the same Archer family – Dan and Doris, their sons Philip and Jack, and their daughter Christine. This time we were listening in to a family New Year's Eve party.

The announcer introduced the characters as 'children of the soil, and like most workaday folk they have their joys and troubles'. At the end of the scene, Dan proposed a toast to 'the coming year'.

'May we all go on being as happy and united a family as we've been up to now, and may the weather be a bit kinder to all farmers.'

Reading the old scripts, I realised the programme's creators had been incredibly daring. The BBC already had a successful radio drama series in the spy thriller *Dick Barton – Special Agent*. This had pioneered features that were to become soap hallmarks, such as the 'hook' at the end of each episode. The *Archers* team decided to apply the same techniques, not to an adventure series, but to a domestic drama set in an English village.

What was destined to become Britain's most successful drama series ever had stuck a marker in the ground. It was to be about farming and family. Sixty-five years later, I was following the path set by those early writers. The least I could do was make certain this special episode remained true to their vision.

The first creative team had offered listeners something priceless in that austere, post-war nation of bomb sites and family tragedy – the comfort of being part of an unchanging community in the English countryside.

This spirit was captured in a famous *Radio Times* cover picture in January 1951. The four members of the Archer family are gathered at the fireside, Dan and Doris, and their grown-up children Philip and Christine. Doris is knitting; the others hold newspapers and magazines. Christine smiles as they break off from reading to share a family moment.

The picture is reproduced on the cover of William Smethurst's unofficial history, *The Archers: The True Story*. It conjures up feelings of security, belonging, caring. These were the elements the *Archers* creators somehow managed to build into their drama. Somewhere beyond the Cotswold Hills was an unchanging community that had always been there and probably always would be. Everyone was invited to be part of it. All you had to do was tune into the BBC's Light Programme every day.

It was the same spirit I wanted to capture in the anniversary episode. It would be set in the same farmhouse as that first scene back in 1951, and those around the table would be members of that same family. Here's a flavour of it.

INT. BROOKFIELD KITCHEN.
FRIDAY 11.35AM

DAVID When I think about the hours we spent going through the breeding catalogues.

RUTH Yes, I know.

DAVID Choosing exactly the right bull to go on our best cows.

JILL You've built such a beautiful herd.

PIP And look how well they're milking. They're flying at the moment.

JILL How can you bear to think of letting them go?

RUTH Think back, Jill. When Phil was pushing Dan to switch over to Friesians.

JILL Oh well . . .

RUTH Don't tell me Dan wanted to do it. What, get rid of his beloved Dairy Shorthorns?

JILL No, of course not. But he could see that times were changing.

RUTH Exactly. It was a different world. The Shorthorns were fine before the war. Good grazers. Nice economical cows to run. Then we got the Milk

Marketing Board, and after the subsidies came in. Suddenly the market was transformed.

DAVID I can see where you're going with this.

RUTH That's when everyone started getting hung up on yields. So in came the Friesians.

JILL You're right, Phil was always saying that. I can hear him now. We've got to go for yield.

RUTH Well, guess what? The world's changed again. It's time to go back to the earlier model. What is it Joe Grundy's always saying? It all comes round again.

PIP (SARCASTIC) Great, so we're going back to the thirties. The industry's moving to robotics and milk sensors, and we're heading for hay carts and milk churns. Brilliant.

RUTH Oh, Pip.

PIP (DISGRUNTLED) We might as well be.

It's fair to say reaction to the episode was mixed. In social media there was a good deal of mocking at the lack of dramatic incident. For many listeners the highlight seems to have been a line of Jill's midway through the episode: 'I think I'll make that coffee. And I'm sure we could all do with a piece of fruitcake.'

'Four voices, tea and fruitcake in the farmhouse kitchen and a proper discussion about dairy cows. Just like *The Archers* used to be,' tweeted one happy listener. 'Jill's best line all year,' chortled another. 'Fruitcake – worthy of the Royal Shakespeare Company.'

In the *Telegraph*, radio critic Gillian Reynolds was firmly on our side. She had no time for those she called 'sensation seekers' with their complaints about the lack of action. 'We true *Archers* fans are perfectly happy with what happened,' she said. 'We rejoice at the return of proper farming.'

Many more on social media took this view, which came as something of a relief. It was clear from the outset that we weren't going to please everyone with our nod back to the 1950s, but at least there were some listeners who'd enjoyed it. Whatever the audience reaction, the fact is we were being faithful to the show's origins. It had been conceived as a drama about a farming community, and in this anniversary episode we were simply acknowledging that history.

The Archers is sometimes lampooned as an escapist fantasy, a make-believe land where the air's clean, there's hardly any crime and everyone looks out for each other. None of this is true. From its very beginnings the programme has featured gritty storylines, including a number of violent crimes.

But the show offers something else, something of universal appeal – a sense of belonging. When in its first decade 15 million people regularly tuned in, they weren't there to escape to some imagined rural idyll. They wanted to be part of the village community that appeared solid and unchanging. The farming life was an essential part of this.

Far from seeking an escape, that first audience wanted reality. In its early publicity, the BBC implied that the characters were real people on a real farm. After the years of uncertainty and change, here was a community that seemed to have been around forever. Its members were mostly related, different generations or branches of the same family, adding to the sense of stability and permanence.

Farming is one of those occupations where it's impossible to separate working life from personal and domestic life. All become seamlessly intertwined in day-to-day events on and around the farm. On this occasion our central family were facing a possible marriage breakdown plus the failure of their main business enterprise, the result of falling profits from dairy farming.

In the anniversary episode I wanted them to find a way through so they'd see clear water ahead in both their relationships and their business affairs. I also wanted to reinforce the sense that this family were at the heart of this disparate community of village characters.

After the episode went out, I thought long and hard about whether I might – or should have – written it differently. Could there have been more humour, even though it had been dealing with serious issues? Had I copped out of showing raw emotion by letting the old farming journalist in me take over? Was it just a bit too *Farmers Weekly*?

Maybe I'd become too close to this fictional family in the twenty years or so I'd been helping to shape its destiny. When I joined the programme, the twenty-five-year-old David was starting to challenge his father Phil over the running of the farm. Though I was sixteen years his senior, I identified with Brookfield's heir apparent. Not for his social and love lives, though these were interesting enough. What really made me want to be David Archer was that he'd soon be running close to 500 acres of English farmland.

I suppose you'd call it a kind of 'farm envy', a common complaint among the farming journos I've known. Most of us have wanted to be farmers at some time in our lives. David Archer would be deciding the destiny of a stretch of countryside in a beautiful part of England, its plants and its animals. He'd have the chance to make the hedges and woodlands ring to the sound of birdsong; to create meadows that echoed with the buzz and rasp of bees and insects.

He'd also have the chance build herds of amazing cattle and graze them in pastures full of clovers and herbs. He'd grow fields of golden corn in which the crop sprayer was seldom seen and in which beautiful arable flowers like corncockle and pheasant's-eye (neither of which I've ever seen) were no longer rare.

All this was fantasy, of course. There's no way the editor was ever going to let him do these things. David was a creature of the BBC, not mine. They guarded his character jealously. Along with the other Brookfield residents, he was part of the show's central family. They were as crucial to its future as they had been to its past. It was an immutable law of Ambridge that the farmer running Brookfield had to be mainstream in all things; to be decent, well-meaning and ordinary, but certainly not organic. He could never be allowed to become too radical, in farming or in any other aspect of life.

In his book, *Being David Archer*, actor Timothy Bentinck hinted that the character he'd played for more than thirty years might not have been the most exciting of personalities. I can assure him it's not because we writers never imagined him as a daredevil risk-taker. Far from it. We were full of brilliant storyline ideas to make him cool and sexy, especially in his early years. Unfortunately, to keep our jobs, we knew we had to keep him out of trouble and just a little bit dull.

So my fantasy of him as pioneer of a kinder, more wildlife-friendly way of farming was going to stay just that, a fantasy. Every so often I might get a chance to nudge him in a slightly greener direction, but he was destined to remain the decent, reliable, likeable David, the one Archer character guaranteed never to set the world on fire. Maybe now Pip and her brothers are starting to take things over, David and Ruth will be permitted to become more edgy. They're surely entitled to by now!

Over the years, as I got to know the character, I became conscious of the gulf between his background and mine. While our family were constantly moving house – most traumatically for me when we left my beloved council estate – David grew up in a place that offered stability and security. Nothing much was likely to change in and around his home for the whole of his lifetime, or if it did, it would be of his making.

Then there was the matter of our two dads. Mine had been volatile, often remote, always on the edge of anger as he battled his inner demons. It's not that he didn't love us. It's simply that he had no energy left to show it. In contrast, David's dad had been steady and reliable – at least he'd become so by the time I got to know him. Player of the church organ and justice of the peace, he'd surely have been a calm and reassuring influence on David and his three siblings as they grew up.

More than thirty years after meeting David Archer, I'd been required to write him out of trouble, which had been largely of his own making. He'd be the first to admit he'd made mistakes in the months leading up to the family summit at the kitchen table. Chief among them was his autocratic decision to pull out of the planned move to a new farm in the north of England. His wife Ruth had been deeply upset that he hadn't even bothered to discuss it with her before pulling the plug on the move.

[*Reality check. The move was obviously never going to happen. It would have been madness to write out the show's central family. Most listeners knew this too, but sometimes there's pleasure in thinking the unthinkable only for it not to happen.*]

At the kitchen summit, it was Ruth's turn to make the decisions. She set out the future for the dairy business while laying down new ground rules for better communication within their marriage. David, conscious of past failings, was only too happy to agree. Normality was restored, peace and harmony returned to the Brookfield fireside. It was the 1950s all over again.

To be honest, after more than three decades in Ambridge, I'd almost reached the point of seeing myself as a resident of Brookfield. Through David I could live my life in the English countryside, close to nature, while being part of the ideal community I'd always wanted. It was a bit like being back on the estate at Emmer Green, but without the family rows and with a farm. Was something similar going on in the hearts of other *Archers* fans, I wondered. Deep down didn't we all share a longing to be part of a village community close to the land?

I suspect *Archers* creator Godfrey Baseley knew this intuitively. I never got to meet him, but hearing the tales of early cast members, he seems to have invoked admiration and fear in equal measure. As far as I'm concerned, the man was a genius. He'd grown up with an intimate knowledge of a close farming community in south Worcestershire and, in a moment of inspiration, he'd realised it would make great drama.

At that time, Britain was a nation of small farms and market gardens. They were served by an army of traders, dealers, auctioneers, hauliers, vets, shopkeepers and publicans. Village England was not, in those days, a leafy place for retirement or for weekend escapes from the city. It was a collection of working, trading, gossiping, independent-minded, neighbourly communities of great strength and resilience.

Baseley's genius was in seeing that if you put one of these communities on a big stage, the war-weary people of austerity Britain would want to be part of it. As it happened, their response exceeded even his lofty ambitions. Suddenly everyone wanted a second, surrogate life in village England.

His second act of genius was to make the central family of the saga, Dan and Doris Archer of Brookfield Farm, dairy farmers. To be accurate, they were small, mixed farmers with a range of crops and livestock, including a dairy herd. When I moved to Ambridge in the mid-1980s, the next generation – Jill and Phil Archer – were still mixed farmers, though the farm itself had grown to about ten times its original size.

Baseley understood that dairy farms had a special place in the English countryside. When *The Archers* began, there were almost 150,000 of them. Except in the most difficult farming areas such as the hills and moorlands, practically every rural parish had at least one dairy farm. Some had two or three.

It's fair to say that dairy farming was one of the main drivers of the village economy. Unlike other farm crops, milk was produced daily and paid for monthly, so dairy farmers enjoyed a regular cash income, much of which was spent locally. It was the money from milk that helped energise the rural economy. Dairy farmers were often at the heart of their communities, which is why I wanted to make heroes of David and Ruth.

Early in my time in Fleet Street I got sent to spend a working day with a dairy farmer near Wincanton in Somerset. The features editor had commissioned a top news photographer to produce a picture-story of a typical day on the farm. I got dispatched to follow him round and write a short piece to wrap around his images.

We booked into the local pub and set our alarms for five-thirty. We arrived on the farm next morning just as Gavin, the farmer, was about to start milking. As the cows stood quietly in the collecting yard awaiting their turn, the ace photographer began clicking away. Fifteen hours later he was still at it. So was Gavin.

Milking the thirty-eight cows in the herd – in the morning and again in the afternoon – was just one of a dozen tasks to be completed that day. After the cows had gone from the milking parlour, it needed to be cleaned and sluiced down. Next the yard had to be cleaned by tractor and rubber scraper. Bales of hay had to be heaved to cows, calves and heifers in the yard.

After breakfast the field work began. Gavin hitched up the tractor and trailer and drove to where he'd trimmed a hedge the day before. Fork-loads of blackthorn and bramble were loaded onto the trailer and hauled to an area of rough ground to be burned. After lunch there was another round of livestock feeding, before his one opportunity of the day to spend time with wife Debbie and their three young children, just back from school.

Twelve hours after morning milking, Gavin got the cows into the collecting yard for the second session of the day. It was nine-thirty in the evening before he was back in the kitchen for a well-earned cup of tea. I was feeling knackered and all I'd done was watch. I asked Gavin if the day had been in any way unusual.

'Not really,' he said. 'Pretty well every day's full on, except perhaps Christmas Day. Having said that, we had a downer cow last year so we had to do split shifts over Christmas lunch, didn't we, love? The kids were not impressed.'

'We wouldn't change it though, would we?' said Debbie.

'If I get eight score draws on the pools, you just watch me,' replied Gavin with a smile.

I still have the double-page photo-spread from that mid-seventies issue of *Farmers Weekly*. I've never been back to that Somerset dairy farm, but I'd like to think one of the kids is now running it while their parents enjoy a well-earned retirement. I wouldn't bet on it though. Most of those small family dairy farms have long been replaced by large-scale, factory-like operations. I was determined that something of that family-farm spirit would live on in *The Archers*.

I'd been writing scripts for the show for more than twelve years when Tony Parkin decided to retire as farm minister for Ambridge, or 'agricultural story editor' as the BBC liked to call him. Though there were tedious parts to the job, I reckoned this would be an opportunity to influence the direction of the show.

As a scriptwriter I'd been devising a lot of my own farming stories, though most had to start and finish in my own week of episodes. If I took on the agriculture job, there'd be the chance to develop bigger stories across all four Ambridge farms. The other writers would be feeding in story ideas too, but for the four farming families at least, my stories were likely to get priority.

By this time, Vanessa Whitburn was running the programme. I'd worked with her during her earlier time on the show, when she'd been an assistant producer. Since then, she'd spent a year as producer of the TV series *Brookside* before returning to Ambridge as editor. I knew she'd enjoyed the farming stories in my scripts. I assured her that if I were agricultural editor, there'd be a lot more stories like that in the show.

She had one reservation. I'd made no secret of my support for organic farming so, not unreasonably, she wanted my word I wouldn't try to use the show as a propaganda vehicle. As she reminded me, there were BBC impartiality rules to be considered.

I'll be honest, this always seemed like a nonsense to me. Political impartiality, of course, but in a drama about farming? *The Archers*' success had been built on creating a fictional community of small family farms. It was the BBC itself that helped undermine this structure by using the programme to promote the government's rural agenda, which was to encourage the spread of large, mechanised farms, where human skills were replaced by machines and chemicals. Where was BBC impartiality when characters were reciting Ministry of Agriculture press releases?

I didn't actually say this to Vanessa, though. I assured her that of course there'd be no bias for or against any particular farming system. We already had an organic farm in the series, Bridge Farm, run by Pat and Tony Archer. Obviously, they'd stick up for organics, but I'd make sure there were equally robust arguments on the other side from farmers like Brian Aldridge, who practised what he liked to call 'scientific farming'.

To be honest, I was perfectly happy with these rules. Technical arguments on organic versus conventional agriculture didn't make great drama. Hopefully I'd find rather more interesting ways of challenging the farming status quo.

Brookfield Farm was the key to everything. Godfrey Baseley had set up Dan and Doris at the centre of the drama, the very heart of the community. Two generations on, Ruth and David Archer were now running the place. While there might be other dramas happening in their lives, given the opportunity, I was determined to evoke the spirit of that 1950s fireside whenever we went to Brookfield.

Here's an early attempt. It's a sunny Sunday morning in June and Ruth's having a lazy breakfast. It's her thirty-fourth birthday and later, in the field, there's hay to be made.

INT. BROOKFIELD KITCHEN. SUNDAY 10AM

DAVID You've got butter on your chin.

RUTH Oh, have I? Look, I don't want to rush you, but it's ten o'clock.

DAVID So?

RUTH Should you go and see what the troops are up to?

DAVID I know what they'll be up to.

RUTH Yeah?

DAVID Eddie'll be swearing at the baler because he can't get it set up right. It'll take him at least an hour.

RUTH Tricky job though.
DAVID And all the time Bert'll be telling him what he ought to be doing. Which'll slow up the process even more.
RUTH Isn't it about time we gave up small bales?
DAVID We don't make that many.
RUTH Even so is it worth all the hassle?

At this point nine-year-old Pip enters with a birthday card she's made for her mum. It's a picture of her daddy feeding hay to the farm's Hereford bull. Her picture includes a small hay bale. Following parental compliments on her artistic skills, Pip exits the scene.

DAVID Pip's got it right about small bales too. Sometimes they're more convenient.
RUTH You sure it's not just nostalgia?
DAVID As if.
RUTH Golden days of childhood. Tea out in the hay field. All that stuff.
DAVID Listen, all I remember is the damn stuff getting down my pants and itching like billy-o.
RUTH Big event, wasn't it? In those days. Hay-making.
DAVID Even more so in Dad's time. You want to hear him going on about it when he was a lad. Pre-silage that was. In those days it was massive.
RUTH I suppose.

DAVID Like getting ready for the D-Day landings. Gran used to bake for over a week beforehand.

RUTH For all the casual workers?

DAVID On a Sunday afternoon they'd have had half the village up here. Anyone capable of lifting a bale.

RUTH And now it's all gone.

DAVID It won't come back either. We're an urban culture these days.

RUTH Never mind, we've still got the old team. Bert, Eddie and Tom.

Later in the same episode there'll be a scene in the hay field. Bert and Eddie will be arguing about how to fix the broken-down baler. The talk will be about obscure baler parts like knotters, tensioners and guide rings. Young Tom Archer will wonder why they're relying on such an antique machine. David will be trying to stack bales in case of a sudden shower, even though there's not a cloud in the sky.

At this point Ruth will drive the Land Rover into the field, bringing lunch. Everything will stop and there'll be pasties, pizza slices, sandwiches and cans of beer among the sweet-smelling hay bales. Chatter and laughter will spill across the meadow. Community spirit will break out again in Ambridge and 5 million listeners will know that all's well in the other England, just as 15 million did in the 1950s.

I loved days like this in Ambridge. A birthday, a family event, a moment aside from the unending engagement with nature that is life on the land. To me it seemed the perfect existence. Firstly, to belong, to be part of a close community, and at the same time to join in the great, all-encompassing adventure that is farming. In reality I don't suppose it's ever quite like this, but it was the life I imagined through my surrogate family at Brookfield.

While the writers and producers were constantly dreaming up momentous new stories, fresh tribulations to heap on the family, I was content, for the most part, to tell small tales of laughter and sorrow. It seemed to me the daily events this family encountered added up to a big enough drama in their own right.

Among those stories was Phil and Jill's retirement. In exchange for a cash settlement, they agreed to move out of the farmhouse, handing it over to the next generation, Ruth and David and their growing family. Unfortunately, the move led to a lot of rancour in the family, especially from David's sister Elizabeth, now married to Nigel Pargetter and living amid the fading splendour of Lower Loxley. She felt she'd been cheated out of her rightful share of the Archer inheritance.

Then, later in the year, Ruth discovered a lump in her breast which turned out to be cancerous. She was told she'd need a full mastectomy followed by chemotherapy. The treatment was successful, but her recovery was slow and difficult. For the time being the family put aside their quarrels and gathered round to support her through the crisis.

The following year the family was hit by a real-life crisis. In the spring, foot-and-mouth disease broke out in Britain and soon spread to large parts of the country, including the English Midlands. As images of burning pyres of cattle corpses filled the newspapers, Brookfield Farm enforced a strict hygiene regime. When the disease was confirmed in the nearby village of Little Croxley, the family went into complete lockdown. Even farmworker Bert Fry was confined to his bungalow for six weeks.

To be honest, I was relieved to get back to important matters like the great escape of Molly the pig. It's harvest time and we're in the yard at Brookfield in late afternoon. Practically everyone's there – Ruth and David, David's sisters Shula and Elizabeth, his brother Kenton, and his cousin Debbie, who's there to run the Brookfield harvest. They're all waiting in the yard for Phil and Molly, his Large White sow.

Phil's getting ready to enter the pig in the local Borchester Show and he wants her to get used to having crowds of human beings around her. So he's asked the family members to stand close by, laughing, chatting and generally behaving like socialising *Homo sapiens* while he gently encourages Molly to brave the crowd. All is going well until Kenton decides that, to better recreate an agricultural show atmosphere, he'll start up the yard tractor.

The roar of a diesel engine is too much for the nervous sow. Squealing loudly, she bolts for the farm entrance, sending Shula flying in her panic.

'The silly fool,' says Phil, remarkably restrained in the circumstances.

'Kenton, you stupid idiot,' shouts David, not remotely restrained. 'Are you ever going to grow up?'

For a while everyone is out scouring the fields and hedgerows for the missing pig, but there are more pressing things to get on with, like the cereal harvest. In the gathering twilight only Phil and Elizabeth are left to search in nearby Lower Wood. Phil is sanguine about the incident.

'She'll turn up,' he says, 'I'm not particularly worried.

If she's got herself into one of those thickets we could be wandering around all night and still not find her.'

'She'll be having a brilliant time,' says Elizabeth. 'Her great night of freedom. She'll be telling her next litter of piglets all about it.'

'We might as well call it a day. I'll ring round some of the neighbours. Someone will see her tomorrow, I expect.'

Though there was no time to include it in the episode, I imagine Phil went home, helped himself to a glass of sherry and sat listening to Mozart on the stereo. It's what I often had him do at the end of a stressful day. I'd think of my dad and the way he'd also find an escape from life's turmoils in classical music, only with him it wouldn't have been Mozart. It would have been something loud and Russian like Tchaikovsky or Rimsky-Korsakov.

Molly's freedom lasted just twenty-four hours. I have her turn up the following day, having got in with Tom Archer's pigs at nearby Bridge Farm. Together David, Phil and Tom manage to corner her and bring her safely back home to her pen in Brookfield orchard. It was a simple enough story; not the kind that gets picked up by the press, but one that is somehow both everyday and extraordinary at the same time.

As I began to feel at home in Brookfield, I looked for opportunities to bring out the hero in David. Not in a loud, flashy way, but in a quiet, unassuming, matter-of-fact sort of way. In my years visiting farms, I'd come to see most farmers like this, even those whose industrial methods I didn't particularly care for. It seemed to me that as a group they were resourceful problem-solvers with a wide range of practical skills. Those with livestock – like David and Ruth – I believed to be particularly dedicated.

So in one winter episode I had David wade into a river in flood to rescue a heifer that had fallen in. Someone had to get a rope around the terrified animal and David knew it had to be him.

Later, when a favourite cow called Bluebell slipped in the yard and 'did the splits', he had no intention of taking the advice of vet Alistair Lloyd that it was time to put the animal down. Though there were no bones broken, the cow had ended up with severely torn muscles. It was possible that she'd recover but not without regular manipulation, day and night, for two weeks or more. Most farmers wouldn't have had the time but I was determined David would make the time.

By week two, he's close to exhaustion. While Ruth admires his devotion, she wonders if he isn't postponing the inevitable. Bluebell's showing little sign of improvement. Sooner or later he's going to have to let her go. Still David won't hear of it. At the end of the week, he's in the farm office, talking over farming issues with Brian Aldridge. Ruth bursts in to tell David he has to come at once.

We cut to a straw-covered loose box where Bluebell is at last on her feet and pulling hay from the rack. David is jubilant. Brian, who has heard about his valiant efforts, congratulates him.

'It's a rare thing in this day and age, good stockmanship.'

David gets a kiss from Ruth, which makes him feel slightly awkward. She doesn't care.

'You're a remarkable man, David Archer, do you know that?' she says. 'It's why I love you.'

In seventy years of *The Archers*, this particular story – or variations of it – must have been told a dozen times. Yet at each telling it sounds fresh, I suppose because it's about something we're all fascinated by, that remarkable bond between humans and animals.

It's also about something bigger and universal, the matters of life and death over which farmers are often on the front line. Just a few months after Bluebell's recovery, David's skills are called upon again, only this time the outcome matters rather more.

<u>INT. BROOKFIELD KITCHEN. FRIDAY 6.10PM</u>

RUTH	I just need to sit down, that's all.
DAVID	Whatever you want. Here . . .
RUTH	No, not on the chair.
DAVID	Oh, love. On the floor?
RUTH	(SITS DOWN) That's better. (BREATHES DEEPLY)
DAVID	I'm going to call Sandra.
RUTH	Good idea. (NUMBERS PUNCHED ON MOBILE PHONE) We didn't really plan for this, did we?
DAVID	Nope.
RUTH	Mind you, we never planned any of it, did we? From the night we rode on the hay cart. It all just happened.
DAVID	(TO PHONE) Oh, come on . . .
RUTH	So why should this bit be any different?
DAVID	Where the hell is she?
RUTH	Oh, David, your face. It's an absolute picture.

DAVID (TO PHONE) Sandra? . . . It's David Archer at Brookfield. Look, we're still here but we think it's started . . . (RUTH BREATHING DEEPLY AS ANOTHER CONTRACTION STARTS).

CUT TO:

INT. BROOKFIELD LIVING ROOM. FRIDAY 6.20PM

RUTH (ANOTHER BIG CONTRACTION) David! (BIG BREATHING, HOLDING ON TO DAVID)

DAVID OK, love, breathe. (LOOKING) Ruth! Ruth, I can see the head! You're nearly there. Oh, Ruth.

RUTH Here it comes. It's . . . (BIG PUSHING NOISE)

DAVID You're doing brilliantly . . .

RUTH (PUSHING) Ooo . . .

DAVID That's it, love. Push.

RUTH (PUSHING) What the hell do you think I'm doing?

DAVID You're doing great.

RUTH (EFFORT, NOISE)

DAVID (EXCITED) Heh, it's coming. You're nearly there. One more! Go on!

RUTH (PUSHING) Aaaaah! . . . (BABY BORN INTO DAVID'S ARMS)

DAVID Brilliant. Hello, little one . . . Hello!

RUTH (BREATHLESS) Is it alright? Is everything alright? (BABY CRIES A LITTLE)

DAVID Come on, little one . . . That's it. Ruth, it's a little boy.

RUTH Oh. (VERY NEAR TEARS) Is he OK?

DAVID (ALSO NEAR TEARS) He's wonderful. There you go. You snuggle up to your mum.

RUTH Hello, my little darling. Oh!

DAVID Isn't he amazing?

RUTH He's wonderful.

DAVID Hang on, let's get you a towel. (CLEAN TOWEL GRABBED) Let's wrap it round you so you're nice and warm . . . There.

RUTH He's so beautiful. I can't get over it.

DAVID (ARMS ROUND RUTH AND BABY) Well done, love. You were terrific.

RUTH I was, wasn't I?

DAVID I'm proud of you. And you, little one. (DOORBELL RINGS OFF)

RUTH There's Sandra.

DAVID Just in time. Because I really don't have a clue what to do next!

As I write this, twenty-year-old Ben Archer is struggling to come to terms with the consequences of a drunken one-night stand with Chelsea Horrobin. After their encounter, Chelsea became pregnant and decided to have an abortion. These events, along with the reactions of family and friends to the news, have left Ben deeply disturbed. Right now everyone's worried about him, especially his parents, David and Ruth.

While it's traumatic for all concerned, it's just one

more drama in the unending family saga which is *The Archers*. Central to the story are the generations that occupy Brookfield Farm.

The highest ground on the farm is on Lakey Hill, which rises to 250 metres on the north-east side of the village. It's a famous local landmark containing several prehistoric burial mounds. Many locals walk their dogs up there, especially on a Sunday morning, taking in the panoramic views it offers across the Am Vale at the very heart of England.

I like to think that David and Ruth sometimes stroll there, especially when there are sheep that need checking on in some of the higher fields. When they do, I hope they sometimes reflect on the timeless drama they're part of; not just the family events but the bigger drama that all of us are involved in, whether or not we ever stop to think about it.

6

Revolting Peasants

WHILE BROOKFIELD GAVE ME a chance to live out my farming fantasies, Grange Farm, home of the Grundy family, was where I belonged. I knew that almost as soon as I arrived in Ambridge, and I suppose I have my grandfather to thank for it. Or perhaps a picture by a celebrated Victorian artist that hung on his wall.

The original oil painting, called *February Fill Dyke*, hangs in Birmingham Museum and Art Gallery, where it's a great favourite with Brummies. Thousands of prints were made in the early twentieth century. One of them hung above the fireplace in the former sitting room occupied by my uncle Alan in Granddad's house, where we lived.

Looking back, it might have been a kind of self-indoctrination. When I was four or five, my brother and I would go into Alan's room each evening for a bedtime story. As Alan told his stories, I would stare at the picture. I grew to love the scene and imagine myself in it. To this day the images stay with me – a waterlogged English lane, a thatched cottage and tall, skeletal trees standing stark against a wintry sky.

I can still see the figures, too – two children with their dog, heading home through pools of water; a woman collecting firewood in front of the cottage; a farmer standing at the gate to his fields. Night after night I stared at that picture. I suppose I must have listened to my uncle's stories, though I have no memory of them. All I know is I longed to go and live in that cold and beautiful place.

The picture, which gave me my first glimpse of rural England, was by the Victorian artist Benjamin Williams Leader. He spent much of his life painting landscapes in his home county of Worcestershire and around the Severn Valley. This was the land that a century or so later was to become *Archers* country.

February Fill Dyke first appeared in the Royal Academy's Summer Exhibition of 1881. Unlike most Victorian landscapes, it presents an unsentimental view of rural life. Nature is shown as immense, cold and indifferent. By comparison, human beings appear as of little significance. While many artists of the period were selling rose-tinted images of rural life, Leader dared to capture a moment of wintry bleakness.

I really loved that picture. Somehow, I found comfort in it. I imagined the cottage to be warm and cosy inside, and the sky with its streaks of brightness seemed full of hope.

Which of my grandparents chose the painting for their sitting room wall, I never knew – but my guess would have been my granddad. Though he lived most of his life in the town, his heart seemed to have been forever in the English countryside of his childhood. Sadly, I know little about his history. I didn't ask the right questions when he was around and now, when I'd really like to know, I've found there's remarkably little about him on record. For some reason he doesn't appear in either the 1901 or the 1911 censuses.

All I have are my memories, a few family stories and a set of medals, one of which is inscribed 'The Great War for Civilisation'. He often referred to himself as 'a farmer's boy', which I took to mean he'd grown up on a farm. My guess is he'd lived in a tied cottage at a time when more than a million people were still employed as farm labourers.

Among the things I'm fairly sure about is that he was born near Chesham in Buckinghamshire and in his late teens he moved into lodgings in west London after securing a job in Whiteleys department store in Queensway. He belonged to the doomed generation who, in the early twentieth century, left the poverty of life on the land to look for opportunity in the city, only to find themselves thrown into a terrible war.

In 1914, he'd stepped up at once, joining the Middlesex Regiment. As part of what Kaiser Wilhelm had called 'that contemptible little army', he saw action in the first few weeks of the conflict. In 1915, he was brought home to recover from wounds inflicted by chlorine gas. Then in 1917, he was discharged with wounds that included a lump of shrapnel embedded in his skull.

Throughout his life he suffered from recurring spells of dizziness together with chronic bronchitis. He and his wife May had four children, including my mum, who was born the year after he returned from war. Somehow the couple managed to keep their family fed and clothed through the Depression of the 1920s and 1930s, though at times it must have seemed an impossible task.

My granddad's name was Herbert, though my dad, my uncles and just about everyone else called him Tom, I suppose because Great War soldiers were generally known as 'Tommies'. After the war, Tom's life was mostly confined within the boundaries of his house and garden, though he never stopped dreaming of wide-open spaces and a life on the land.

He became fascinated with the story of the Oklahoma Land Rush of 1889, when 50,000 people lined up in their wagons and buggies for the race to claim a share of 2 million acres the government had opened up for settlement.

He must have wondered how different his life might have been if, instead of heading for London as a young man, he'd emigrated to America. He could have been on his own prairie homestead rather than putting his life on the line for a few yards of Flanders mud. His consolation was the garden of his council house. He made it just about as fertile and productive as any patch of ground in the land.

His dream of life on the prairies never died. After we moved to the other side of town, I'd sometimes visit him with my mum. In old age he became a big a fan of country-and-western music, artists like Hank Williams, Gene Autry, Slim Whitman and Tennessee Ernie Ford. Cowboy songs would ring around the very English living room with its willow-pattern china, a stuffed red squirrel in a case and framed family photos of Edwardian men and women.

I don't remember exactly when it happened, but at some point after my arrival in Ambridge I got the idea that Joe Grundy spoke for my granddad and his generation of country people. There was no logic to it. According to the archives, Joe had been born in 1921, so he was of a later generation. Even so, I started to think of him as the voice of the rural dispossessed, a lost English peasantry, which is how I'd come to think of my granddad.

It was an idea that played to my own view of English history. It also gave me a more interesting take on Joe and the rest of the Grundy family. To me, their voices were echoes from a time when English freedoms were enshrined in our rights to land, rights which were steadily eroded over the centuries by acts of enclosure instigated by landowners and Parliament.

The character of Joe had been introduced as a comic figure, a successor to Walter Gabriel, the original incompetent small farmer. The reasons were, of course, political. Once again, the small, supposedly inefficient farmer was being unfairly compared with the large, mechanised 'modern farmer'.

Most of the time we writers didn't think too much about the reasons for Grundy grievances. We took it all as a bit of a laugh as we sat in script meetings dreaming of ever more bizarre ways of reinforcing the caricature, Joe. He was supposed to hold a long-standing grudge against the Archer family. One of the reasons was that Phil and David had once reported him to the animal health authorities for failing to dip his sheep properly, as was required by law.

Farmers were supposed to immerse each animal in an insecticide solution by putting them through a dip, a sort of bath for sheep. Joe hadn't done this. He'd merely sprinkled the stuff over them with a watering can, which counted as a failure to comply.

It was a ludicrous storyline, but the writers played along with it. Everyone enjoyed poking fun at Joe's foibles, especially his disdain for the Archers, Phil in particular. Here's a scene from the mid-1980s, not long after the imposition of 'milk quotas' by the European Union. Dairy farmers, even those with small herds like Joe and Eddie, had a strict limit put on the volume of milk they were allowed to produce and sell.

In this scene, Joe is complaining about another dairy farmer, Mike Tucker, setting up a Christmas turkey enterprise in competition with the Grundys. It's not long before the criticism has switched to the old enemy, the Archers.

<u>INT. GRANGE FARM KITCHEN. SATURDAY 6PM</u>

JOE You can see what's behind it, can't you, Eddie? It's them milk quotas again.

EDDIE You reckon them big dairy boys are filling up their sheds with turkeys?

JOE Course they are. They're rushing into everything. They've spoiled the milk job for us small guys, now they're out to ruin our little sidelines like the turkeys.

EDDIE You could be right.

JOE Phil Archer'll be the next one into some fancy new scheme. Always ready to snatch the crust off the small man's table is Phil Archer.

EDDIE (LAUGHING) I reckon he's got other things to worry about at the moment. Now his daughter's in trouble.

JOE Trouble? She ain't been out pinching cars again with that Nigel Pargetter?

EDDIE Not Shula. Elizabeth Archer, this is. She's only been chucked out of her school.

JOE (GLEEFUL) Oh dear, oh dear. Chucked out, eh? What's she been at, then?

EDDIE	The way I heard it, she was found with three blokes in her room at two o'clock in the morning.
JOE	Oh dear, oh dear.
EDDIE	Smoking and drinking cherry brandy.
JOE	And her old man a magistrate too.
EDDIE	They say her locker was stuffed full of gin and vodka. Apparently, she was selling it off to the younger kids in empty shampoo bottles.
JOE	Exploiting the little 'uns, eh? That's typical of them Archers.
EDDIE	Now she wants to go to Borchester Tech college, but I can't see them having her. Not when all this comes out.
JOE	It won't come out though. It'll be all hushed up.
EDDIE	You can't hush up something like that.
JOE	You can if you knows the right people. Phil Archer will pull strings with the college heads, you can be sure about that. Freemasons the lot of 'em, I shouldn't wonder.

We'd led the listeners to believe Joe's hostility was the result of his incompetence as a farmer, but there was another way of understanding his resentment. Under the post-war policy, public subsidies were paid according to the amount of food produced, whatever it was, beef or lamb, wheat or milk. The more a farmer produced, the more she or he was paid. To take full advantage, many abandoned traditional mixed farming with its small fields, grazing animals and crop rotations.

There was more money to be made by grubbing out hedges, felling woodlands and ploughing up old meadows. The land could then be sown with cash crops and so maximise the income from government subsidy. Farmers who were able to expand their output in this way often became wealthy enough to buy out their smaller neighbours.

As a tenant renting his land from a large estate, Joe wouldn't have been able to join the party even if he'd wanted to. At the same time he had to watch his neighbours – including Dan and Phil Archer – turning away from what had always been considered 'good husbandry' and joining in the land rush.

The Archer family were part of this countryside revolution. When the programme started in 1951, Dan, like Joe, was a small tenant farmer. By the time I'd moved to Ambridge in the mid-1980s, Brookfield had expanded to nearly 500 acres and was owned, not rented, by the Archer family. As well as persuading his father to buy out the tenancy, Phil must have done his share of hedgerow removal and land acquisition.

Watching all this would have been galling for Joe. As a result of the government-led boom, the price of farmland soared, which meant farm rents went up, too. They usually follow the land price. Joe found himself having to pay more rent on his small farm even though he was excluded from the rural jamboree. It's no surprise he felt resentful towards his upwardly mobile neighbours.

He'd also had to watch the steady break-up of the village community he'd grown up in. Along with the thousands of small farmers, the pre-war countryside supported many more skilled farmworkers and craftspeople. Under the new policy, most were to be put out of work. Farming had to be efficient, Whitehall decreed, which meant replacing people with machines and chemicals.

No wonder Joe was angry. He'd watched the bureaucrats putting village people out of work. He'd seen families that had been part of the community for generations robbed of their livelihoods, their homes sold to incomers. Through six years of war, the might of Hitler's army and air force had failed to break England's rural communities. Now Whitehall was achieving it by stealth.

Far from being the loveable rogue the show had made him out to be, I began to think of him as a tragic figure. Heartlessly and unjustly, we writers had mocked him. We were constantly giving him and Eddie crazy ideas for making their fortunes, then ensuring they failed. Garden gnomes, ghost walks, caravan hire, ferret racing, garden compost, pop concerts and garden patios were just some of the litany of hare-brained schemes we dreamed up for them.

Inevitably they'd turn out to be money-losers rather than money-spinners. With each new project their hopes soared. This was going to be the scheme that made their fortunes and changed their lives. And each time we'd bring the enterprise crashing down. We'd chuckle to ourselves that once more fickle fate had shattered their dreams. But heh, what can you expect? They're Grundys. They never learned, never grew wiser.

The more I thought about this, the more illogical it seemed. Joe can't have been a bad farmer or his business wouldn't have survived either the pre-war recession or the post-war boom, when the subsidies were going to his bigger neighbours. Whatever else he lacked, Joe had survival skills. To consistently portray him – and Eddie – as stupidly incompetent made no sense to me. I was determined to make the Grundys the more rounded and complex characters I believed them to be.

Here's how I had Joe deal with a difficult calving in the small herd run by part-time farmer Oliver Sterling. By this time, the Grundys had lost their beloved Grange Farm. Sterling was the new owner. Needing help with an ailing cow, he'd already put in a call to David Archer, whom he considered to be an experienced and competent livestock farmer. David was on his way over, but before he arrived, I had Joe unexpectedly turn up. He immediately rolled up his sleeves.

INT. CALVING BOX AT GRANGE FARM.
7.25PM. (COW ON STRAW MOOS OCCASIONALLY)

OLIVER Here it comes . . . (CALF PLOPS OUT) Well done, old girl.

JOE There you are, look. Nice little heifer calf.

OLIVER Splendid, isn't she? Let's just make sure her airways are clear.

JOE It's always the way. Soon as you get the head in the right position she'll calve in no time at all.

OLIVER You were right, Joe. I'm very grateful.

JOE When you've calved as many of 'em as I have.

OLIVER (TO CALF) There you go, little one.

JOE Right now, drag her round so her mum can see her.

OLIVER Come on then . . . (CALF DRAGGED OVER STRAW. COW MOOS) Alright, Mum, we're not taking her anywhere.

JOE She's quite a weight. She ought to do well.

OLIVER (TO COW) There you go, girl. There's your little one. (COW LICKS CALF)

JOE She'll be alright now.

OLIVER Wonderful sight, that. Mum licking her calf. It doesn't matter how many times you see it.

JOE You're right there. If I had a shilling for every time I've been here, I'd be a wealthy man.

OLIVER I bet.

JOE I mind one night, matter of fact it was in this very shed. Christmas night, it was. Goodness knows how many years ago. She was an old Dairy Shorthorn. She'd been trying to calve all the afternoon, just like this one of yours---

DAVID (APPROACH) How's it going, Oliver?

JOE David Archer. You're a little bit late.

DAVID Yeah, I'm sorry, Oliver. I came as quick as I could.

OLIVER I'm sure. Thanks so much for coming.

DAVID No problem.

JOE You've had a wasted journey, though. The job's done as you can see.

```
A nice heifer calf. Now me and
Oliver are about to go for a beer,
isn't that right, Oliver?
```

To me, the Grundys represented that disappearing farm culture, rooted in the English peasantry, combining independence and resourcefulness with a deep knowledge of animals, the land, the weather and nature's cycles. Trying to reflect their history didn't mean I wanted to sanitise the Grundys, far from it. They'd still have ferrets and tractor parts littering their kitchen floor, but occasionally we would catch a glimpse of country wisdom passed across the generations.

If there was one part of their business that demonstrated their dogged determination to succeed, despite a lifetime of setbacks, it was the Christmas turkey enterprise. To be fair, this probably owed more to Eddie's long-suffering wife, Clarrie, than to the men.

Over the years I've known a number of farms where they reared Christmas turkeys and sold them direct. Though it was usually run as a sideline to the main business, it could be an important income-earner.

To me this was proper farming. No government subsidies were involved. No supermarket deals or corporate supply chains, just farmers on their own initiative producing food that local people wanted to buy. It was definitely no route to riches. A lot of work was involved in rearing the birds, with the whole process ending in the frenetic and mucky business of killing them and preparing them for the oven.

I always liked to make a big production of the Grundys' turkey days. The first act was when the birds were slaughtered and the second when they were made 'oven ready'. I wouldn't want to come across as a Scrooge-like character, but I have to be honest: I quite enjoyed serving up a cold dash of reality in the middle of all the seasonal glitz and sentimentality.

These were my mind pictures. Clarrie's at the centre of them both. In the first, she sits in a plastic patio chair at the front of an old shipping container which also serves as a cider store. Under a faded yellow 'hoodie' she's wearing five layers of woollen jumpers against a brisk and biting wind. On her lap is a newly killed turkey from which she's pulling the feathers.

Beside her is a small table with more dead turkeys lying on it. On the other side of the table sits her elder son, William. He, too, is warmly dressed against the cold. They're listening to an upbeat version of 'The Holly and the Ivy' on a portable radio.

CLARRIE Don't let them blow all over the place. They're meant to go in the bin.

WILLIAM It's not easy in this wind.

CLARRIE Well, try harder. It's not good for the customers to see feathers all over the field.

WILLIAM How much are you and Dad charging for the birds this year?

CLARRIE Same as last year.

WILLIAM That's crazy. They ought to be double.

CLARRIE Oh yeah, very smart that is. And everyone goes down the shop and buys Susan's frozen ones. Thank you, William.

Mind picture number two, a week or so later. This time Clarrie's standing at the kitchen table on which there's a heap of plucked turkeys. She's reaching inside one of them to pull out the guts and drop them into a large plastic tub at her side. She then removes the gizzard, liver, heart and neck, dropping them into a plastic bag, which she stuffs back into the turkey. The radio's playing 'Jingle Bell Rock' by Bobby Helms.

The back door opens and Eddie comes in with half a dozen more plucked turkeys, carrying them on a red plastic tray. He pushes the door shut with his shoulder.

EDDIE	Brrr, it's brass monkeys out there, love. (TRAY DOWN ON TABLE) There you go, that's the last of 'em.
CLARRIE	Put the kettle on, will you, Eddie? I need a break.
EDDIE	How's it going?
CLARRIE	We're getting there.
EDDIE	(OFF) Nice lot of birds this year, I thought. (KETTLE FILLED)
CLARRIE	They don't look no different when you're pulling their guts out.
EDDIE	(OFF) You know, love, there's something about seeing you at that job. It may sound daft but that's when I start feeling really Christmassy. (KETTLE SWITCHED ON)

Simple scenes from country life. They might have come from Hardy or Dickens, or even from a Bruegel painting. I don't know what the listeners thought of them, but to me they were as important to the Ambridge calendar as the annual flower and produce show or Lynda's Christmas production. No TV soap can touch *The Archers* for its portrayal of the eternal round, the ebb and flow of life that lies outside the realm of rulers and kings.

The Grundys at Christmas were the perfect antidote to the seasonal craziness of the high street, a reminder of the things that really mattered – home, belonging, family ties.

Bizarrely, it was these things that made them great candidates for bankruptcy. Since the audience were so attached to them, having them chucked out of their home would be high-octane emotional drama. It would also make a powerful point about the haves and the have-nots in today's countryside.

It seemed all too plausible that Joe and Eddie might go bust and be unable to pay the rent. They'd been trying to make a living from a small herd at a time when the dairy industry was heading in the direction of mega-herds. Supermarket pricing policies were demolishing the notion of milk as a healthy food and promoting it as low-cost commodity.

None of the listeners would be surprised if the Grundys went under. We'd taken them to the brink many times before. Tipping them over the edge now would surely be seen as bowing to the inevitable.

Not everyone on the production team was happy with the idea. They argued, understandably, that taking the Grundys out of Grange Farm with its chaotic kitchen (despite Clarrie's tireless efforts) would greatly disappoint our audience. It would be like taking the Steptoes out of their junk yard or Basil out of Fawlty Towers.

I got that. As characters, the Grundys were twenty-four-carat gold, but so was the dramatic potential of getting them evicted. Besides, we were a soap. It would be perfectly possible to come up with a storyline for bringing them back to Grange Farm at some time in the future. In effect, we'd be giving the audience a double dose of gut-wrenching stories, paradise lost, then paradise restored.

So we drove the Grundys into bankruptcy. Their new landlords, Borchester Land, refused to give them a rent holiday, and the bank refused to extend their credit. The farm's assets – livestock and 'deadstock' (equipment and feed) – would be sold by auction, after which the family would have to move out of the farmhouse that both Joe and Eddie had grown up in. I was determined to wring every bit of anguish from the tragedy.

Here's part of a scene with Eddie and the assessor sent by the auctioneers to list the items that will go into the sale and to give them all lot numbers. When we pick up the action, the assessor, called Waring, is itemising a set of hand tools.

INT. GRANGE FARM BARN. TUESDAY 11AM

EDDIE What about all them hand tools? The hay rakes and the pitchforks? Who's going to buy that sort of stuff?

WARING They'll go alright. No trouble at all. The heritage industry. It seems to be insatiable.

EDDIE (CONTEMPT) Oh heritage, is that it?

WARING You've seen these themed pubs. They're always on the lookout for genuine artefacts.

EDDIE Funny, ain't it? It wasn't many years ago they wanted every last bit of food we could turn out. Now all they want is heritage.

WARING Let me give you a piece of advice, Mr Grundy. Try not to look on this experience as a disaster. Try to see it as an opportunity. A chance to make a fresh start . . .

EDDIE Great. I'll go and put it on my CV. Maybe they'll give me a smock and a pitchfork and stick me in a museum: British farmer - extinct.

The auctioneer's man is having a hard time and there's more to come. Eddie hasn't finished with him yet. He grabs one of the pitchforks and thrusts the worn wooden handle close to the intruder's face.

EDDIE See them initials? There, look . . . G.G. Shall I tell you who that was? George Grundy. My granddad. And you see it's all worn down round the base. Any idea how it got like this?

WARING From repeated use, I imagine.

EDDIE That's right. Work. Pitching up hundreds of tons of hay ten foot up on the back of a cart. Then pitching it off again onto the elevator. Summer after summer. Year after year. To keep twenty pedigree Shorthorns in milk.

WARING I appreciate it's got a history.

EDDIE And I'll tell you where that milk used to go. Out on the streets of Borchester to feed poor little beggars whose mums didn't have the money to put boots on their feet. And I'll tell you sommat else. It didn't matter a toss to them folks if they stuck antique hay rakes on the pub wall or if they didn't. Just so long as their little 'uns never had rickets.

WARING I think you've made your point, Mr Grundy.

EDDIE This lot's coming with me. (TOOLS GATHERED UP) You can stuff your lot 33.

WARING I'll mark it withdrawn.

EDDIE You do that. And you can tell them money-grubbing vultures you work for, one of these days when they've put the last little farmer out of business, this country's going to go hungry again. Only it'll be too blimmin' late. And who'll be sorry then?

It was a powerful polemic from the usually amiable Eddie. When I listened to it on-air I wondered if I'd gone a little over the top. It was a relief when Trevor Harrison, the actor who played Eddie, later told me he'd enjoyed developing this new side of the character.

To be honest, I was starting to use that same angry voice outside Ambridge. In 1997 my book, *The Killing of the Countryside*, attacking industrial agriculture and the impact it was having on wildlife and small family farms, had caused something of a stir in the media. Supporters called it 'passionate', the other side – including former colleagues in the farming press – rubbished it as an angry rant against progress.

I'd also had an afternoon play on Radio 4, *A Small Plot of England*. A young, self-employed farm contractor, an early exponent of the gig economy, suddenly and unexpectedly (to his wife) turns feral. Pitching his tent on a stretch of common land near his home, he declares it 'The New Commonwealth of England'. We discover that his action is inspired by a group known as the Diggers, or True Levellers, who, in the year 1649, occupied common land at St George's Hill in Surrey and called it the New Commonwealth.

The Diggers were led by a charismatic character called Gerrard Winstanley, whose radical writings greatly appealed to me. As his followers began cultivating a small corner of leafy Surrey, he published a pamphlet headed 'The True Levellers Standard Advanced'.

> The Earth (which was made to be a common treasury of relief for all, both men and beasts) was hedged into enclosures by the teachers and rulers, and others were made servants and slaves; and that the Earth, which is within this creation a common storehouse for all, is bought and sold and kept in the hands of a few. Whereby the Great Creator is mightily dishonoured.

Inspirational stuff, I thought. A high point in the story of English radicalism. What was being said in the mid-seventeenth century seemed to match what I'd seen going on in rural Britain in the second half of the twentieth century. I had my contemporary hero, Steve, take on the persona of Winstanley. He'd become an angry voice calling out for land reform in the English countryside.

I was starting to think of Joe and Eddie in the same terms. For all their comic adventures, they were contemporary victims of a process very like enclosure. The economic odds had been stacked against them. They were about to lose their farm and so had become, like many thousands of country people before them, a modern version of a dispossessed peasantry; at least, that's how I chose to see it.

As the storyline unfolded, the dairy herd and trappings were sold off and the family were finally evicted. The council rehoused them in a cramped flat on a notorious Borchester council estate called Meadow Rise; nothing at all like the estate where I'd grown up.

Joe immediately fell into depression. Forbidden by the council from keeping pets, he resorted to killing his ferrets. One episode ended with a series of thuds as he dispatched them with a hammer, a sound effect that drew much criticism and provoked the newspaper headline 'Doom di doom di doom'. Fortunately, we found a way to bring the family back to Ambridge, at first to live in a caravan, then shortly before Christmas, in a rented cottage.

We even invented a storyline for moving them back into their beloved Grange Farm thanks to the generosity of the new owner, Oliver Sterling. However, with less than half the land remaining the farm was no longer viable. The era of the Grundys as small farmers was over. The storyline that ended their land tenure was tragically real. It was a drama that had unfolded thousands of times before across the quiet English countryside.

*

I often wonder how different *The Archers* might have been if its creators had set out to make heroes of their small farmers rather than undermining them; if it had simply told stories about this close-knit rural community and their fight to survive in the face of hostile government policies.

As it happens, that policy was highly controversial even at the time, especially among farmers. Not far from the fictional county of Borsetshire, on the edge of the Cotswold Hills, farmer and author George Henderson had been campaigning against the government's agriculture policy since the war ended. His bestselling book, *The Farming Ladder*, had been particularly popular among former servicemen and women settling down to civilian life after VE Day.

Inspired by the book, many dreamed of making a living in the English countryside. In a nation of small farms there were limitless opportunities for keen new entrants. Henderson argued that they'd bring vitality, enthusiasm and new ideas into agriculture.

Clem Atlee's post-war government had other plans. Lobbied by the big farmers, they introduced subsidies which effectively slammed the door on new entrants. It meant that every time a small farm or a piece of land came on the market, it was snapped up by the subsidised farmer next door. Unless they were rich, there was no way for aspiring farmers to get in.

George Henderson was a fierce critic of the subsidy policy. He claimed it would lead to stagnation, waste and inefficiency in a vital sector of the British economy. During the harsh, inter-war years of recession, George and his brother had made their own small farm one of the most productive in the country on a 'per acre' basis.

He compared his output with that of some of the biggest and best-known farms in the land to show that small farms invariably produced more food per acre than large ones.

Far from being inefficient, as the bureaucrats were claiming, Britain's small-farm structure was a priceless national asset, George claimed. Their strength came from their very independence. State control, which was what subsidies amounted to, would render the industry moribund. Though many farmers backed George's view, the government won the argument and introduced subsidies, thanks to powerful support from the National Farmers' Union among others.

Archers' creator Godfrey Baseley would have known all about George Henderson, his book, and his campaign. He'd have heard the arguments of small farmers, especially in the part of south Worcestershire where he grew up. Many of them would have been fiercely opposed to government interference and the threat to their independence.

Nothing I've read about the show's early years leads me to think this very real conflict ever made it into storylines. Today's writers would bite your hand for the chance to dramatise a fight between a small community and a bureaucratic state. Baseley, who until then had been the maker of programmes aimed at 'educating' farmers, seems to have taken the government line, perhaps because the BBC expected it.

The Grundys can be seen as delayed victims of these same policies. National subsidies had long given way to those set by Brussels, but the impact remained the same. Even in the early years of the twenty-first century, public support for agriculture generally ended up helping large farms and corporate enterprises and disadvantaging the small guys. It's no wonder Joe was cynical about the Archers. What's amazing is that he managed to retain such a sharp sense of humour.

Though the Grundys lost their farm, I did manage to bequeath them a lasting legacy – the Cider Club. To be honest, the idea came from a good friend of mine, poet and adventurer James Crowden. In addition to many other interests, James, the author of *Cider Country*, is a serious aficionado of proper cider and the culture around it. Over the years he's regaled me with many tales of the cider dens of Somerset and Herefordshire.

Out of this came the Grundys' Cider Club. I imagined it as a sort of free space for the expression of dissent and subversion in the heart of *Archers* country. If there's ever to be another Free Commonwealth of England, it's very likely to start here. Though the club originally met in a shed at Grange Farm, it subsequently moved to the small field where the Grundys have their barn for raising the Christmas turkeys.

Over the years I've had a few fun times in the Cider Club. One I particularly remember was an occasion when Eddie found refuge there with Lilian Bellamy when their respective partners were trying to keep them off the booze. Here's the scene revisited, this time with an additional guest: me. I'm having my first taste of Joe's famous Tumble Tussock cider.

'Do you know, that's really nice,' I say as I savour the golden liquid.

Eddie's face registers hurt. 'You don't have to sound so surprised. Me and Dad have been at it a long time, ain't we, Lilian?'

'You can say that again,' she says. 'Everyone knows

this is the best cider in the county. I mean why else would I be sitting in a dump like this?'

'Yeah, OK, so it's a bit of a tip. We likes to keep the place informal.'

'There's informal and there's public health hazard, darling.'

It's not the ambience I'm interested in. It's the cider. 'It'll be an absolute tragedy if this stuff doesn't get made any more,' I say.

Eddie's reassuring. 'It'll get made, don't you worry about that. We lost the farm but we can still get the apples from the old orchard . . .'

'As long as Oliver Sterling keeps on turning a blind eye,' adds Lilian.

'Oliver don't mind. He wants the old ways to go on. And we've still got the press next door. As long as that don't let us down, we'll keep on going with it.'

'And what happened to the rest of the land after you got kicked out?' I ask, though I know the answer.

'Winter wheat,' says Eddie. My cue to get up on the soap box.

'It's a bloody outrage, that's what it is. Getting plastered with chemicals. Killing the soil. Killing the wildlife. And they're getting paid sodding subsidies for doing it. After all those years you and Joe had it, growing proper food . . .'

'Not just food, proper milk,' says Eddie, putting me right. 'Grass-fed milk, the very best.'

'Not to mention great cider. Doesn't matter a damn to people like that so long as they make their profit and get their tax breaks. And what do the politicians do? A big fat nothing. Crony capitalism, that's what it is.' That's the end of my rant.

'So when are we putting up the barricades?' Lilian wants to know. She's wondering if she's come to the right place.

Of course, it didn't ever happen like that. On-air the Cider Club conversations rarely strayed into politics, or if they did, only village politics. I'd sometimes share my views at script meetings, but the writers seldom took much notice. There were characters in the show who might well have agreed with me: Robert Snell and Jim Lloyd, for example. They never spoke up, though.

I like to imagine that when the broadcast from Ambridge ends at quarter past seven every day, talk turns to revolution. More than ever rural England needs its radical voices. If they can't be heard in the Grundys' Cider Club, what hope is there for the country?

7

On the Downs

ONE OF MY BEST experiences of the wraparound comfort you get from a small community was in a village of grey-stone cottages nestling in a fold of the rolling Wiltshire downs. I moved there a few years before my trial scripts on *The Archers*, but it turned out to be a great preparation for life in Ambridge.

It came at a particularly bleak time in my life. I was still feeling grief over the failure of my marriage eighteen months earlier. Marion and I had met during our student days in Bangor and parting after eight years had come as a severe blow.

Shortly afterwards, my dad had died at the age of just sixty-one. Right up to the time of his illness, he'd stayed youthful, active and apparently fit. I'd always thought him invincible.

We'd grown a good deal closer over the years. He'd mellowed with age and become less dogmatic in his views, while I'd tried my hardest to throw off the angry teenager. It was work in progress, but progress was being made. We even looked into the possibility of buying a small farm together. He and Mum would sell their house to fund their share of the purchase price, while I'd take a mortgage to cover the rest of it. The aim was to find a house big enough to split into two.

In our search, Dad and I took a number of trips to areas like north Devon and west Wales, where the price of land was relatively low. I look back on those viewing trips around beautiful parts of Britain as some of our best times together. We stayed in local inns and small hotels, spending the evenings in the bar chatting about the places we'd seen and the general economics of agriculture.

In the end I pulled out of the deal, much to his disappointment. I believed, mistakenly, that this would help save my marriage. Whether the farm arrangement with Dad would have worked I don't know, but to this day I have a sense that I let him down. Afterwards he and Mum moved to north Cornwall, where they embarked on another adventure. Dad bought a boat, a sailing cruiser, and moored it off the Roseland Peninsula on the south coast. He took a couple of sailing courses, but sadly became ill before he could put them to use.

At the time he died, I was living in the grey-stone Wiltshire village a few miles from Salisbury. An ex-journalist colleague had a house there, from where he ran his public relations business. In an act of kindness, he asked me if I'd like to move to the village and carry on my freelance work from his office. There was plenty of room for another desk, he assured me.

His generosity went further. He found me a small cottage in the village, coming to an informal arrangement with the local farmer who owned it. He then helped me furnish it with second-hand carpets, table and chairs, plus a few other odds and ends, bought at the auction rooms in Salisbury. That's how I came to be living in a small, thatch-roofed cottage of grey stone in a valley not far from Stonehenge.

In some ways it felt like I was starting over again. My job at *Farmers Weekly* was gone, though I was still writing for them as a freelancer. My marriage was gone. The house my wife and I had bought in Gloucestershire and lived in briefly and unhappily, that too was gone. I was back at square one with precious little to show for my thirty-three years on the planet. But hey, I was a writer and living in a village community at the heart of Hardy's Wessex. From here on in my life was going to be all art.

I quickly got to know some of my village neighbours. There was no shortage of vivid and memorable characters around. Many might have come direct from a Hardy novel. My immediate neighbour, for instance, the ninety-two-year-old Jack, who lived alone in the other half of my semi-detached cottage.

Jack, or Mr Mason as I always called him, had lived in the village almost all his life. He'd never visited London, and only once lived away from the village, a two-year spell during the Great War, when he'd worked for the army at a camp on nearby Salisbury Plain. Over his long life he'd done a variety of jobs, including farm work, road-mending, building and quarry work. As far as I know, he'd never married, and in old age was one of the most cheerful and contented men I've ever met.

While my cottage had a small bathroom installed in what had been a tiny third bedroom, his side had no bathroom or inside toilet. He washed at the kitchen sink and used an outside 'privy' at the bottom of our shared garden. My girlfriend was often there at weekends. When the weather was warm, she'd sometimes sit out in the garden reading. A little ritual developed around Jack's trips to the toilet.

We realised that when he saw her sitting in the garden, he'd stand on his doorstep for a few moments gazing at the sky. Then as if he'd merely stepped out to check on the weather, he'd retreat back inside. We got wise to this manoeuvre and devised a strategy in response.

Whenever he appeared, my girlfriend would close her book and get up from her chair. Giving him a cheerful greeting, she'd mutter something about having 'wasted quite enough time reading' and head inside as if to get on with more important work. Decencies had been observed, ancient moral codes respected. We were both very fond of Jack.

Two or three times a week he'd get a visit from his nephew, who also lived in the village. Trevor Mason was the local builder, who doubled as the village undertaker, as was common in country districts. He had four daughters, ranging in age from mid-teens to early twenties. He was in the process of building a house in the village for the eldest girl and had declared his intention to build houses for the other three, ready for when they flew the nest.

Around the time I moved to the village, one of the girls was going out with an ex-soldier, a likeable guy from a tough estate in Salisbury. Most of the time he went around in faded denim and a well-worn black leather jacket, but once in a while you'd see him in a black top hat and frock coat, so you knew someone had died. He was lean with dark brown eyes and a slightly pinched face, giving him a sad, puppy-dog look. Perfect for walking in front of a coffin, I thought.

As you'd expect, there was a sprinkling of retired professionals in the village, including a brigadier, a surgeon, a bank manager and a former airline pilot. In one of the grandest houses with an imposing entrance and sweeping, tree-lined drive, lived the chair of a large electronics company, an ex-military man. As in Ambridge, there were also a few farmers in the village, along with a number of farmworkers and their families.

The farmers I knew best were the couple who owned my cottage. There was always something happening at their elegant Georgian farmhouse on the edge of the village – a jolly supper party in their spacious kitchen or a boisterous summer gathering beside their pool, to which half the village would have been invited. Though neither I nor they knew it at the time, the couple with their lavish and generous lifestyle were to become my model for the Aldridges of Home Farm.

Thirty years later, Jennifer would be hosting sumptuous parties in her magnificent new kitchen thanks to a Wiltshire farmer called Barbara. And thanks to her husband Edward, Brian Aldridge would be at a farmers' meeting somewhere, complaining about the price of wheat, while his daughter was tipping coloured dye into the family swimming pool at a wild teenage party that had got out of hand.

The other farming couple I got to know pretty well were unusual for Wiltshire in that they didn't actually own land. This hadn't stopped them building up a sizeable sheep flock, by temporarily renting parcels of land on the mainly arable farms in the area. Farmers would agree to sow a couple of their fields with pasture each year, and, on the contracted dates, Robert and Sally would truck in their itinerant sheep.

It was what's called a share farming agreement, now common but unusual at the time. 'It's an arrangement that suits both parties,' as I put it in a feature for *Farmers Weekly*. My friends got grazing for their ewes and a fresh crop of lambs each year, while the host farms benefited from the massive fertility boost only sheep can bring to those thin, chalky soils.

It's why there's a long tradition of sheep-grazing on the pastures of the Wiltshire Downs. Sheep had mostly gone from the Downs by the time I moved to the area. A combination of EU subsidies and chemical fertilisers had made it more profitable to grow wheat, but at least my village friends were reviving the tradition with their pop-up sheep business. They even employed their own peripatetic shepherd to look after the animals wherever they happened to be.

Shepherd Mike had a cottage in the village and, when he wasn't up on the Downs somewhere with his sheep, he was likely to be in the village pub. Six months before I arrived, his wife had moved out, taking their two kids with her to a house she'd rented in Shaftesbury. From what I could gather, life for Mike had carried on much as before. He'd either be up on the downs with his sheep or quaffing pints in the White Horse.

He was a popular figure in the village, especially with those who frequented the pub, which included me.

I enjoyed our conversations. I'd become particularly interested in sheep and the way an itinerant flock could improve the environment on the open downlands. There was always the chance I'd pick up some snippet of news that I could turn into a story for the farming press. Better still, he might even give me a lead for a possible colour feature in *Farmers Weekly*, a real money-spinner.

It wasn't all financial self-interest, though. I'd developed a genuine fascination for the lives of the old downland shepherds ever since I'd met one of the last of them on the farm in Dorset. I'm not saying Mike's life had much in common with those of the old-time shepherds. For them, shepherding was a way of life, practised seven days a week, fifty-two weeks a year, often from childhood to retirement. In the late twentieth century, no one lived like that any more. Even so, Mike and his daily work on the high downs provided a link to that far-off world.

Soon after arriving in the village, I'd read one of the classic works of nature writer W. H. Hudson, *A Shepherd's Life*, published in 1910, which had been set near where I now lived. Hudson portrayed the downland shepherds as naturalists, as interested in the wildlife they encountered as in the sheep and sheepdogs in their care.

I was starting to think about the old ways of farming that didn't involve the wholesale destruction of wildlife and habitats. Most of the farmers I wrote about seemed uninterested in the wildlife on their land. Their aim was to maximise profit. They'd marshal their forces – tractors, workers, combine harvesters, fertilisers, crop sprayers and the rest – in much the same way as a general preparing for battle. It's as if they stood outside the 'theatre' of operations, manipulating the various elements in a godlike way from above.

The contrast with the old shepherds couldn't have been greater. Hudson's semi-fictional shepherd, Caleb Bawcombe, was engaged in the business of farming too, but in a way that didn't destroy his environment. He didn't see himself as standing outside nature, controlling and manipulating. Instead, he saw himself as 'a creature of nature' along with the other plants and animals on those wild and desolate hills.

In Bawcombe's home village, the fictional Winterbourne Bishop, believed to have been based on the Hampshire village of Martin, Hudson writes of the intimate association between man and nature.

> The final effect of this wide, green space with signs of human life and labour on it, and sight of animals – sheep and cattle – at various distances, is that we are not aliens here, intruders or invaders on the earth, living in it but apart, perhaps hating and spoiling it, but with the other animals are children of nature, like them living and seeking our subsistence under her sky, familiar with her sun and wind and rain.

I loved that approach to farming the land. It was surely the answer to the mass destruction going on in the fields of England? Unfortunately, no one seemed interested in the old ways, including Mike, the shepherd.

There are many more vivid characters I remember from those village days in Wiltshire. People like Ernie, who'd been abandoned as a baby at the local workhouse in the first year of the twentieth-century. A born entrepreneur, he'd started work in the village brewery at the age of ten. During the Second World War, when a number of Italian prisoners of war worked on local farms, he was said to have loaned them shotguns so they could pot a few rabbits, which he would then sell, giving them a share of the proceeds.

Then there were Stella and Madge, the Misses Lacy, two middle-aged women who'd made their bungalow home a shrine to a little-known Victorian artist who'd specialised in the landscapes of Wiltshire. I never went inside, but they were said to have had more than a dozen pictures of Stonehenge alone. I was told by 'a usually reliable source', as we journos used to say, that there were three of them hanging on the walls of the downstairs toilet.

Another villager I'd never forget was Stan, a retired tractor driver with an obsession for growing potatoes on any vacant plot he could find, including a corner of the churchyard, to the annoyance of some worshippers. To me, it seemed a great idea. I wasn't averse to cooking up a few holy chips myself.

All these people remain powerfully in my memory. No doubt each of them contributed in some way to storylines and dialogue during my years in Ambridge. The lasting legacy of that downland village was the sense of belonging it gave me at a time in my life when I needed it. For the first time since I'd left the estate at Emmer Green, I felt part of a real community.

It's not something I'd moved to the village explicitly looking for. I'd been offered a place to work and the chance to make a fresh start, that was all. Yet somehow the community had closed around me, pulling me into its invisible web of ties and obligations. This may sound a touch coercive. It was never that. As far as I could tell, no one got drawn in any deeper than they wanted to be. At the same time, you were left in no doubt that, as a village resident, you owed something to the community.

I suppose it started when my journalist friend and I decided to put on a harvest supper in the village hall. There hadn't been one for years, so we thought we'd revive the tradition. I was cautious at first. I didn't want to look like one of those newcomers who starts trying to take over everything. I needn't have worried. Everyone loved the idea. Soon offers of help were pouring in.

On the night, the army captain's wife turned up with a large cauldron of pumpkin soup. Whoever has a cauldron these days? A dozen other village women heaped the long table with cold meats, hams, quiches, an assortment of salads, baked potatoes, plus an array of puddings, both traditional and exotic. Afterwards, the tables were cleared away and the ceilidh band struck up, bringing everyone mobile onto the floor. The pub darts team ran a lively bar, and at the end of the evening Dave and I were given a rousing cheer.

The following day I received invitations to join the darts team and the gardening club, even though I was useless at darts and my patch of garden had been commandeered by Stan for his next crop of first earlies. A couple of days later I was asked if I'd take over as treasurer of the annual flower and produce show, which I did.

Though I couldn't know it, my preparation for Ambridge was underway. Lynda Snell's imperious style could hold no fears for me after a couple of years on the village show committee. If you've ever had to decide who should win the cup for the highest number of winning entries following an unfortunate tie, you'll know all about the loneliness of power.

I'd wanted a sense of belonging and soon I was caught up in a tide of it. But it didn't end the moments of bleakness and loss. There were still nights when I'd lie awake listening to the mice – or rats – scratching in the roof space above my head, feeling nothing but emptiness, that awful sense of being alone in a cold, uncaring universe.

I'd had nights like this in childhood, at Emmer Green. I remember the desolation of that dismal place, as I lay in bed with the music of Tchaikovsky drifting up from my dad's radiogram down below. There'd been nights like it at university, too. Now, despite the busyness and friendships of village life, they'd returned to trouble me again.

I found comfort in imagining the generations of families who'd lived within those ancient stone walls. Their daily existence would have been hard, uncomfortable and haunted by the fear of poverty and the workhouse. Filled with so many everyday concerns, would they have had time, or even the physical energy, to worry about such abstract fears, I wondered.

Among the many attachments I'd established in my new village home was a special relationship with a couple who were destined to become lifelong friends. Like me, Sarah and Rob were from working-class backgrounds. They'd grown up and married in Rochester in Kent. Sarah had trained as a nurse, Rob as a boat builder. They'd hatched a plan to move to Cornwall but only made it as far as Wiltshire. She now worked as a district nursing sister specialising in end-of-life care. He'd taken a job with a boat-building firm in Salisbury.

They lived in one of three Victorian cottages set on high ground overlooking the main village street. I met them in the pub one evening, and we quickly found we had a lot in common. Like me, they were enjoying the novelty of village life and the chance to know people whose entire lives had been spent in the English countryside. Like me, they'd also been surprised to discover that so many of the old class divisions still flourished here.

We shared political concerns too. Like me, they were unhappy with the social and political changes taking place, particularly the rise of Margaret Thatcher and the Tory right. We'd all grown up in a post-war climate of social justice and equal opportunity. We believed in the big society, in fine council estates, a well-funded health service and good schools for everyone. In the new politics, all that seemed to be under attack.

These weren't things we were comfortable talking about in the pub, so we'd usually head back to their cottage, sometimes with other kindred spirits, for a few more beers and a heated political discussion. Or it would have been heated if we hadn't all agreed with each other. We were a radical cell in the English shires, the heartland of conservatism. Perhaps it was an early forerunner of the Grundys' Cider Club, who knows?

Just as urban politics were being transformed, so big changes were going on in the countryside. Tragically, they were generally invisible to our city-focused media. One of my favourite haunts on the Wiltshire downlands was a large, prehistoric earthwork called Yarnbury Castle, between Warminster and Amesbury. Hudson mentions it in *A Shepherd's Life*. In the mid-nineteenth century it was the site of one of the biggest sheep fairs in the country, even though it was remote and far away from any population centre. Castle Sheep Fair, it was known as.

I drove there often from my village home. Although it lay right beside the busy A303 trunk road, as soon as you climbed the massive circular earthworks, you could easily believe yourself to be in the most remote place on earth. In the autumn it was a brilliant place for collecting mushrooms, while in summer the thousand-year-old turf put on a stunning display of chalk-land flowers.

From those walls you got a magnificent view across Salisbury Plain and the downlands. Sadly, there wasn't much of the old, flower-filled grassland left. Much of it had been ploughed up by government edict during the war years. Now, in Mrs Thatcher's Britain, the war on nature had resumed, with the finance coming from Brussels. By this time, the European Economic Community had created a vast surplus of wheat.

Even so, European farm ministers, including our Minister of Agriculture, continued throwing money at farmers, incentivising them to spray more pesticides and grow yet more of the stuff on fragile chalk soils. The grain would all be hidden away in secret warehouses, known as 'intervention stores'. They'd become part of the notorious EEC grain mountain, to be sold off later at a knock-down price to the Soviet Union.

The government appeared perfectly happy with all this. They saw political advantage in farmers clawing back as much money as possible from the UK's contribution to the European community. They seemed oblivious to the reality that British citizens were effectively being taxed to pay for the destruction of their own wildlife and countryside.

All this I saw going on from my lofty perch on the ancient walls of Yarnbury. Not far from here, at a place called Parsonage Down, a particularly upsetting episode was playing out, one that I would later write about. Since the early 1920s, the land had been owned by Robert Wales, a thoughtful farmer who believed, like those who'd gone before him, that the best way to manage the thin, drought-prone soils was to keep them under pasture and graze them with cattle and sheep.

This he did until he died in 1979. The policy didn't make him rich, but it gave him and his staff a living and produced healthy, grass-fed meat for the nation. When he died, his little corner of English downland was as rich in wildlife and chalk-land flowers as when he'd taken it over nearly sixty years earlier. Now it was under threat.

As farmers scrambled to take the 'prairie' option and get their hands on the European cash, fertile grassland like this was in great demand. On the open market the farm was likely to fetch millions.

Farmer Robert had foreseen the danger. In his will, he'd offered it to the nation at a knockdown price of just one-fifth of its market value. Environment Minister Michael Heseltine agreed to put up the money for the purchase, but insisted it had to be paid back to the Treasury within twelve months. This meant the Nature Conservancy Council would have to resell part of the farm at the full market price to recoup the money.

On the day the deal went through, the tractors were lining up in the lane ready to plough up these last fragments of ancient chalk grassland in order to grow more wheat for the European grain mountain. Sometime later, I went to the official opening of the new Parsonage Down nature reserve. Afterwards I wrote a piece for the countryside press about the betrayal of farmer Robert Wales.

'I can't believe what we're doing to our countryside,' I ranted to my ever-patient friends, Rob and Sarah. 'It's totally crazy. Nothing short of vandalism.'

Sarah smiled sympathetically and opened a bottle of Merlot. As we sipped our drinks, she passed on a snippet of news. Apparently, the BBC were about to start filming a dramatisation of Hudson's *A Shepherd's Life*. The chosen location was Bowerchalke on the downs.

'Let's hope they can find the odd patch of grassland with a few wild flowers left in it,' I said.

Ironically, I was doing rather well out of the destruction of the English countryside. Such was the enthusiasm for wheat growing, sales of chemical fertiliser and pesticides were booming. This meant that from March through to October, *Farmers Weekly* was printing super-size issues to provide space for all the chemical companies who wanted to advertise with them. In those days their products had macho names like Commando, Dagger, Avenge and Stomp. What were these toxins avenging, I wondered? What were they stomping on? Song birds? Wildflower meadows?

Since the publishers liked to maintain a constant ratio of advertising to editorial, there were a lot more pages to fill. Freelancers like me were called on to make up the shortfall, especially when it came to features. I'd bought myself a Pentax 35mm camera. If I came up with a 2,000-word feature and supplied a few half-decent colour pictures to go with it, I could earn good money.

I went out of my way to find softer stories with an environmental angle. I found a farmer near Stonehenge who was feeding his cows a forage crop that had been grown on his farm since 1750. It was called sainfoin, he told me, and a century before it had been grown throughout the chalklands of southern England. As a legume, in the same family as peas and beans, it fixed its own nitrogen with the help of soil bacteria, so no chemical fertilisers were required.

Grazed or fed to cattle in silage, it produced remarkable growth rates and milk yields, while growing it built up carbon reserves in the soil. No other crop stood up to drought as well. In summer its beautiful magenta flowers were a magnet for butterflies, bees and other pollinators. As far as I was concerned, it was a better friend to farmers than anything the chemical companies had to offer.

The farmer gave me some good quotes and I got some passable shots of the crop in flower with sheep grazing it. When the feature appeared in the *Weekly* a couple of weeks later, I took great satisfaction from knowing the pesticide companies had paid for something that would ultimately undermine their sales.

There were plenty of other journos filing pro-chemical stories, of course, or pretty quickly the companies would have taken their advertising elsewhere.

Soon afterwards I wrote a feature on the traditional water meadows in a river valley near Salisbury. Each winter these meadows were deliberately flooded by a system of sluices and ditches. The idea was to 'harvest' the fertility being carried by the adjoining chalk stream when it was in spate. The winter 'drowning' of the meadows produced a surge of spring growth, again without the need for chemical fertilisers.

It also produced stunning landscapes, much to the delight of artists like John Constable.

By the late 1970s I'd become interested in the organic movement, led by its founders, the Soil Association. There'd been something of a coup in the movement, with a group of young farmers taking over from the old guard. The new team had grown out of the hippie movement of the 1960s, when a number of young idealists had headed for west Wales to set up their organic farms. The successful ones were now aiming to inject more dynamism into the movement.

I started going to their annual conference at the Royal Agricultural College (now a university) at Cirencester. The event always took place the week after Christmas, before the students returned for the spring term. The Association must have done cut-price deals because there never seemed to be any heating. We'd sit in the conference hall shivering in coats, sweaters and woolly bobble hats. The talk was of transforming society by boosting soil fertility and growing more nutritious carrots. It was heady stuff.

In the evening we'd all drink copious amounts of real ale and organic wine and party until the early hours. Then at nine the following morning we'd appear, red-eyed and padded out like Michelin men, for another round of world transformation. I loved it. I'd found no other group in farming with their zeal, energy and sheer optimism about a better future.

When, a few years later, I joined *The Archers*, organic farming was regularly featured in the show. The farm chosen was Bridge Farm, the dairy farm run by Pat and Tony Archer. In one of my early scenes I had them both going to an open day on an organic farm to see what it was all about.

EXT. FIELD IN WEST WALES. 4.30PM

PAT I'm glad we came today.
TONY So you don't think it's such a barmy idea?
PAT I never did. I wondered if it was going to pay the bills though.
TONY It must be paying the bills for these people.
PAT I suppose. And even if it is a bit of a struggle today, I'm sure this is the way things will go in the future.
TONY And what about our future, Pat?
PAT I think we might just make it work, don't you?
TONY Come on, let's find that tea van. Try a real organic brew-up.

From my time in the Wiltshire village, I began to associate organic farming with the whole idea of community. To me, it wasn't simply a prescription for the way we produced our food, without pesticides or chemical fertilisers. It was also a celebration of everything local. While mainstream farming was fast becoming locked into the global economy for both its inputs and its markets, organic farmers saw themselves as firmly embedded in their local communities.

My models for Pat and Tony at Bridge Farm were a farming couple I'd got to know across the border in Dorset, in a village not far from the giant carved in the chalk at Cerne Abbas. Like Pat and Tony, they'd had a kind of conversion moment. It happened just after they'd taken delivery of a lorry-load of nitrate fertiliser. As they looked out on the huge heap of chemicals in their plastic sacks, they decided there and then they wouldn't chuck any more of this stuff on their land.

Their farming was changed forever. They started processing and cartoning their own milk, creating jobs for people in the local village. They had their wheat stone-ground into premium flour and sold in wholefood shops. They even had their crop harvested by traditional binder so the straw could be used for thatching. Everything was geared to adding maximum value to their products, so as to create jobs and retain wealth – the wealth of the soil – within the local community.

This was the future I wanted for the Archers of Bridge Farm, and when I took over as agricultural story editor in the late 1990s, I got the chance to speed their progress. They were already heading in the right direction with Pat's farm-made yogurts, but I wanted them to go further in developing local markets. Ambridge Organics would go on to become a successful brand, with the products sold first through daughter Helen's shop in Borchester and later through a new shop on the farm. The range of products would grow as Helen's cheeses and Tom's processed meats came on stream.

I wanted the Bridge Farm team to influence community life in other ways, too, not just through food. I'd put Pat Archer at the heart of 'Transition Ambridge', the drive to make the village more 'resilient' at a time of climate change. Now I had Pat take on local business tycoon Matt Crawford and his plans for an industrial solution to the climate challenge. These were the two contrasting visions for the future.

Matt's vision, which later became Justin Elliott's, too, was that 'resilience' would come in the form of big-scale animal factories – a mega-dairy and giant pig factory – supported by anaerobic digesters feeding power into the grid. It reimagined the farm as a kind of industrial estate, a world of concrete, steel, humming motors and security lights. To make it happen there had to be huge capital investment along with government grants. The profits would go mostly to corporate investors and the operation would be fully integrated in the global economy.

Pat's vision (and mine) was rather different. She believed that nature had better and cheaper solutions to the climate challenge, with the benefits going to local people rather than remote corporations. In her new world, sunlight would provide the power for change, working through plants and trees to enrich the soil and build fertility. She'd create a carbon-rich landscape of woodland, grasslands, hedgerows, wetlands and food crops that sustained the soil rather than impoverishing it. It would be a landscape of beauty, diversity and healthy, nutrient-rich foods.

Pat Archer, who'd been an organic farmer for more than thirty years, was well aware of the power of nature and the need to harness it on the farm. She was also keen to find ways to strengthen ties with the village community. Behind all this reforming zeal was the tragedy that took the life of her son John at the age of just twenty-three.

On his brother Tom's seventeenth birthday, he'd gone out on his father Tony's vintage tractor to repair a fence. Later, when he didn't turn up for the party, Tony went looking for him. He found John's lifeless body lying beneath the overturned tractor. The tragedy left deep, long-lasting wounds on every member of the family, no one more than young Tom. This may help to explain why, the following year, he ended up in the Crown Court on a charge of criminal damage.

At the time, a fierce argument had been going on over the supposed benefits and dangers of genetically modified (GM) crops. Leading the campaign against them was the organic movement. Organic farmers feared that if they were introduced, even on an experimental basis, they'd quickly contaminate all farms as their pollen was spread by bees or on the wind.

In Ambridge, Tom Archer was still struggling to come to terms with the loss of his brother. He'd been trying valiantly to keep John's organic food business going. To him, the prospect of GM crops in the village seemed to threaten everything his brother had worked for. I suggested to editor Vanessa Whitburn that we run a story in which Tom and a few friends trash an experimental GM crop on his uncle Brian's farm. He would then stand trial for criminal damage.

While we were still discussing the story, we had a stroke of luck. A well-publicised trial of two women accused of criminal damage to a GM crop was due to be heard in Plymouth Crown Court. On the day the trial opened, the prosecution withdrew their evidence and the case was dropped. In the popular press there were dark hints of political interference. The government hadn't wanted the facts about GM crops to be heard in open court, at least, that was the speculation.

It was great news for us. I contacted the Crown Prosecution Service in the south-west, and they outlined the case they'd intended to bring at Plymouth. I then got in touch with the London solicitor who'd been handling the defence case for the two women. He met me and explained the new and, as yet, untried defence they'd planned. Since the case was no longer to be heard in a real court, everyone was happy it would now get an airing in the crown court at Felpersham.

In Ambridge, word got around the village that Brian Aldridge was growing a GM oilseed rape crop on the estate. Organic farmer Tony Archer was angered that his brother-in-law seemed prepared to risk Bridge Farm losing its organic status as a result of cross-contamination. If pollen from the GM crop were to fertilise plants – wild or domesticated – it could spell the end of the farm as an organic business.

The Ambridge campaign against so-called 'Frankenstein foods' gained momentum. In a protest meeting in the village hall, Brian came under withering attack. Tony spoke up on the risks associated with GM crops. Embarrassingly for Brian, one of his sternest critics turned out to be his daughter Kate.

Then, one evening, David and Ruth Archer surprised a

group of masked saboteurs attacking the GM crop with sickles and machetes. Incensed at seeing a farm crop being damaged, David stormed up to the attackers yelling threats. A brief fracas followed, during which David took a punch in the face. At this the saboteurs made a hasty retreat.

In the village gossip that followed, Kate Aldridge became the number-one suspect. There was shock all round when, a few days later, the police turned up at Bridge Farm and arrested her cousin Tom. It seemed he'd been identified as the driver of the van used in the attack.

Before the drama went out on air, I got a call from the solicitor who'd been helping with the defence case. He could no longer work with us, he explained, as he'd now be defending a real-life anti-GM campaigner, Peter Melchett, head of Greenpeace. His defence team was likely to be using the same legal arguments as Tom in our fictional court.

The Mail on Sunday ran a top-of-the-page story under the headline 'Is the Archers' everyday story of eco-warriors too close to the truth?'.

A few weeks later, Tom Archer appeared in the Crown Court charged with criminal damage. If found guilty, he'd face a prison term. Vanessa and the production team decided we would dramatise the trial and run it over a full week's episodes. I wrote the trial scenes, giving equal weight to arguments for and against GM crops. I wanted Tom to be found not guilty, but the programme managers said they'd decide on the verdict once they'd read the scripts.

Everything was set for a week-long drama in Felpersham Crown Court. Here's a glimpse of how the case unfolded.

MONDAY 25 OCTOBER

10AM

PROS BARRISTER Members of the jury, Tom Archer is no selfless environmental hero. He acted, not out of high ideals or honest belief, but out of bravado and hot-headedness. He is, in fact, a common criminal whose selfish act has caused widespread distress and upset.

CROSS TO MIKE 2. PUBLIC GALLERY:

PAT (WHISPERED) Oh, Tony . . .

TONY (WHISPERED) It's alright, love.

PAT (WHISPERED) It's not alright, it's awful. I knew it would be.

TUESDAY 26 OCTOBER

10.30AM

PROS BARRISTER Tell me, Mr Archer, did you recognise any of these people?

DAVID ARCHER No.

PROS BARRISTER They were all strangers?

DAVID ARCHER They had their faces hidden. With balaclavas.

A couple of them had scarves. You know, wrapped around their faces.

PROS BARRISTER So there was no recognition of any of them?

DAVID ARCHER Not really.

PROS BARRISTER Well, was there or wasn't there?

DAVID ARCHER Somebody shouted something. It sounded a bit like someone I knew.

PROS BARRISTER And who was that?

DAVID ARCHER Tom Archer.

<u>11.15AM</u>

DEF BARRISTER You saw a group of youngsters setting about your neighbour's crop with sickles and machetes. Presumably you felt angry?

DAVID ARCHER I did, I admit it. It's instinctive for a farmer. You see someone destroying a perfectly good crop. Never mind what it is. You just flip.

DEF BARRISTER And that's what you did? You flipped?

DAVID ARCHER Well, I wasn't going to suggest we all sit down and talk about it over a cup of tea.

DEF BARRISTER Are you saying you were aggressive?

DAVID ARCHER Yeah OK, I was aggressive. I asked for it. If I'd been a bit more sensible I probably wouldn't have got thumped.

<u>2.45PM</u>

EXPERT ONE It's true that any new gene construct can lead to the production of new proteins. And in rare cases these might lead to allergic reactions. But in the case of a rape crop it's the oil that's going for human consumption. The protein would be removed during processing.

PROS BARRISTER So in your view, the public are already well protected against any possible health risk?

EXPERT ONE I believe they are.

<u>THURSDAY 28 OCTOBER</u>

<u>10AM</u>

DEF BARRISTER Dr Finch, as a geneticist would you say genetically engineered crops were 'safe'?

EXPERT TWO	I'm afraid I wouldn't. We have too little understanding about the impact of these plants on the environment. That's why we should proceed with the utmost caution.
DEF BARRISTER	You're not against research per se?
EXPERT TWO	Not at all. But I don't think we should be doing it in an open environment. Not without taking all necessary precautions to prevent gene escape. Once they're out there, there's no getting them back.

<u>FRIDAY 29 OCTOBER</u>

<u>2PM</u>

PROS BARRISTER	The defence has tried to present the genetic modification of crop plants as a hazardous and unpredictable technology. You've also heard from scientists who are convinced this technology has huge potential benefits for mankind. And that it's being introduced with all proper caution.

The defendant, Tom Archer, thinks he knows better. He has taken it upon himself to make the decision for us. He and his pals are doing their best to trash these trials before they can produce any useful results. From beginning to end, this whole adventure was furtive, ill-considered and sordid. Those who took part were criminals - selfish and totally indifferent to the interests of others.

<u>3PM</u>

DEF BARRISTER It's difficult for us, ladies and gentlemen of the jury, to comprehend the anxiety and concern felt by this young man, the defendant, Tom Archer. He had seen his father made sick with worry at the situation. He had watched his father's desperate attempt to rally opposition to this crop by calling a protest meeting in the village hall. But to no avail. The concerns of local people appeared to have no affect at all on the landowner, Mr Aldridge, or the owners of the crop.

What was the defendant to do, faced with what seemed like the wanton violation of everything he held dear? Well, we know what he did. Out of concern for the consequences of what he considered a foolhardy experiment, he joined with a group of equally worried youngsters to try and remove the danger. He did it because he cared passionately about the environment we all share. He may well be wiser than the rest of us. So how on earth can we condemn him for it?

<u>CROSS TO MIKE 2. PUBLIC GALLERY:</u>

TONY (WHISPERED) Great, eh, Pat?

PAT (WHISPERED) Yes. But now it's up to the jury.

TONY	(WHISPERED) It's going to be Monday, I should think. By the time we've had the judge's summing-up.
PAT	(WHISPERED) It just goes on and on.
TONY	(WHISPERED) It's nearly over now.
PAT	(WHISPERED) Is it? We don't know that. What if this is just the start?
	(SIGNATURE TUNE)

Pat needn't have worried. On Monday, following the judge's summing-up, the jury delivered a 'not guilty' verdict, as the BBC management had decided. It's the outcome we'd all wanted. I like to think the 'suits' had been led to the same conclusion by the evidence presented in Felpersham Crown Court.

To me, it was a great result. We'd dramatised one of the most contentious issues of the day and presented the facts in a totally even-handed way. To balance the pros and cons of the GM debate, we'd measured the airtime devoted to each side to the very second. Even so, at the end of it I felt we'd struck a blow for a greener Britain. In the Commons, one MP commented that he'd learned more about the GM argument from the *Archers* storyline than anything he'd read in the media.

A few weeks later, Peter Melchett went to trial for the offence Tom Archer had been charged with. His legal team used the same defence, and like Tom he was acquitted. It felt like a triumph, not just for organic farmers, but for the whole nation. The interest of the community had, for once, won out over the forces of globalisation and rural decay.

I stayed three years in my cottage below the Wiltshire Downs. Before I left, I took a drive south to the downland village of Martin, now in Hampshire. This was Hudson's Winterbourne Bishop, the home of shepherd Caleb Bawcombe. I called in at the little church, walking among the moss-covered tombstones in the churchyard. I was delighted to find a small sheep flock grazing in a fenced-off section.

In the centre of the little lawn, an ancient headstone had been re-erected in a position easily visible to worshippers walking toward the church porch. Though the letters were worn and half-covered in lichens, it was still possible to make out the words.

Shepherd of the Wiltshire Downs
William Lawes
Died December 14 1886

William Lawes had been the inspiration for Isaac Bawcombe, the father of Caleb, in Hudson's *A Shepherd's Life*. Close by the stone, sheep tugged at the churchyard grasses in the early evening light. Beyond the village the first mists of autumn were settling on the high downs. It was reminiscent of the time when the way the land was farmed left plenty of room for nature.

Would we ever see such methods used again? Who could say? If I had my way, we'd certainly be seeing them in Ambridge, though. As a soap writer I should have known better. As in a Hardy novel, fate was to intervene.

8

Paradise Postponed

IT WAS TELEVISION THAT put paid to my Ambridge ambitions, which I suppose you could say was quite fitting. Back in the 1960s, TV-phobia was a common complaint among *Archers* editors, convinced they were losing audience through the pulling power of shows like *Coronation Street* and *Emergency Ward 10*.

Editors, too, found themselves drawn by TV magnetism. I'd only been on the show a couple of years when William Smethurst deserted Ambridge and headed off to Crossroads Motel, taking half the writers with him. I was in the half he didn't take.

Three decades later, Sean O'Connor shocked us all with the bombshell announcement that he was off to Albert Square and the East End. The news put paid to my as-yet-secret plan to restore the English countryside to its former glory.

It wasn't all bad, though. Before he left the show, O'Connor gave me two parting gifts. The first was a second-hand copy of a beautiful book, published in 1948, called *The Golden Year.* It told the story of a small Welsh farm and the life around it, as seen through the eyes of a naturalist and poet called R. M. Lockley. It's a beautiful account of the countryside and rural life before industrial farming began its demolition job.

Sean's second gift was a conversation we had during a car journey from Hay-on-Wye to Hereford. It was about the psychology of the Second World War bomber crews and the strain they were under, a subject he'd researched for his own remarkable book, *Handsome Brute*. This was the harrowing and at times moving story of a highly decorated wartime pilot who went on to become one of Britain's most notorious murderers.

Sean's insights made me determined to find out more about my dad's wartime history, especially the events that seemed to trouble him through his life. It would become my new mission, but first there were upheavals in Ambridge to take care of.

The year was 2016 and everything in the village had been looking just fine. Life was getting back to normal after the Great Ambridge Flood. Fortunately, there had been no casualties, except for Freda Fry, and as her voice was never heard, grief was fairly muted. In fact, the flood seemed to have brought out the best in everyone. Even the detested wife-abuser Rob Titchener had displayed considerable personal courage in rowing his little boat in total darkness across the swirling floodwaters to rescue Shula Hebden Lloyd at the riding stables.

On the farms of Ambridge, preparations were going ahead to protect the community against future climate emergencies. At Home Farm, Adam Macy was monitoring the performance of his herbal leys, the herb-filled pastures that are super-charged to remove carbon from the atmosphere.

In Adam's view, this was the future of livestock farming, an answer to the jibe that grazing with cattle and sheep were as bad for the planet as torching rainforests. Whether he'd ever get his stepfather Brian Aldridge to come round to his way of thinking was debatable.

Over at Brookfield, his cousin Pip Archer was also taken with the idea of putting flowers back into pastures. Not to be outdone, Helen and Tom Archer were planning green changes at Bridge Farm, their organic place. They'd decided a productive farming landscape ought to contain more trees. Agroforestry is the name for this kind of farming – a combination of orcharding and conventional farming where the food output per acre is generally higher than both. And as with Adam's herbal leys, more carbon gets captured and stored in the soil.

Whether BBC programme managers picked up on these subtle changes to the Ambridge landscape, I've no way of knowing. Each month they received my latest set of 'Agricultural Notes', but I doubt many of them were read. To be honest, it didn't matter much to me. Editor Sean seemed happy and that's all I worried about.

From the moment he took charge at *The Archers*, he'd made it clear that farming was to be at the heart of the programme. But this wasn't simply a convenient mantra to be parroted to the media as evidence that the programme remained true to its roots. Sean genuinely believed that our connection with the land was what gave the show its enduring appeal. In his view, British identity was still linked to the countryside; its land, and its landscapes. It was an emotional bond he wanted woven into the storylines. This suited me just fine. I intended to make the most of the opportunity.

Though I hadn't totally taken Sean into my confidence, I'd made plans to nudge Ambridge in an even more radical direction. I was toying with the idea of turning Bridge Farm into a 'local food hub'. From their fields and orchards, I'd have them producing an ever greater range of foods, from apples, pears and nuts to all kinds of meats. Along with their cheeses and processed dairy foods, they'd be sold through the farm shop.

It would become a major food-retailing destination, breaking the stranglehold of the supermarkets with their food miles and plastic packaging. The Bridge Farm shop would link people with their local landscape in a way which would bring a new enchantment to everyday foods. Ambridge would lead the world.

My plans for Brookfield were equally ambitious. At some time or other, I intended to have Pip and Josh Archer replace the grazing paddocks for their dairy cows with herbal leys, as demonstrated by Adam Macy. I knew a farm manager in the Cotswolds who'd been grazing his dairy herd on these flower-filled pastures for about ten years. In that time he'd captured, or 'sequestered', massive amounts of carbon, taking it out of the atmosphere and storing it in the soil.

I'd visited his farm a couple of times. It was situated on a high, cold plateau that had once been a wartime aerodrome. Now it was producing nutrient-rich milk from super-healthy dairy cows on their salad-bar nutrition. Plus it was making a serious contribution in the struggle against climate change. If that weren't enough, its flowering fields created a sweet spot for bees, butterflies and other pollinators. Each summer there'd be clouds of them drifting above the cow pastures.

If this could work on a cold, Cotswold hilltop, why not in leafy Ambridge? I wanted the show's central farm to be leading the way in returning nature to the British countryside. There needed to be bees and butterflies in the cow pastures of Brookfield, too. When listeners tuned into *The Archers*, they should be immersed in the sights and sounds of a wildlife-rich countryside, even if the sights were in their mind's eye. It was our job to put them there.

I never quite got round to talking through these ideas with Sean, but I felt sure that if I introduced them carefully, respecting the characters involved, he'd be up for it. By this time he'd been in the job three years, and he and I were writing most of the five weekly storylines between us. He worked out the relationship stories. I devised and wrote up developments around the farms.

Within the BBC, Sean's stock was just about as high as it could be. His 'gaslighting' story – the cruel demolition of Helen Archer's personality and identity at the hands of her sinister husband Rob Titchener – had sparked massive media courage and won much praise. The idea that a sixty-year-old radio drama could portray an abusive marriage more shockingly than any other media show seemed to have come as a total surprise.

Following the success of this story, Sean was free to do pretty much what he wanted, such was the confidence he enjoyed from programme managers. What he most wanted was a few more plaudits from the BBC along with a modest increase in the show's budget. When Godfrey Baseley, the show's creator, was given the go-ahead for a three-month trial run in 1950, he'd famously been allowed £47 an episode.

Something of that same penny-pinching attitude still persisted. Even though the show had long been the most influential drama in the British media, working on it felt a bit like being on a daytime TV show about rug-making. There was a touch of make-do-and-mend about it.

It's not that Sean expected the show to be showered in riches. But as he said, it would be nice to plan a story without worrying the actors might suddenly go 'non-available' because they'd taken a couple of well-paid days on *Casualty*, or that a writer might head for Coronation Street or Albert Square, not for the prestige but for the money.

Sean's view was that *The Archers* was just about the most successful and influential drama in the history of broadcasting. Professionals ought to be queuing up for a job in Ambridge and, having landed one, should feel immense pride and a sense of achievement. How could there be pride in the job when the programme managers appeared to hold it in so little esteem? That it happened to be a radio drama was no reason for running it on the cheap.

Confident that the good times were on the way, I started to think big. I dreamed up bold new policies for the Ambridge farms. I would repair this damaged and industrialised landscape and return to what you could call 'nature's default'. This was my logic. *The Archers* had been inspired by a community of mostly small, independent farms. Together they'd created a vibrant and nature-rich countryside, a land of immense beauty as encapsulated in *The Golden Year*.

In the English Midlands, the chosen setting for the drama, the countryside had once been a mosaic of small fields, hedgerows, woodlands, wetlands and flower-filled meadows. Many of these features had now gone, swept away by the fetish for technology and chemicals. *The Archers* had played its part in this rural revolution. The show had made heroes of modernisers like Phil Archer and poked fun at the 'traditionalists' like Walter Gabriel and Joe Grundy.

Surely the policymakers would now have to reverse the process. Modern, intensive agriculture had thrown up too many unintended consequences – biodiversity loss, soil erosion and most damaging of all, the release into the atmosphere of millions of tonnes of carbon that had formerly been locked up in the soil and in those traditional landscape features.

Faced with these problems, the government would surely have to start paying farmers to put carbon back into the landscape. Sooner or later, they'd realise that carbon capture through a change in land use was the most effective and practical strategy available for countering climate disruption. Techniques like 'mob grazing' and the planting of herbal leys could capture and store carbon as effectively as growing trees. In the business it's known as 'regenerative agriculture'.

What if Pip and Josh Archer were to take up these methods at Brookfield? What if, instead of using electric fences to set up their grazing paddocks, they were to plant new hedges? The paddocks would instantly become small fields.

As organic farmers, Tom and Helen Archer would surely follow a similar path. They'd already decided on tree-planting as part of an agroforestry enterprise. Wouldn't they now be thinking of new hedges as well? And ponds? And wetlands?

Before long I was imagining the landscapes of the 1950s, the ones I remember from around the Reading housing estate where I lived. I was also imagining feature articles in the *Daily Mail* and the *Telegraph*. I could see the headlines: '*The Archers* returns to its roots'.

I felt sure the listeners would love it: the re-creation of an older England, its wildlife restored; a land echoing to birdsong where, in the mind's eye, we'd see brightly coloured butterflies dancing across flower-filled summer meadows.

My rural vision knew no bounds. I even began thinking of restoring some of the old rural politics. The common thread in the history of these islands was enclosure, the relentless removal by a powerful elite of the people's rights to land.

The consequences were there for all to see, even today – homelessness, income inequality, soaring rents, inadequate housing and poverty. All these social ills could be linked to the process – begun in Tudor times – of denying peasants their long-treasured land rights. Shouldn't a soap rooted in rural England find new ways to tell these stories of ancient wrongs and how they impacted on communities today?

A bold new storyline began to form in my head. Joe Grundy would have been the obvious lead character. He was endlessly complaining about long-forgotten injustices perpetrated by the Archer family. Everyone had heard Joe's rants and no one took much notice of them. They were simply his way of making sense of a world in which misfortunes seemed to be heaped randomly on some, while others prospered.

What if, for once, there was truth in one of Joe's complaints? What if Jennifer Aldridge, the village's resident historian, were to uncover a piece of land skulduggery? Here's how it might play out. She's in the local studies section of Borchester Library studying enclosure settlements for a blog she plans to post on the village website. She's scrutinising a copy of a nineteenth-century document when she spots something that doesn't make sense.

She reads it again, more carefully this time. It concerns

a piece of land she knows well – perhaps it's part of Brookfield Farm. Oddly, the boundaries set out in the document don't match up with those of the field today. There's a block of twenty acres that's now part of the field but which, according to the old document, shouldn't be there.

I was warming to the idea. What a great story for Joe or Eddie, or maybe the next generation, Ed and Emma. Joe had been right all along. Some long-forgotten member of the Archer family had robbed a long-forgotten Grundy of a parcel of land, and in doing so had changed the course of Ambridge history. If it hadn't happened, who's to say the Grundys wouldn't still be the tenants of Grange Farm? Maybe they'd never have gone bust.

I could see the drama unfolding. Ed and Emma Grundy would take on Pip and Josh Archer in a bid to get their land back. Their action would undoubtedly split the village, always a good starting point for an *Archers* storyline. Even better, it would have implications out there in the real British countryside. Who really owns our land? For whose benefit is it being managed?

It was the kind of story the media might go for. There'd certainly be a Twitter debate. Perhaps the *Guardian* would run a feature on land reform. There might even be questions in the Commons. It had happened before with *Archers* storylines. There was the famous case of Susan Carter, imprisoned for helping her brother Clive, the arsonist, following his escape from custody. That led to questions in the House.

I was convinced the Ambridge Land Grab was going to become another iconic *Archers* story. That's when I got the call from Sean. My brilliant storyline was about to explode like a banger on Bonfire Night.

SEAN Hello, it's Sean. How are you?
ME I'm OK, thanks.

For some reason, I hear Joe Grundy whispering in my ear.

JOE Why's he calling you today? He never calls on Monday.
SEAN I thought I ought to call you. I've got some news . . .
JOE Said so, didn't I?
SEAN I shall be leaving the programme at the end of the month. I don't suppose you want to hear that.

My mind's temporarily scrambled. I'm trying to work out what this means.

SEAN I've been offered the job at *EastEnders*. In many ways I wish it hadn't happened. It's been a really hard decision, I can tell you.
ME You're going to *EastEnders*?
SEAN It's not something I went looking for. I've loved working in Ambridge, you know that, and I really appreciate the job you've done.
ME What about all our stories?
SEAN They'll go ahead as we planned them. At least until the new editor starts. After that it'll be up to her or him.
JOE He's never leaving Ambridge? He wouldn't be so daft.

ME So when are you going exactly?
SEAN Like I said. End of the month.
ME OK.
SEAN Don't worry, it'll be fine. The show's in really good shape.
JOE So what does he want to leave the village for?
SEAN It's really important what we've been doing here.
JOE So why's he going then? He's as bad as the old squire. Tells you he's got the village at heart. Don't stop him feathering his own nest when he gets the chance though.
SEAN Like I said, I wish the offer hadn't come right now, but it has. I honestly feel I've got to take this opportunity. I hope you can understand that, Graham?'
ME Well, good luck anyway.

Soon Sean was gone and with his departure went my plan to launch a rural renaissance from the BBC Mailbox building in Birmingham. Looking back, I shouldn't have been totally surprised. I knew his high profile had brought him to the attention of the TV soaps. I'd had a foretaste of what might happen during the car journey we'd shared during the summer.

We'd both been speaking at an *Archers* event at the Hay Festival. Afterwards, I drove Sean to the station in Hereford, where he was due to catch a train back to London. During the journey he took a call from ITV. I gleaned it was some sort of job offer. When he'd hung up, he said in a matter-of-fact way: 'They want me to go and run Corrie.'

He must have seen the look of panic on my face because he quickly added: 'Don't worry, I won't be taking it.' The reason, he told me, was he still had big plans for *The Archers*. The show was riding high, and he wanted to bring back a former producer, Kate Oates, who'd left a few years earlier to go to *Emmerdale*. Kate, who'd been a brilliant storyliner, was now executive producer and was rumoured to be ready for a change.

'I think I may be able to persuade her to come back,' said Sean gleefully. As well as creating great stories, Kate had a warm and fun-loving personality, making her one of the most popular people on the team. If she came back to Ambridge, this really would be the show to work on.

Kate didn't return. A couple of weeks' later we heard she'd taken the vacant job on *Coronation Street*. This came as a blow to Sean. I guess it was one of the reasons he took the job at *EastEnders*. In the big world of TV drama, it felt like he was being left behind.

Back on that drive to Hereford station, I mentioned to Sean about my dad's wartime trauma and the mystery surrounding it. I can't remember how the subject came up, but Sean had plenty to say about it.

The Air Ministry recruited pilots with a distinct psychological profile, he told me. The sort of men they wanted might be described as headstrong, impetuous, arrogant, devil-may-care. These all seemed to fit my dad, though I was well aware that there was another, softer side to him, one he dared not show the world.

'I'm thinking about writing to the MOD and asking for his service records,' I told Sean. 'Apparently they'll now release them to next of kin.'

'You should,' he said. 'Let me know what you find out. I'll be interested.' I found out a great deal but I never had a chance to tell Sean. He'd gone to Albert Square by then.

For the next few months there was a sort of interregnum in Ambridge, with the show being run by 'direct rule' from London. The head of radio drama was drafted in from Broadcasting House to keep things ticking over. It wasn't a great time to be working on the show. For the time being at least it wasn't going anywhere, and somehow I knew my days in Ambridge were numbered.

In the summer that year there came another shock. The British people voted to leave the EU. For years I'd ranted against the European Common Agricultural Policy and how it was killing our wildlife, contaminating our food and generally wrecking what had been a productive and sustainable farming system.

Now the hated policy was to go. I ought to have been ecstatic but I wasn't. Instead I felt ashamed that we were abandoning our friends and neighbours across the Channel. How could we so easily have forgotten the suffering of two world wars?

By coincidence, the next day's post included a package from the Ministry of Defence. I'd written to them requesting my father's wartime service record. The package contained copies of two record sheets, with handwritten entries detailing the progress, or otherwise, of Peter Harvey, trade – u/t pilot (under training). Below were recorded his date of birth and civilian occupation: solicitor's clerk.

In a separate box were the basic details of his marriage to my mother, Rhonda Waters. The wedding had taken place in Hastings in March of 1940. I knew my father had been posted to the Sussex town early in the war.

Though there's no surviving photograph of the wedding, there's a family picture of Dad posing in his full flying kit on what appears to be a hotel balcony.

He looks incredibly young and handsome, every inch the dashing English air ace. I can understand how my mum fell for him. I tried to imagine what their big day would have been like in that forlorn seaside town in the winter of 1940. Who would have been there to celebrate with them, I wondered. Had any of their three surviving parents made it down from Reading and Abingdon?

I couldn't imagine my mum's father making the trip, suffering as he was from his Great War disabilities. So who would have given my mum away? Perhaps it was one of Dad's air force mates. What had been the couple's hopes for the future at a time when the lives of either of them could have been snuffed out in an instant?

Lower down the page was a huge black blob. Someone had tipped over the ink bottle while making an entry. The stain, shaped like someone's leg with a boot at the end of it, stretched almost to the bottom of the sheet. The anonymous clerk had written the word 'ink' alongside the blob. I felt a rush of anger that someone should have been so careless as they recorded my dad's fate.

I wondered if it was the same hand that, in a box headed 'Miscellaneous', had written the words: 'Relinquishes the authority to wear the observer badge.' Here it was, officially recorded. Confirmation of the family story that Dad had been grounded and shamed.

He'd been stripped of his coveted aircrew status. Although he'd enlisted as a pilot, he'd retrained as an observer/navigator and was crewing the legendary

Mosquito, the fast, twin-engined fighter-bomber known as 'the wooden wonder'. The prized observer badge was as much a mark of courage and honour as the 'wings' of a pilot. Now he'd suffered the shame of losing it because he'd been unnerved by too many hazardous operations.

Elsewhere on the record sheet was a box marked 'Time Forfeited'. It recorded the days that would be added to his five-year engagement in the RAF, which had begun in August 1939, before war had even been declared. In this box were just two handwritten entries. As I read them, I grew even more angry.

The first entry recorded four days of lost service. The time would be added to his service before his official discharge. The reason for the lost days was given as 'Close arrest' and lasted from 4 October to 8 October 1943. The second entry recorded ninety-one days of lost service, from 13 October 1943 to 12 January 1944. This time the reason was 'Detention', presumably following a court-martial. The period covered the time of my birth on 1 November.

I tried to imagine my mum's state of mind while this was going on. All she knew was that there'd been no communication from him for weeks. She told me she'd feared he had been killed. She believed the Air Ministry were withholding the information, knowing that she was soon to give birth.

Now I knew the real reason for his silence. He'd been locked up in a military gaol. Even though he, like all RAF aircrew, had volunteered to fly, he'd been punished for losing his nerve. He'd apparently panicked under the unimaginable stresses of air warfare. Today it would be called 'combat stress'. Back then you were branded a coward and humiliated. LMF – lack of moral fibre – was stamped on your passbook.

The truth is he'd been a very brave man. I have the evidence in the combat reports he wrote up in his observer's log. Each entry, in his own meticulous handwriting, is a record of courage in a unique set of combat conditions. Sadly, the evidence appears to have counted for nothing. It didn't protect him from public humiliation or a gaol sentence.

As far as I was concerned, the court-martial had been an inhuman act. I was convinced it had been a major cause of the demons that haunted him and which blighted our family life. I was soon to discover that events in those far-off wartime days were rather more complicated.

In Ambridge, we were still working without a permanent editor. I sent in my five weekly storylines as usual. Adam Macy would take delivery of a high-tech seed drill. This amazing machine would do away with the need for ploughing and cultivations, he'd explain to his less-than-enthralled mother Jennifer. There would be enormous benefits for the soil. Carbon levels would steadily rise, helping to stabilise the climate. Jennifer would become marginally more interested.

Meanwhile, Tom Archer would apply for a Nuffield travel scholarship. This would give him the chance to study how farmers around the world were diversifying into the organic baby-food market. This he saw as 'the next big thing'.

Over at Brookfield there'd be another instalment in the emerging love triangle between brothers Toby and Rex Fairbrother and the object of both their fancies, Pip Archer.

All pretty routine stuff, but it was hard to be inspired when the programme seemed rudderless. It's as if we writers were crewing a high-speed clipper ship that suddenly found itself in the doldrums. We were drifting around on ocean currents waiting for trade winds in the form of an editor with a vision for the future.

Perhaps anticipating my departure from the show, I decided to drive up the motorway and take a walk in *Archers* country. In more than thirty years in Ambridge, I'd never once visited the countryside that's supposed to have inspired it: the farming country to the south and east of the old Midlands spa town of Droitwich. It's surprisingly easy enough to find this fabled land. You simply drive north on the M5 motorway from Worcester until you see the twin lattice-steel masts of the Droitwich radio transmitter, and you know you're there.

I must have passed those masts a thousand times in my journeys to and from *Archers* script meetings in Birmingham. Opened with much razzamatazz in 1934, the long-wave transmitter broadcast the BBC's 'national service' across much of Britain and a sizeable slice of western Europe.

I don't remember the serendipitous moment when the connection dawned on me. Those skeletal steel towers beside the motorway were the technology that broadcast the daily happenings of an English village to the nation. At the same time they acted as way-markers to the very part of England that had inspired the show. How wonderful was that!

On my Ambridge day out, I left the motorway at the next junction and skirted around the edge of Droitwich, taking the old Roman road, the Salt Way, heading east. I knew that somewhere to the left of me was a farm called Summerhill, once owned by the sister-in-law of *Archers* creator Godfrey Baseley. This is said to have been one of the farms that inspired the programme's Brookfield.

The road leads through what was once the ancient royal hunting forest of Feckenham. Soon after crossing the Worcester and Birmingham Canal, I turned off on a side road signposted to the village of Hanbury. After a short distance, I drove into the car park of the National Trust's Hanbury Hall, a large Queen Anne-style stately home standing in parkland.

I had no intention of visiting the house. To be honest, it's not a place I felt particularly comfortable. Hanbury Hall has long been thought of as the model for Lower Loxley Hall, home of Elizabeth Pargetter and the twins, Freddie and Lily. In our fictional world it had been the family home of Nigel until his untimely death. It was here that the amiable, scatty, passionate environmentalist and devoted family man fell to his death while trying to take down a banner from the roof.

A sizeable section of the audience was outraged. Some vowed never to listen to the show again. The reaction caused us all to reflect on the decision we'd made. It was clear we'd completely underestimated the affection the character was held in. While the decision to kill off a character is never taken lightly, it's happened a number of times in the programme's history. Sometimes there are good dramatic reasons for doing it. After all, the sudden death of friends or loved ones is an experience most of us have shared.

Even so, the distress caused by Nigel's accident made many of us question our motives for endorsing the storyline. I had a special reason for feeling uncomfortable.

Those feelings came flooding back as I stepped out of my car at Hanbury Hall.

Pushing such thoughts from my mind, I walked away from the grand house and took a well-marked footpath across the fields, following the signs to Hanbury Church. The weather was hot and the sky an azure blue. I strolled across a couple of pasture fields, passing a series of ancient oaks in their full summer foliage. Under one of them about seventy sheep lay tightly packed together, making use of every patch of shade. Together they traced exactly the shape of the ancient tree.

After a mile or so, the path opened onto a steep, narrow lane leading up to the thirteenth-century hilltop church. Hanbury Church has long connections with *The Archers*. In 1951, the carol service in the show's fictional St Stephen's Church was recorded here. Villagers packed the pews to sing along with members of the cast. The following Easter the church was the setting for the wedding of George Fairbrother and Helen Carey.

The most momentous event of all took place three years later, when the young farm manager Philip Archer married his great love Grace Fairbrother, a marriage that was to be cut tragically short. In those austere times it was the showbiz wedding of the year. You could almost call it a 'royal' wedding. The Archers were, in those days, a sort of second-division royal family.

On the day of the great event, more than 500 well-wishers packed the church pews. Outside, the lane was blocked by dozens of cars. The BBC's outside broadcast vehicle got stuck in the traffic queue and the real-life rector of Hanbury had to call out the registration numbers of the cars that needed to be moved.

There were no crowds on the day I walked up to the church. No vehicles passed me in the tree-lined lane. After its brief frenzied moment under the nation's gaze, this quiet corner of England had returned to its usual slumber. Even so, the steep climb in the summer sun turned out to be well worthwhile. Built of handsome red sandstone, the church of St Mary the Virgin, Hanbury is a beautiful place occupying a dramatic position overlooking the Worcestershire countryside.

From the church gate I took the path through the churchyard with its lichen-covered gravestones. While some of the grassy areas had been mown, most had been allowed to grow tall and lank, presumably to encourage wildlife. Bees and butterflies drifted among the grass seedheads. A large, tiger-striped cinnabar moth caterpillar chewed on a ragwort plant.

At the edge of the churchyard, a grassy bank dropped steeply away to the south, providing a spectacular view across *Archers* country. The Ordnance Survey map told me I was looking across Worcestershire towards Evesham and the River Avon, with the distant Cotswold Hills to the south-east and the distinctive spine of the Malverns to the south-west.

This was what the map said, but I know the truth. I was in the county of Borsetshire, location of Ambridge, Penny Hassett, Loxley Barrett, Darrington, and a host of other villages whose names were known only to Radio 4 listeners. Seen from the churchyard, it was a land of gently rolling hillsides, pasture fields and crop-lands, hedges, copses and slow, meandering waterways. Scattered across this landscape were a number of farmhouses and cottages, many of the black-and-white timbered variety or of mellow red brick.

In the warm July sunshine, it was easy to imagine this landscape hadn't changed in centuries, though I knew it had. When butcher's boy Godfrey Baseley cycled across it delivering his dad's meat, most of the dwellings would have been occupied by farming families. It was overwhelmingly a landscape of family farms. They'd created a mosaic of small fields, hedges, orchards, meadows and pastures, plentifully stocked with cattle and sheep.

Though many of the small-scale features of that pre-war landscape would have gone, enough remained to reveal the English treasure it must once have been.

When the war came, Baseley again travelled the countryside, this time promoting the government's 'Dig for Victory' campaign and later making farming programmes for his new employer, the BBC. Rural south Worcestershire was a land of thriving village communities. Later, when he started planning his new radio drama set in just such a community, the centuries-old pattern was beginning to unravel.

Sitting in the grass of the ancient churchyard, I couldn't avoid thinking of my dad. He must have got to know this landscape intimately as he converted from pilot to air observer/navigator. In January 1942, he'd been posted to Bomber Command's navigation school at RAF Staverton in Gloucestershire and then at nearby Moreton Valence aerodrome. For the next twelve months he'd criss-crossed the country on training flights, mostly in the twin-engined Avro Anson.

Except when bad weather made it impossible, the working day included at least two hours flying. Each trip was written up in his log book with the care and neatness you'd expect from a trainee solicitor's clerk. The early entries are filled with navigator's jargon: *Staverton to*

Llanbedr. D/F Fixes. W/V Air plot. TR and GS. Or: *Air Plot No. 4. W/V 3 Drifts Fixes 02. Compass.*

Later, the entries simply refer to a 'Navigation Exercise'. Daytime flights were written in black, night exercises in red. One navigation exercise in August involved a five-and-a-half-hour flight and took him and Pilot Officer McIver over Great Ormes Head, Newtownards in Northern Ireland, and RAF West Freugh in south-west Scotland. However, most of the training flights lasted around two hours and generally stayed closer to home.

As I sat amid the grasses, I wondered what he'd have made of the countryside below – that's if he'd had a chance to look away from his plots and drifts. His life until now had been mostly spent in the town, chiefly Reading. What would he have made of this world of small fields and hedgerows? He's certain to have known the hilltop church so close to his Gloucestershire base. A prominent landmark, it was probably used for his 'fixes'.

At the end of February 1943, he was posted to the Mosquito Training Unit at RAF Marham in Norfolk. For a few weeks, training flights were conducted in the twin-engined bomber, the Blenheim. Then, on 13 March, the first log-book entry for the legendary Mosquito appears. The entry reads: *Cross Country. Low Level Bombing*. Through the spring the Mosquito training intensified, both by day and by night. In mid-April he was posted to a Mosquito squadron, number 105, also based at Marham.

By the end of the month he was carrying out active operations. The entry for 27 April reads: *Low level attack on Julich. 4 x 500 bombs. No flak observed*. On the following day: *Wilhelmshaven. Night attack. 4 x 500 MC Bombs. Inaccurate heavy flak observed*. On 1 May he records: *Recall owing to bad visibility. Crashed aircraft.*

Despite the crash, the log-book entry for the following day shows that he and his pilot, Flying Officer Coyle, were back in action flying the same aircraft: *Low-level attack Thionville. Stbd engine u/s over enemy coast. Flak over coast and Yvetot.*

Each time I read these entries I'm struck by the obvious courage of my father and the pilots he flew with. Their days involved a few hours of extreme danger followed by a return to near normality, a pattern repeated day after day. For some, the constant pressure becomes too great to bear.

In June he was posted to a newly formed unit known as 1409 Met Flight, based at Oakington near Cambridge. The codeword PAMPA began appearing in his log book. This was the time of massed night-time bomber raids on German cities. Experience had shown up the deficiencies in weather-forecasting methods for the chosen targets. Weather conditions could make the difference between a successful raid and a catastrophe in terms of aircraft and crew losses.

Air Ministry strategists believed PAMPA (Photo-recce and Meteorological Photography Aircraft) would be the answer and 1409 Flight was set up to test it. A couple of hours before the bombers set off on a raid, a crew from the flight would fly over the chosen target, first at height, then for a second time at low level. The aim was to give the bomber crews and their controllers an accurate assessment of weather conditions. If the flight's assessment was that conditions were unsuitable, the raid would be abandoned.

It could be dangerous work. Unarmed Mosquito aircraft were generally used, relying on their speed to get them out of trouble. On reaching the target, the duty crew would have to descend below the cloud base, which might be as low as a hundred metres. This would often put them in a highly vulnerable position. One former pilot wrote of emerging from cloud to be confronted by eleven enemy fighters.

According to war historians, the atmosphere at Oakington was unlike that of a bomber station. Crews remained on call day and night, and there was little chance of getting away from the scene of operations. Because the work concerned future bombing raids, security was of special importance. This may be why many of the PAMPA entries in my father's log book contained no destination details.

The book records that on 15 June he and his pilot – Flying Officer Becker – returned with the port engine 'u/s'. Eight days later, in a different aircraft, they crashed in a field at Histon, near Cambridge. The following month, Dad flew on PAMPA missions to Amsterdam, Essen, Hamburg then Essen again. There were three more missions that same month to unidentified targets.

During August he flew on four PAMPA missions, three of them to northern France. The fourth was to an unspecified destination, one that required double the flying time of the French missions. That was the last. There were no more log-book entries. Flying for the month was signed off in the usual way by the officer commanding 1409 Flight, Flight Lieutenant Hatton, and that appears to have been the end of Dad's flying career.

For me, it left a lot of unanswered questions. His service record shows he was placed under close arrest on 4 October, so when did his breakdown occur? What happened in September? Had he been taken off flying duties before the crunch point? Was there another flight during which he lost control and panicked? Or was it that he simply refused to board the aircraft at all?

From the hilltop churchyard I looked down at a peaceful countryside. A few wisps of cloud were now streaking the blue sky. The only sounds were from bees and crickets performing their own timeless dramas among the wild grasses. The events of wartime Britain seemed a world away. Even so, I knew I'd have to find some answers.

For now, though, I had more urgent matters to attend to. I looked across to the distant outline of the Cotswolds, partially obscured in the heat haze. I was soon to meet a remarkable woman on a small farm on the edge of those distant hills. I believed she would give me an insight into the spirit of village England in the momentous post-war years that produced *The Archers*.

I needed to find out if the show's creators had been right to settle on their chosen scenario. Or had they missed the far bigger story that might today have led to a happier and healthier land?

9

A Duty of Care

I DROVE THROUGH THE Oxfordshire countryside in a state of high excitement. It was a trip I'd been planning for weeks to a farm I'd first read about years earlier. At the end of the Second World War it had been the best-known farm in Britain and its owner a national hero. I suppose you'd call my trip a kind of pilgrimage.

I passed through the village of Enstone with its honey-coloured houses and cottages, then took a country road that led across farmland. After a couple of miles I turned into a quiet lane. I saw immediately what I'd been looking for – a simple sign with just two words that made my heart leap. Oathill Farm. Turning into the driveway, I drove onto a concrete track leading to the main house and buildings. From here I got my first clear view across the farm.

I found I had to stop for a moment. I was becoming quite emotional. This was a view I'd come to know intimately from a plain black-and-white picture in a book I'd looked at a hundred times. The caption read: *A general view of the farm.* Now here I was, thirty-plus years after seeing it for the first time, looking across those same fields. It was all a bit overwhelming.

Much had changed, of course, since that wartime photo had been taken, not least the arrival of a Formula One racing team headquarters alongside the farm. There were a lot more buildings around the farmhouse and, most strikingly, the cattle, sheep and chickens had gone from the fields. There were no cereal crops either. Most of the land had been sown to grass. Even so, I knew the place instantly. In an odd way it felt as if I'd come home.

Over the years I've collected several copies of the wartime classic *The Farming Ladder*, but the copy I treasure most is the one I discovered by chance forty-plus years ago in William Smith, second-hand booksellers of London Street, Reading. I'd pulled it from the Agriculture section, attracted mainly by the title. Though by then I was working as a farming journalist, I still clung to the idea that one day I'd get my own small farm. It was this same dream that had helped make the book a bestseller among young people caught up in the great conflict.

In his preface, written in 1943, George Henderson explains why he wrote the book. It was 'to demonstrate how a happy, secure and useful life may be spent, on what were a few barren acres, without the toil and drudgery which are usually associated with smallholding, and that a financial return may be obtained comparable with that in any other business'.

To a wannabe farmer like me, the words seemed scarcely believable. They went against every conventional view of farming – that you needed to do it on a big scale, to invest a lot of money, and to have a low expectation of ever making a decent profit. All that was being turned on its head.

George went on:

> The methods used, none of which are clever or unusual, will show that in peacetime depression or in wartime prosperity the creative work of the farmer can have its just reward, independent of tariffs and subsidies, if directed on the right lines; that great capital, special knowledge or skill are not essential, only energy, patience and a thorough grasp of the underlying principles.

What war-weary young English man or woman with a hankering for a life on the land could pass up on a promise like that? Even thirty years after the war ended, when I first read those words, it still had the power to make the unattainable seem possible. To me, this is what gave this plain wartime publication, printed on thin, economy-standard paper and bound with rough-edged pages, such huge and enduring potency.

The book's main adornment in those times of utility was a stylised plan of the farm printed in two colours on the inside covers, at the front and at the back. Drawn by artist C. F. Tunnicliffe, it shows the buildings, hedges and fields, the crops they grew and the animals they raised in the year before publication. The picture is of a small, mixed farm, the sort you'd often find in children's books.

The fields, which are tiny by today's standards, all have names – Duck Field, Spring Field, Garden Ground, Barn Field, Radford Hill. I loved these names. They gave the farm its own, distinct personality. They're a mark of human engagement and care for the land before it all got lumped together in some great, anonymous dirt factory.

Equally charming are the artist's tiny, hand-drawn icons of cattle, sheep, chickens and wheat sheaves, used to indicate what each field was growing or being stocked with in that year. Around half the land was in wheat and cereal crops, while half was down to grass and was being grazed by cattle and sheep, or pecked over by poultry.

It's an idealised picture of what was, at the time, a typical small farm growing a range of crops and livestock. In reality this little farm was anything but typical. According to official stats, it was producing more food per acre than almost every farm in Britain, large or small.

I could never understand why *Archers* creator Godfrey Baseley and his writers hadn't told this story. They'd imagined a village community based around a couple of small, mixed farms. Yet they'd ignored their greatest attribute – their ability to feed large numbers of people, in wartime and in peace. To me, Henderson's story was inspirational. It had enchanted a nation being tested by war. Why hadn't Baseley's team told it to a post-war generation challenged by shortages and rationing? Perhaps now the need was even greater as the world faced climate change and the loss of wild species.

As I drove on down the farm track towards the house, I began to think of how the case for small, mixed farms might somehow be woven into our storylines. The Archers at Bridge Farm could be considered small farmers. They had about seventy hectares in all, small enough by today's standards though double the size of George Henderson's farm.

On the downside, they were organic and, while they already followed many of George's principles, there was a risk the case for small farms might get confused with arguments over the rights and wrongs of pesticides.

The Grundys – Joe, Clarrie, Eddie, Will and Ed – would have been ideal candidates if they'd still been the tenants of Grange Farm. What a story that would have been: Joe using George Henderson's methods in a spirited bid to hang onto his farm. Now it was too late. I was annoyed with myself for having missed the opportunity.

As it happens, I needn't have worried. I was about to meet a remarkable woman who'd show me an even better way of telling the story of this legendary farm and the timeless principles applied here. I didn't know it at the time. I'd simply come for lunch.

I parked in a small space opposite the house and walked up the garden path. As I rang the doorbell, I felt a mixture of anticipation and nervousness. I wouldn't be meeting my farming hero, George Henderson, I knew that. He'd died many years earlier, but meeting his widow seemed momentous enough.

The woman who greeted me put me instantly at ease. Elizabeth Henderson was tall and elegant, with sparkling eyes and a welcoming smile.

'You must be Graham from *The Archers*,' she said. 'We like *The Archers* here. Come in, come in. Did you have a good journey?' She led the way through the hall into a dining room, where sunshine streamed in from the garden. The table had been set for six and I was immediately introduced to Elizabeth's daughter Louise and son Francis, who now ran the farm.

The daily lunch, I discovered, was a free-and-easy affair where any family member who happened to be around simply dropped in. Since a number of them worked on or around the farm, there was often quite a crowd at the table. Even so, there always seemed to be room for the occasional visitor like me. More than six decades after George's book first appeared, people still wanted to see the farm that had inspired it.

'I hope you didn't mind me phoning up out of the blue,' I said as we ate. 'I'd only just discovered you were still here. I just had to get in touch. A hell of a cheek, I know.'

'I'm very glad you did,' Elizabeth assured me. 'If I hadn't done much the same all those years ago, none of us would have been here today.'

Later, over coffee, she told me her own extraordinary story. She'd grown up in Somerset with her twin sister and brother, the children of middle-class parents. Though the family were comfortably off, there had been tough times, too, as there were for many in the 1930s. Her great passion was animals. While still at school she kept goats in the family's large garden.

When she left school in the last year of the war, she joined the Women's Land Army and was sent as herdswoman to a dairy farm five miles from her home. It meant being up at five each morning to cycle there in time for milking. On her birthday, her nineteenth, her mother gave her George's book – already a bestseller. It was a present that was to change her life.

Sitting up late in the family kitchen and reading by the light of a Tilley lamp, she got through it in two evenings. Like thousands of others, she was inspired by George's story. It made the dream of becoming a farmer not only possible, but readily achievable through dedication and hard work. Fired with ambition, she wrote to George and asked him to take her on as a farm pupil, a sort of informal agricultural apprenticeship.

George's response was cool. They couldn't possibly take on girls, he told her. There weren't the facilities.

They had a number of male pupils who boarded in the farmhouse, along with George and his mother Flo. It wouldn't be 'appropriate' to bring a young woman into the household.

Elizabeth wasn't easily put off. She wrote back with an impassioned plea.

'I just have to come and work at Oathill Farm,' she insisted. 'I don't care where I live. A barn, an old hen-house. In Timbuktu if I have to. I just *have* to come and work there.'

George's resistance crumbled. He invited the nineteen-year-old for an interview, then offered her the position of farm pupil. She'd lodge at the nearby Land Army hostel.

As she recalled these far-off events, the eighty-seven-year-old Elizabeth still had a clear memory of her early days on the farm. She recalled the first task she'd been given: scrubbing out the hens' water troughs. She also remembered the shock she felt at getting a marriage proposal from the boss.

It happened during hay-making. Elizabeth had been piling up the mown grass onto wooden frames or 'haycocks', as they're called, to speed the drying process. George came by, ostensibly to check on her work, but clearly with something else on his mind. To her surprise – and dismay – he blurted out his proposal. The forty-year-old farmer wanted to wed his nineteen-year-old apprentice.

Her first response was panic. In a state of confusion, she walked away. Having thought about it for a while, she decided to say 'yes'. 'He was a kind and caring man,' she wrote later. 'I realised we'd have a good future together.'

The wedding took place in Somerset, a small family affair under wartime conditions. George travelled down alone for the occasion. His mother disapproved of the relationship and refused to attend. But the marriage proved a strong one. The couple raised five children on that little farm on the edge of the Cotswold Hills.

During this time, farming was going through a revolution, both political and technical. As partners, George and Elizabeth guided the farm through the momentous changes, and when he died in the early 1970s she continued running it, with family help, until she retired at the age of seventy.

As I listened to her story, I was struck by the quiet strength of this woman, with her twinkling eyes and ready smile. Though elderly and a little frail, her zest for life was clearly undimmed. In that repressive world of male control and regimentation, she'd been determined to make her life an adventure. What courage it must have taken to leave the safety of her Somerset home in wartime and make a life for herself in farming, and on her own terms.

What she shared with George Henderson was a passion for life on the land. In his book, George, a Londoner, wrote that he realised early on there was only one thing worth doing on this earth: to farm it. This is what she responded to as she read his book by lamplight. Over the years it's what many of us have felt as we read it, though not all of us have had the courage to act on it. Elizabeth Henderson had become for me Hardy's Bathsheba Everdene.

As I drove home I found myself thinking about Pip Archer at Brookfield Farm. At sixteen she was becoming a major character in that central farm. I'd written a few scenes with her myself. Mostly she'd played a peripheral role in whatever drama was going on.

When characters were new there was always a temptation to give them short, throwaway lines rather than invent new character traits that would make them more complex. There was a risk the editor might not like your invention and ask you to rewrite the scenes. Writing to tight deadlines was stressful enough without adding needless complications.

Hearing Elizabeth's story made me think afresh about Pip. Elizabeth had become a farmer at a time of momentous change. Wartime farming had been kept under tight state control, then with the peace the government had embarked on a massive expansion driven by public subsidy.

While George had been a doughty campaigner against subsidies and what he saw as state control, Elizabeth hadn't been interested in politics. Even so, her marriage and her partnership in the farm put her at the centre of events at a time of great upheaval. This had been the background to the BBC's new drama about farming families.

Today, our countryside is on the verge of change as great as in those post-war years, or so it seems to me. Climate change and our vanishing wildlife are creating a new reality. Why not put our new young character, Pip Archer, at the centre of events, just as Elizabeth Henderson had been in the 1940s and 50s? In fact, why not take her story to the point where she became the new boss at Brookfield?

She could then lead the farm, and maybe the nation as a whole, into the new era of climate-friendly farming. Put simply, this new, charismatic figure would be taking

The Archers back to its roots. Just as the show had reflected an output-oriented agriculture at a time of food rationing, it would now show a countryside becoming more resilient in response to the climate emergency.

Of course, it wasn't down to me to decide the destiny of the programme's leading characters, but I could have an influence through my storylines. A consensus was already emerging among the production team that Pip, Ruth and David's eldest, would be the next head of the Archer dynasty, based at the tribal home of Brookfield. First it had been Dan and Doris, then Phil and Jill, followed by Ruth and David. Barring upsets, the next incumbents were likely to be Pip and her daughter Rosie.

I imagined Pip bringing the same youthful exuberance and passion for farming the young Elizabeth Henderson had shown. Thanks to the writing team, she'd got off to a pretty good start. By the age of thirteen she was doing the occasional milking, as well as parading young cattle at the local agricultural show. At fourteen she was taking part in decisions about the farm's cattle-breeding policy.

<u>INT. SOMERSET PIZZA RESTAURANT.</u>
<u>MONDAY 12.45PM</u>

DAVID So are we all agreed we want to try out Brown Swiss?

PIP Yeah.

RUTH Agreed.

DAVID Carried unanimously.

PIP Are we going to get a bull?

RUTH I think we should do. AI for the cows and a young bull to run with a few of the heifers.

DAVID Sorted. Hopefully we'll end up with a couple of dozen crossbred replacements, so we can see how they perform.

PIP It'll be ages before they're in the herd.

RUTH Three years.

PIP I'll be seventeen by then.

DAVID Just in time for you to do the milking and me to retire.

PIP OK, you're on.

RUTH Seriously, Pip, this could be the foundation of a new herd. So you've got to be in favour.

PIP I am. I think it's great.

DAVID Let's hope you don't change your mind and decide to be a TV presenter instead.

PIP Don't worry. It's not going to happen.

The following year, Pip was in the cowshed helping her dad carry out a tricky operation on a sick cow. The animal had become ill after giving birth to a healthy heifer calf. Now she was going downhill fast. David was convinced it was mastitis of the most dangerous kind. She needed urgent attention but he hadn't been able to get through to the vet. There was only one thing to do. The cow would have to be given an antibiotic injection directly into the jugular vein in her neck.

The emergency treatment required a steady hand from David and steel nerves from Pip. With a halter on the cow, she had to keep the cow's head rigid so her father could make the difficult injection. The fifteen-year-old was more than up to it. If anything, she stayed cooler in the crisis than her dad. The treatment was successfully administered, and later the vet congratulated them both on saving the cow.

Was this a new leader of Brookfield in the making? Could this be the young woman who would inspire a new generation of environmental activists and take British farming in a new, greener, more community-minded direction? Was this the 'Dan and Doris' for our age? Unfortunately, from her late teens, the character had looked less a cultural icon than a chaser after rainbows.

At the local college she started an affair with an older man, mature student Jude Simpson, much to the concern of her parents. She wanted to go backpacking around the world with him, though in the end he dumped her and went off on his own. Later, at university, she spent so much time partying she almost failed her first year. She surprised her parents by somehow managing to get a degree. She then took a job with a global agri-business company, only to walk away from it after a week.

These were all good soap stories which no doubt reflected the lives of many young people, but they weren't where I wanted to go with the character. Like David and Ruth, I had ambitions for Pip Archer.

Back on the farm, we began to see a more grounded character. In the world outside Ambridge, the price of milk had collapsed. Like many dairy farmers, Ruth and David found themselves producing at a loss. They were starting to think the unthinkable. How long could Brookfield continue as a dairy farm? The idea that the cows might have to go came as a severe shock to Pip. For the first time in her young life, she understood the insecurity felt by her parents and countless other farmers across Britain.

In my storyline for the period, I outlined a scene in which Pip shared her worries about the family's predicament with her mother. This is how I imagined it. Mother and daughter are at the kitchen table, chatting over a coffee. Pip has finished the morning milking but she's wondering if there's a long-term future for her on the farm.

'If I'd stayed in High Wycombe, in the job, you and Dad would've been better off. You could've done without me around pushing up the bills,' she says.

'That's rubbish.'

'No it isn't. I'm just one more drain on resources that you don't need right now. To think that only a few months ago I was trying to persuade you to spend four hundred grand on robotic milkers. Crazy.'

'Yes, well I can't say I'm sorry we pulled the plug on that one.'

'How stupid could I be? That would have just about pushed the whole business over the edge. I'm a total liability round here.'

This is too much for Ruth. She's not going to allow her daughter to talk herself down any longer.

'I'm not having this. When you told us you wanted to come home we were absolutely delighted, your father and I. We still are. We need you here, now more than ever.'

'Really?'

'Yes, really. OK, these are tough times, no one's denying it. But that's precisely why we need you here. We need your energy. We need your bright ideas. This is a family business, that's our strength, and you're a vital part of that. Believe me, we can't get through this without you, Pip.'

'Oh, Mum . . .' Pip is close to tears.

'So let's have no more of this nonsense. We've got to pull together and get through this, right?'

'Right. Thanks, Mum.'

This was a turning point for Pip. Life at Brookfield was destined to get a good deal tougher before it got better. Ruth suddenly decided to go on a study tour in New Zealand. Not long afterwards she called to say she'd be staying on. David was deeply upset and worried she might stay away for a long time. It was no secret that the marriage had been going through a rocky patch following a tumultuous year.

Pip, too, was unnerved by the sudden absence of her mum. At the same time, she'd been thrust into the key role of keeping the struggling farm afloat. Her father's growing anxiety about the marriage meant he was operating at below his usual competence. Ready or not, his daughter had to step up and fill the void. Not only was she required to shoulder the main burden of the farm, she had to somehow keep up her dad's morale and stop him sliding into despair.

In the weeks leading up to Christmas, Pip became the effective manager of Brookfield Farm. She worked with Matthew, the young contract milker, to fine-tune the cows' ration so they were soon performing better. There might not be any profit in the enterprise but, like any farmer, she took much pride and satisfaction in a job well done.

She complimented her father on the quality of the silage he'd made in the spring. It was one of the reasons the cows were milking so well, she told him. It was also why the Hereford beef cattle were gaining weight quickly. She revisited the idea she'd come up with years earlier that they should sell more of their food direct. Fired with a new determination to boost the farm's income, she called on organic farmers Helen and Tom Archer at Bridge Farm to see if they'd be willing to stock Brookfield beef in their farm shop.

When David returned from a visit to the bank even more gloomy about the farm's prospects, she thought up creative ways to cut costs by removing herself from the payroll. She would look for a job near home, one that would give her the time to work part-time on the farm. If she couldn't find anything suitable, she'd set herself up as a self-employed contract worker picking up whatever agricultural jobs were going. Anything to get the farm back into profit.

As it happens, none of these potential remedies were needed. Ruth flew home from New Zealand shortly before the New Year. In the big family meeting, she set out a new direction for the dairy herd, one based on making better use of the pasture. Even during these straitened times, it should bring the enterprise back to profit. To David's huge relief, Ruth also came back fully committed to their marriage.

The pressures on the family and farm had eased. Even so, the young Pip had been prepared to take responsibility during a particularly difficult period. She'd been willing to commit everything to ensure the farm survived. More than that, she'd shown that things like home, family and community mattered to her.

I wasn't content to leave it there, though. I had another, bigger ambition for the heir apparent of Brookfield Farm.

I had the idea that this young character on a popular radio soap might show the world how to overcome the biggest challenge we faced: climate change.

This wasn't so far-fetched as it might seem. Climate scientists argue that our best hope of halting – perhaps even reversing – climate change may be to re-carbonise farmland.

I went to a London talk given by a remarkable Australian microbiologist-turned-climate scientist called Walter Jehne. He showed convincingly that our best – perhaps our only – way of averting climate disaster is to restore soils to peak fertility, with high levels of soil carbon and the ability to hold huge amounts of water. Jehne called it regeneration of the Earth's soil carbon sponge.

With soils re-energised and rehydrated, the natural hydrological (water) cycles that govern 95 per cent of the Earth's heat dynamics would be restored. They would cool the blue planet as they did 420 million years ago. The process is known as pedogenesis. It covers the evolution of soils, their hydrology, our stable climate, resilience against flooding and drought, and the cooling of the planet. Farmers, if we empower them, can make all these things happen.

Listening to one of my science heroes, I started thinking about how to get these ideas into *The Archers*. The show had played some part, a minor one admittedly, in setting Britain on its disastrous transition from small-scale, sustainable farming to industrial agriculture. Now our world was in peril, the programme surely had a role to play in guiding us back to a carbon-intensive, planet-saving agriculture?

Getting such a complex and controversial idea into a

popular soap would be a challenge, though. Understandably, writers aren't keen on storylines around issues or abstract concepts. They know the best drama revolves around conflict and emotion.

So here was my dilemma. I'd discovered a farming system with the potential to bring back wildlife and combat climate change, but there was no denying it was complex. It required a conceptual leap from thinking of farms as factories with measurable inputs and outputs to re-imagining them as complex ecosystems to be managed.

I knew I'd never get away with a detailed explanation of the interaction of soil microbes with the roots of plants, for example. To me, these subterranean events were among the most exciting things I'd learned in a lifetime, but my fellow scriptwriters were sure to ask me: 'What's this got to do with drama?'

Here's the way I usually raised issues in my storyline notes:

> *Adam Macy, who's pretty environmentally aware these days, knows that many of the methods they use at Home Farm are damaging to the planet. He's taken part in plenty of online chats on the subject of ecological agriculture and, as we know, he's had a few run-ins with his stepfather Brian on the subject. Let's try and reflect some of these attitudes in conversations with other characters.*
>
> *It doesn't have to be more than a few lines here and there. Maybe he makes a chance remark to Jim Lloyd, 'the Prof', triggering a conversation on climate change. Adam will know only too well that farmers don't have a great track record in this area. Their extravagant use of chemical fertilisers and*

pesticides have made things a great deal worse over the years.

These products, made from oil and gas, have done serious damage to the life of the soil, especially to the vast population of microorganisms that underpin life on the planet. Adam will argue that he's trying to mitigate these effects through the planting of cover crops and the use of 'no-till' drilling methods. The idea is to rebuild fertility by boosting levels of soil carbon, he'll tell 'the Prof'. He'll admit, though, that farmers have a long way to go before they can claim to be the solution rather than – as they are now – the cause of many environmental problems.

That's the general tone I used in my notes. Measured, reasonable, hopefully balanced. I tried not to let my own enthusiasm for nature-friendly farming appear too obvious. The writers knew my views well enough. They'd heard me banging on about the issues in numerous script meetings. I hoped that when they read my notes one or two of them might be fired up, as I was, with the possibility of a more wildlife-rich and beautiful countryside, one that would give all of us a better future.

A consensus was emerging among environmentalists and many farmers that what was needed were nature-friendly systems. These would deliver healthy, nutrient-dense foods from a countryside rich in wildlife. They'd also produce a variety of 'public goods', including food security, flood protection and climate stability.

As far as I was concerned, *The Archers* needed to reflect this new view of farming in its storylines. Our listeners would surely be interested in this alternative approach.

Sadly, I never quite got my fellow writers to see it this way. Maybe I should have adopted Lynda Snell's directorial style when I wrote my storyline notes:

> *Here's something you need to wise up on. You've got to be the luckiest bunch of writers ever to work on this show. You've arrived in Ambridge at a special moment in history. You have an opportunity to change the way Britain and the world sees farming and food production. If you tell good enough stories, you might even help save the planet from climate catastrophe. Who's not up for that?*
>
> *So here's what you need to know. Farming's got itself in the position of relying on the oil and energy giants for pretty much everything it grows. Brian Aldridge and his business pals on the estate are out there in front as you'd expect, but if you think the Brookfield Archers are on the side of the angels, forget it. They use nitrate fertilisers too, which puts them among the planet-trashers. It's time to face facts. Most of our farming characters make a living by using the oil and gas industry's dodgy products.*
>
> *The good news is we've got a chance to fix things. We need a couple of our farmers to make history by turning their backs on chemicals, especially nitrogen fertilisers. Instead, they need to use techniques that take carbon out of the atmosphere and store it in the soil. Please don't tell me Helen and Tom are already doing this because they're organic. Maybe they are but we never hear them talk about it, which on a radio show is rather pointless.*
>
> *Here's how you're lucky. Climate scientists – some of them anyway – say that if the world's*

farmers produce just one-fifth of their food by these carbon-sequestering methods, they'd reverse climate change and stabilise weather patterns. If you don't think that's worth telling stories about, you're working on the wrong soap. So, let's come up with some great plot ideas and see if we can save our planet.

That's the note I'd like to have written but never did. As far as I was concerned, if farmers were in a position to save the planet, *The Archers* ought to be there with the story. If I wanted Pip Archer to emerge as Ambridge's environmental champion, she'd have to go on a similar journey to mine. Like me, she'd have to discover what a handful of pioneering farms were achieving around the world using methods known as 'regenerative'.

What was needed, I decided, was a storyline that introduced conflict from the very start. Something disruptive. The obvious way in was through the farmers of Home Farm, Brian Aldridge and Adam Macy, who were always arguing over something. The soils at Home Farm were likely to have been in pretty poor shape, I thought. For nearly four decades Brian had been hammering them with chemicals, with the big flood of couple of years earlier also taking its toll.

What if Adam were to come up with a plan to restore the flood-damaged soils, using herbal leys to nurse them back to fertility? Brian would object, of course. The idea of deep-rooting herbs nurturing soil microbes would sound decidedly flaky to Brian the arch-rationalist. Nonetheless, he'd agree to Adam's green experiment, I was sure. Every so often he liked to toss the odd morsel to his stepson for the sake of a smooth-running farm.

So, as per the storyline, herbal seed mixes were sown on a few of the fields at Home Farm. The following summer the blue flowers of chicory and the pink/magenta flowers of sainfoin glowed brightly in the summer sun amid the brown seedheads of the grasses. Eco-warrior Lynda Snell congratulated Adam for laying on such a glorious spread for the local bees. Even Brian was pleased. If nothing else, the spectacular show of pasture flowers added up to some first-class PR for the farm.

It was Pip I wanted to bring into the story, however. If, as I expected, this form of regenerative farming was to be the future for the UK countryside, then the heir apparent of Brookfield needed to make it her own. I invented a story where Adam employed Pip part-time to manage the cattle grazing the flowery leys. Over a season or two, she'd get to see how productive they were and persuade her parents to adopt them at Brookfield. *The Archers* would flag up to its millions of listeners the new countryside revolution that was underway.

As I imagined the spectacular, flower-filled pastures, I started planning how best to make use of them as a location. This was surely a place where love might blossom, there among the waving flower-heads and the flickering butterflies? At the time, Pip was in an on-off romance with artisan gin-maker and wannabe farmer Toby Fairbrother. In my mind's eye I saw the two of them riding their quad bikes over the flower-filled fields of Home Farm, their attachment sealed in a summer of love.

Things didn't quite work out that way. The show's new editor, Huw Kennair-Jones, had plans to make Pip Archer anything but a heroic leader. He wanted a story about an outbreak of a highly infectious livestock disease that Pip could be blamed for spreading. So I came up with IBR, infectious bovine rhinotracheitis. The virus would first appear in dairy cattle at Brookfield. It would then spread to all the herds in the village as a result of Pip's carelessness in allowing a bunch of cattle to escape.

She would go on to make things a great deal worse by trying to cover up her mistake. Brookfield Farm and Pip in particular would be vilified in the Ambridge farming community. Inside the family, David and Ruth would be deeply angry that Pip had lied to them.

Not quite the heroic character I'd been trying to portray, but a good story nonetheless. I consoled myself with the thought that flawed heroes often go on to achieve great things. Sadly, the herbal leys at Home Farm hardly get a mention these days. I'm still hoping the story will re-emerge sometime.

Following my meeting with Elizabeth Henderson, I was so inspired by her story I decided to turn it into a stage play, a one-woman show called *No Finer Life*. In it, the young Elizabeth recalls her life on that small Cotswold farm in the momentous days of Britain's recovery from war. In the final soliloquy, Elizabeth is determined to remain hopeful after George loses his battle to save Britain's small mixed farms from the clutches of the Ministry of Agriculture.

```
ELIZABETH  Later we walked through the snow
           to the top of Radford Hill, just
           as the last wintery rays of
           sunlight were fading beyond the
           far hills. Far away a curl of
           smoke rose up from a field. Just
           another hedgerow being ripped
           out, said George. He seemed
```

> resigned to it. It looks like the world isn't interested in our story of hope, he added. Not yet perhaps, I said, but it will be one day. And when that day comes, we'll have to make sure this little farm is still here to show the way, won't we? George put his arm round me. The wind was picking up, a cold one from the north. And together we turned to walk back home. Spring and new life would not be far behind.

That day has now clearly come. How brilliant if *The Archers* were to champion George Henderson's style of farming, having signally failed to do so in its early years.

10

Out of the Blue

IT'S A WET SATURDAY in early March 2015, and the rain's coming down in stair rods. Every so often the gusty wind hurls torrents at the windows of Brookfield farmhouse. No one inside takes much notice. They have other things to fret about.

Following David Archer's autocratic decision to call off the planned move to a new farm in the north-east, everyone's feeling hurt and angry, especially Ruth and Pip. As the rain lashes the window panes, the atmosphere in the kitchen is toxic. Resentment hangs in the air, as thick as the aroma of Jill's weekend baking. As I eavesdrop on the family's discomfort, I can't help but feel a small glow of satisfaction. It's me that's brought them to this. Not a bad job, if I say so myself.

Though they don't yet know it, the family is about to suffer a blow far more momentous than the dashing of their removal plans. Their land and home are about to be engulfed in a flood that will put their lives in danger and severely test their courage and resourcefulness.

It won't be just this one family that are put at risk. The entire village community is about to be hit by the deluge, making dozens of them homeless and calling for the wartime spirit of dogged grit and determination to see them through. We're about to test our characters to destruction, to put them through an ordeal that will change their lives for ever.

It had been the idea of *Archers* editor Sean O'Connor. He was keen that, early in his tenure, we should remind ourselves and our listeners of what you might call the show's 'founding myth'. Somewhere out there in the green and leafy shires there existed a rural community which enshrined all those virtues we like to think of as particularly English – tolerance, humour, courage, endurance, self-sacrifice.

We would put our characters under extreme pressure and show how they more than rose to the challenge. We'd see a resurgence of the wartime spirit – a sense of 'whatever gets thrown at us, we'll all pull together and come through'. There'd be individual acts of heroism, kindness and generosity. Characters we thought we knew would behave in unexpected ways to help others. We'd remind ourselves that when the chips are down, we English can be relied upon to come together and help one another.

Sean shared my view that farming communities had their own distinctive qualities. There aren't many jobs where your home is also your place of work and where, if you have animals, you're required to be on top of things for 365 days a year, rain or shine. There aren't many jobs where a seemingly random natural event like an outbreak of cattle disease can threaten both your livelihood and your home. Such things give farmers special qualities of resourcefulness as well as strong family bonds.

It was a farmer who once told me that there was nothing in nature so hard to change as the farmer's mind. It's a job where people live daily with the possibility of disaster. The chance may be small but it's always there. You'd want to make sure those aspects of your life and business you could control were securely locked down.

Now we were about to present our central farming family with the biggest challenge of their lives, a sudden, catastrophic flood that would reveal the fearsome power of nature and show how easily it could overwhelm the flimsy defences of riverside communities.

Sean and I had planned a year-long build-up to the story. The idea was to set up a totally different threat to the farm, a diversionary tale, a false plotline that would ultimately lead to rancour and dissent within the family.

The aim of the story was to point up the quiet strength of this ordinary village community. To do this we had first to reveal its fault lines. Its strengths would emerge at a moment of danger, just as it had at the outbreak of war. The more arguing and in-fighting we could see in the days and weeks leading up to it, the more heroic the response would seem.

The first challenge was to come up with a plausible threat to Brookfield Farm, one that would undermine family morale. We needed them to be at a low point when catastrophe struck. Sean's idea was for a road scheme. Short of the natural disaster we had in mind, what could be more terrifying than a letter from the council proposing a new road through the middle of the farm?

Here's what might make the family contemplate leaving Brookfield. They were the show's First Family, *Archers* royalty: farmers Ruth and David, their offspring Pip, Josh and Ben, plus David's mum, Jill, Brookfield's own 'Queen Mother'. For the family to move from the farm would be like the King leaving Buckingham Palace. It was inconceivable. Britain would never be the same.

Yet somehow, we had to believe the family might actually take the momentous step. To the BBC's programme managers, it would have been unthinkable, of course, but we who lived daily in Ambridge had to take our characters to that point. If the farm were about to be bisected by a new, fast road, running the place would become a nightmare. A shock proposal like this might just be enough to persuade the family to move.

We'd have them start by joining the village campaign to fight the monstrous plan, but in the end they'd decide that moving to a new farm in Northumberland – close to Ruth's family home and where her mother Heather still lived – would give them a better future. We also had to convince Archers fans that the move might really happen. I'm not sure we achieved this, but at least they seemed content to go along with the story and see where it led.

The key was to ensure each character had his or her own iron logic for wanting to make the move. By the time David made his high-handed decision to pull the plug on the plan, everyone except Jill would be in favour. If I'd been able to call in at Brookfield and interview the key characters about their hopes for the future, these are the kinds of things they might have said.

Pip Archer, 22. It's not great leaving all my friends and family. But I've got to be realistic. Farming's my future, I know that. And doing it on a farm that's been split in half by a stupid road makes no sense. With the compensation and the sale value we get on this place, we'll have enough cash to put up a brand-new, purpose-built dairy building on the new farm. Which I'll get a chance to design. And since it's me that's going to be running the business before very much longer, it's a no-brainer.

Ruth Archer, 46. It's going to be a wrench leaving here, obviously. What with Jill and the family all around us. Not to mention all the wonderful friends we've made over the years. But thinking what's best for the future – especially for Pip and Josh and Ben – we've got no choice really. It's got to be a fresh start. And to be honest, it'll be a great relief living close to Mum. She's getting quite frail these days and I'll be able to take better care of her.

David Archer, 55. Quite honestly this has been the hardest decision I've ever had to make in my life. My grandfather Dan set up this farm. My father Phil spent his entire life looking after these fields. And now I've decided to walk away. It'll be like tearing a bit of my heart out. But farming's about hope and the future, not being stuck in the past. That's why I know it's time to move on. Besides, it's not about my generation any more. Our time's coming to an end. The land needs a new generation now – Pip, Josh and Ben's generation.

Josh Archer, 17. Moving to the new farm's going to be a great opportunity. To be fair, I'm still going to be spending a lot of time in this area. I'll be keeping the business going, you know, doing the used farm machinery. Only now I'm going to be able to set up a branch up north, maybe based at Hexham Market. There's a whole untapped market up there. This is going to be getting me close to national coverage. The sky's going to be the limit. I don't want to big it up too much, but I reckon there's a good chance I'll be retiring by the time I'm forty.

Jill Archer, 84. I'm going to miss them all terribly when they go, I know that. But there's no question of me going

> with them. I couldn't dream of leaving Ambridge. It holds too many memories for me of life with my Phil. We've shared so many good times – and hard times too – in this village. And now he's buried at St Stephen's, where he played the organ for so many years. How could I possibly leave this place? I wish them all the luck in the future, obviously. But it can't be with me.

So everything was in place for the Archer family to make their historic move from Brookfield and from Ambridge. A new farm had been chosen in Northumberland and contracts were being drawn up. The sale of Brookfield, under threat from the new road scheme, was being arranged by the local auctioneers. A fleet of specialist cattle lorries had been hired to move the dairy herd north.

Everyone was getting excited about the new chapter that was about to open up in the life of the family. Then David dropped the bombshell. He had changed his mind. When it came to the crunch, he couldn't actually contemplate walking away from the ancestral family farm. He'd come across an old farm diary of his grandfather Dan. It had reminded him of the continuity of life on the land. A commitment of care lavished on a small corner of England that went on from generation to generation.

He'd also discovered a model farm, a favourite toy from his boyhood. Here was a reminder of his own personal promise to care for the land at Brookfield, in good times and in bad. Whatever the difficulties imposed by the new road – if it went through – he had a duty to make the best of things. To go on farming the land as best he could.

This was the reason for the toxic atmosphere at Brookfield on that wet Saturday afternoon in March. David had announced to the family that the long-planned-for move to the new farm was off. Like it or not, they'd be staying at Brookfield. Understandably, the family were enraged with him.

For Ruth it was a decision that undermined the whole basis of their marriage. Their lives together had been a partnership, in the farm business as well as in family matters. That he'd been prepared to backtrack on an agreement arrived at by the entire family amounted to a betrayal. Pip saw it in much the same way. Her own hopes and ambitions for their farming future had been dashed by her father's decision. Only Jill, the family matriarch, was pleased to learn of David's last-minute change of mind.

As the rain lashed against the window panes of the solid red-brick farmhouse, the family tensions looked set to explode into outright hostility. Capricious fate had another shock in store though. A breathless Pip came bursting into the kitchen screaming an alarm. Floodwater was gushing up through the drainage system of the milking parlour. At the rate it was coming in, the whole place would soon be under water.

As it happened, I nearly missed the Great Ambridge Flood Disaster. A couple of years earlier I'd stepped down from my job as agricultural editor after eighteen years non-stop. I was feeling in need of a break.

Don't get me wrong, I loved the job. For a farming nerd like me, who also happened to love *The Archers*, it would have been hard to beat. I got to shape the lives and destinies of characters I'd come to know so well they were like good friends. I also got to be a sort of fantasy farmer, a role I found endlessly interesting.

At the same time, working on a daily soap can at times feel like walking a treadmill. Each month I was expected to produce half a dozen or so new storylines. This meant coming up with the initial ideas, researching them in fine detail, then turning them into crafted storylines that the scriptwriters could grab hold of and build into their weekly story structures.

After eighteen years, I was finding the stories harder to unearth. I asked Vanessa, the boss, if I could go back to my old job as scriptwriter. But fate was to intervene again when Sean took over from Vanessa as editor in 2013. He'd worked on the show as a producer twenty years earlier. He called me up to ask if I wanted to work on some new storylines, especially the big one about the Ambridge flood. It was hard to turn him down.

I knew from his first spell on the show that Sean was a gifted storyteller with a wide literary knowledge. I also knew he had an instinct for producing powerful dramatic scenes, sometimes when they weren't exactly appropriate.

He'd once directed a scene of mine in which Adam Macy, farmer and strawberry-grower, had got a team together to unroll the polythene covering over the metal frames of a polytunnel. To protect the covering from winter damage, it gets taken off in the autumn and put back again the following spring. It's a job that's best done when there's little wind.

I'd written a note that there should be a light breeze blowing. Sean read the scene and decided it had untapped dramatic potential. He turned it into the storm scene from Hardy's *Far from the Madding Crowd*.

'We need to give it more jeopardy,' Sean told the actors. Sound effects for gales were called up. Polythene sheeting was brought into the studio and flapped about wildly. The actors were directed to deliver their lines as if they were shouting over the storm.

When editor Vanessa Whitburn listened to the end

result, she was horrified. 'It's ludicrous,' she told him. 'Adam would have heard the forecast and waited for a better day. This makes him look an idiot. You'll have to record it again.'

While Sean's tempest gave the writers a laugh, we all knew his instinct to go for maximum dramatic impact might make life on the show interesting. And so it turned out.

The Great Flood was his first big story as editor. In researching it, he and I went with scriptwriter Tim Stimpson on a series of visits to farms bordering the River Severn, all of which had been inundated in recent times.

On one beautiful farm on a loop in the river close to Upton-on-Severn, farmer Oliver Surman told us how floodwater had once filled the farm drainage system and come gushing up into the pit of the milking parlour. This is the sunken part where the milker stands, giving him or her eye-level contact with the business end of the cow.

With the usual initiative of farmers, Oliver and his herd manager found a novel way of halting the inflow of water. They had to move fast. If the floodwater had reached the vacuum pump, the milking machine would have been rendered unusable, causing much distress and discomfort to the cows.

In the middle of the farmyard was a large drain cover over a concrete chamber. This was where the floodwater was entering the drain from the parlour. Instead of taking washing water out, the drain was now providing an entry point for the floodwater. If a way could be found to block it, the ingress of water would be halted. But how? In the heat of the moment the only possible plug Oliver could find was his young son's toy football. Partially deflated, it might just jam into the drainpipe and be held there by the pressure of the floodwater.

To fit the makeshift plug, Oliver had to hold his colleague – who happened to be of slighter build – by the ankles, then lower him head-first into the chamber. Somehow the young manager succeeded in stuffing the toy ball into the drain. It worked a treat. The flow of water into the milking parlour all but stopped.

In the Ambridge flood we re-enacted this story exactly, with Eddie Grundy being dangled by his ankles as he blocked off the drainage pipe. Recording the scene in the studio, actor Trevor Harrison tried hanging upside down from a table while being held in place by a studio manager. The idea was to reproduce the sort of strangulated tones of a human being in that contorted position.

As he waited to deliver his scripted lines, Harrison quipped: 'I haven't checked, but I'm pretty sure that performing upside down isn't mentioned in my contract.'

To which the studio manager retorted: 'Stop moaning or we'll start chucking water over you. Let's go for total realism!'

The Ambridge flood set out to show how an ordinary village community would cope when faced with an existentialist threat and with no help coming from the outside world. In a foretaste of life in our new, overheated world, the floodwaters of the River Am rose higher than at any time in the past. Or so farmer Adam Macy concluded as he pulled drowned sheep from a field that had always been considered safe from flooding.

Today scientists confirm Adam's observation. Climate-enhanced flood events, they report, have already started happening in Britain.

To add to the drama of the Ambridge flood, the soap's

usual time convention was temporarily dropped. In normal times, an *Archers* episode covers events that have happened in the previous twenty-four hours. For this particular storyline, a whole week's episodes – by this time six – were used to cover a period of just eighteen hours, from Saturday afternoon until Sunday morning.

To further ramp up the drama, scriptwriter Tim was asked to abandon the soap's usual writing style. *Archers* dialogue is unlike everyday speech in that characters tend to speak in complete sentences and allow space for the other side to reply. In telling the story of the flood, characters would speak in half-formed sentences and phrases, as in real speech. And they'd frequently talk over each other, just as people do in everyday conversation, especially at moments of crisis.

The flood drama, when it aired, proved as inspirational as it was gripping. Faced with sudden danger, our village heroes revealed depths of courage and resourcefulness we'd seldom glimpsed before. Here are some of the stories that were played out on that fateful weekend.

Helped by her cousin Tom Archer, farmer Pip had to stand waist-deep in the rising floodwater as she struggled to disconnect the milk pump from the wall of the flooded milking parlour. Meanwhile David braved the storm as he moved cattle to higher ground and safety. He then drove his tractor to the village and helped rescue villagers trapped in their flooded cottages.

Jill ran an emergency refuge centre in St Stephen's Church, which remained, miraculously, a little above the floodwater. Alan, the vicar, tolled the church bell, a call of hope to the distressed villagers. There was safety and some comfort to be found beneath the ancient tower.

Farmer Adam Macy saved estate manager Charlie

Thomas from drowning after he'd become trapped in the grating of a flooded drainage culvert. He then carried out resuscitation on the young manager.

Alan pulled the elderly Freda Fry from her crashed car after it had been swept away by the rising waters. Even Rob Titchener, later to be exposed as the cruel abuser of his wife Helen, showed courage in rescuing Shula Hebden Lloyd from the rising waters.

On the morning after the night of storm and flood, David Archer and daughter Pip – newly reunited after the dramatic events of the night – walk together on Lakey Hill, where they've gone to check on the Hereford cattle. The storm clouds have gone and the sun has started to shine through. There's the sound of a distant helicopter. The outside world is at last coming to the aid of the beleaguered riverside community.

Together, father and daughter look down on the village, where many of the houses and cottages are now surrounded by water. They're horrified that so many of their friends and neighbours have been made homeless. At the same time, they know this is the place they belong. For all the appeal of a fresh start, far away from the everyday troubles of life in Ambridge, this is the land they are bound to, by ties that are stronger than their dreams and ambitions.

The story had had its moments of melodrama, no question. All the same, I was proud of what we'd done. We'd reminded ourselves and our audience of the strength of our communities. When adversity strikes, people draw closer together in an instinctive need for comfort and to offer help to others. It's not an especially British virtue. People respond to adversity in much the same way everywhere. It's a mark of our common humanity.

That said, the community spirit always appears strong in Britain at times of crisis. We saw it at work in the country during the dark days of the Second World War. When the peace came, we saw it resurge again in the clamour for a socially reforming government. It re-emerged powerfully in a series of flooding events in the decade after 2007, and during the Covid emergency its outpouring was extraordinary.

I was proud of our story for another reason. It was a reminder that, for all our smart technology and brilliant science, we remain at the mercy of elemental forces of nature. Our complex and sophisticated societies can still be paralysed by storms, deluges or a tiny virus. In this sense the Great Ambridge Flood was pure Thomas Hardy. Fate had arbitrarily intervened to thwart the plans and hopes of men and women.

It set me thinking. What other consequences might this catastrophic event have on the residents of Ambridge? Could it have set in train a series of seemingly unrelated events that nevertheless arose from that first catastrophe? Might the village be in for a run of misfortunes? The idea began to seem pleasingly Hardy-esque.

A few months after the flood, cows in the mega-dairy at Berrow Farm were struck with a mystery disease. Dozens of animals suffered a kind of muscular paralysis, and many died, despite the heroic efforts of manager Charlie Thomas to save them. Joe Grundy pronounced it 'a terrible plague' that would sweep through the village, taking who knows how many animals.

The plague turned out to be botulism, a muscle-wasting condition caused by a bacterium that proliferates in decaying carcasses. The source was traced to a batch of silage containing the rotting corpse of a dog. It seems the dead animal had been swept up with the grass during silage making. The only missing dog reported in the village had been Lynda Snell's beloved mongrel Scruff, which had disappeared during the flood, much to its owner's distress.

Out of kindness, no one told Lynda the cause of the mystery cattle disease. Everyone was convinced the beloved pet had drowned in the flooded pasture, only to be concealed when the grass grew up around him after the floodwater had receded. It was a gruesome story but somehow it illustrated the apparently random acts of fate.

There was a happy outcome of sorts, though not for the infected cows. A few weeks later, on Christmas Eve, Lynda heard a scratching sound against her back door. When she opened it, there was her beloved Scruff, bedraggled and emaciated, but alive and clearly overjoyed to be home.

So far so Thomas Hardy, but by then I'd had another idea. I'd long been intrigued by the character Michael Henchard, the Mayor of Casterbridge, the impoverished hay trusser who sells his wife to a sailor at Weydon Fair. Decades later, when he's become a wealthy corn dealer, the shocking event of his past returns to haunt him and bring about his demise.

In my days as a farming journalist, I met a lot of country characters like Hardy's mayor. Mostly men, they'd risen to great prominence in their local areas, usually as a result of running a successful rural business. Often they'd been dealers in farm machinery, livestock or agrochemicals.

Sometimes they were simply farmers whose land had been earmarked for development – an instant route to riches, better even than winning the lottery. I know a couple of farmers who ended up as big property tycoons simply because they owned land near an expanding town. Most were well-meaning if flawed characters, much like the rest of us.

In Ambridge, I'd always thought Brian Aldridge had a touch of Michael Henchard about him. Both were successful in their agrarian ventures. Both were highly esteemed in their local communities – Henchard in Hardy's Wessex and Aldridge in the BBC's Borsetshire. Both were also deeply flawed.

There were obvious differences, though. Henchard was a man of humble origins, who happened to make good through hard work and business acumen. Aldridge, on the other hand, had a head start. The son of well-off farmers, he was privately educated. While it's not clear exactly what help he got to start farming on his own, we do know he was in a position to buy 1,500 acres of prime West Midlands farmland without a mortgage at the age of just twenty-eight.

There's also the matter of past indiscretions. Early in his working life Henchard shockingly sold his wife at a fair. As *Archers* regular listeners know, Aldridge has long been a serial philanderer and womaniser. Not quite the same, I know, but it got me thinking. What if there were something shameful in Aldridge's past? Something that even today might bring him down.

When I took over as agricultural editor, my predecessor, Anthony Parkin, told me that in financial terms Aldridge was 'bomb-proof'; so secure financially as to be protected from the everyday vicissitudes of farming life. He seemed to enjoy a charmed existence in his private affairs, too.

Back in 2001, when I was still getting to know Brian, we sent him on a study tour to Hungary. He joined a group of businesspeople who were thinking of investing in Hungarian agriculture. On his way home he stopped over in Brussels for a secret assignation with the latest object of his desire, Siobhan Hathaway, the village doctor's wife.

I'm watching them from a discreet distance as they have dinner in a smart Brussels restaurant. Outside the streets are bright with the lights of Christmas. Siobhan seems bemused that Brian has been able to track her down to her hotel.

'You really are the most extraordinary man,' she tells him. 'There aren't many who'd have dropped in on the off-chance.'

'I was on my way home. It seemed rather a waste to fly on when I knew you'd be here on your own.'

'And I always thought you farmers were stick-in-the-muds?'

'That's where you're wrong. Farmers are risk-takers. Some of the biggest empires in history have been built by agricultural societies. It's because we have a mission to tidy up the planet. It starts with the farm next door. Then the neighbouring village. And so it goes on.'

'Until you've taken over the world?'

'Exactly.'

'And is that what you're doing now? The trip to Hungary?'

'Let's just say I'm eyeing up the prospects.'

'And how are they looking?'

'Very promising I'd say. In fact, I'm actively considering an investment.'

He gazes into her eyes, judging the reaction. The waiter comes by with their cognacs.

'*Monsieur-dame.*' He sets them down on the table. Brian reaches into his pocket and places a small box in front of her.

'For me?'

'Of course. Well go on, open it.'

Siobhan removes the lid and takes out a jewel-encrusted brooch. Its beauty makes her gasp.

'Oh, Brian,' she whispers.

'I'll pin it on. There we are . . .'

'How does it look?'

'Splendid. It suits your elegant jacket.'

'Thank you. You're very sweet.'

They kiss. Then Brian proposes a toast.

'So, what should we drink to?'

'How about a spirit of adventure?'

'Perfect. May it lead us to unexpected places.'

It leads them in fairly quick time to Siobhan's hotel room. And then to a passionate, clandestine affair that lasts many weeks. And finally, the following autumn, to the birth of a baby boy, Ruairi.

Eventually Brian is forced to confess all to his wife Jennifer. He has no choice. His stepdaughter Debbie has pieced together the story from snippets she's learned from her friend Siobhan. She tells Brian if he doesn't come clean to Jennifer, then she will tell her mother the truth.

A bitterly hurt Jennifer gives Brian an ultimatum. Either he agrees not to see Siobhan again or their marriage is over. After a wretched few days of soul-searching, Brian makes his decision. At Birmingham Airport he bids a final farewell to Siobhan and Ruairi as they depart for Ireland and the embrace of her family. Brian drives home to his anguished wife.

But the emotional turmoil is not yet over for Jennifer. Four years after the birth of Ruairi, she and Brian learn that the boy's mother is terminally ill. The only options for his upbringing are Siobhan's career-minded sister, Niamh, or his eighty-year-old grandmother. Not ideal, either of them. But there's no one else. Unless, of course, Jennifer will agree to raise Brian's love-child as if he were one of their own.

Under pressure from Brian, she does agree. The boy makes his home in the grand farmhouse – except when he's away at his posh boarding school, that is.

Now that things had been settled for a few years, I wondered if this might be the moment for fate to deal a cruel hand to Ambridge's own sun king. Not for his personal indiscretions – that was a family matter. But the way he'd been abusing his soils, that was very much my business.

As the closest Ambridge has to a specialist arable farmer, Brian had sprayed more tonnes of toxic pesticides on his land than any other Ambridge landowner. Since Home Farm also held the contract to farm the estate land for many years, he had spread his poisons far and wide. Over the four decades he'd farmed in Ambridge, the chemical broadsides would have done enormous damage to the soils and wildlife of the village.

What act of retribution might have the ring of poetic justice about it? I thought back to my days as a farming journalist in the seventies. I must have visited dozens of farms where they'd maintained unofficial dumping grounds for old bits of machinery, empty chemical containers and sometimes old oil drums. Often these alternative tips were located on former quarry faces or filled-in ponds.

As the regulations on the disposal of industrial wastes were tightened up, stories began to appear in the press about haulage contractors and landowners being fined for illegally dumping and burying toxic waste.

What if the young Brian Aldridge had been part of such a scam, I wondered, back at the time he started farming, when cash flows were probably tight? What if the Ambridge flood of three years earlier had disturbed some long-forgotten stash of rusting oil drums? What if their contents had started to spill out and contaminate the ground water?

On a cold, bright January day, Kirsty Miller – a keen wild swimmer and conservationist – is skinny dipping in the River Am with her friend Roy Tucker. Suddenly they become aware that they're surrounded by dead fish. Environment Agency investigators are called in. The experts quickly identify a substance known as TCE – a highly toxic industrial degreaser. It's soon traced to a hidden dump of chemical drums at Home Farm.

Brian's reputation crashes to earth like a burned-out rocket. The clean-up costs are soon heading towards £4 million. In a subsequent court action for 'causing or knowingly permitting' the discharge of contaminants into the river, he pleads guilty and so narrowly escapes a gaol term. What he can't escape is the vilification of his neighbours and the village community.

He's fired from his post as chair of Borchester Land, the consortium that owns much of the land around Ambridge, and in a final ignominy, he's forced to sell off the family home to pay part of the debt. He and the long-suffering Jennifer are obliged to rent a small cottage next door to Kirsty Miller, who'd been the first to find the poisoned fish.

Unlike the heroes of great novels, popular soap characters seldom show any great contrition after their guilty secrets are revealed to the world. Audiences and scriptwriters like them to stay much as they are, eagerly anticipating the next act of mischief. So while Aldridge lives in straitened circumstances, he doesn't show much remorse. Just annoyance at having been found out.

Thanks to Sean, I'd succeeded in bringing something of Thomas Hardy into my storylines – the impact of a cold and merciless fate. I'd used it to spread fear and confusion through village life, and to demolish (temporarily) one of the community's most powerful characters. What I didn't know was that fate was about to strike me a shattering blow, too.

It was a grey, autumn day when I caught the train for Kew, a journey of three hours from my home on Exmoor. As I stepped from the Tube at Kew Gardens, the sun was starting to break through, gleaming on the bronzed leaves of the trees around the station approach. I crossed the narrow footbridge over the railway and followed the signs for the National Archives.

The route took me down a quiet, tree-lined avenue of smart Edwardian villas. I felt a sense of mounting excitement. I was about to discover the dark secret that had cast a shadow over the lives of our little family back on that estate at Emmer Green. At least, that's what I hoped. There was a distinct possibility that I'd find nothing. The letter from RAF Hendon had warned me that many wartime records had been lost or destroyed.

Whatever I found, or didn't find, I knew it wouldn't alter the truth – that my dad had been a hero. I had the proof in his observer's log book. Around the time I was born, he and his pilot had taken off daily in a plane made of plywood. They'd carried out daring, low-level bombing raids and reconnaissance missions. They'd been shot at by fighters and anti-aircraft guns, suffered multiple engine failures, and crashed twice. After each flight they'd taken off the next day and done it all over again.

To me, this had been the life of a hero. If at some moment he'd been unable to take it any longer and refused to fly, or had panicked mid-flight, it didn't alter that fact. A court-martial might have found him guilty of cowardice, or LMF, 'lack of moral fibre' as they called it, but I knew the truth. Whatever I found or didn't find in the records, my dad was up there with the best of his generation.

The National Archives are housed in a pleasant, low-rise building set in attractive parkland. I checked in at reception and was photographed for my reader's ticket. I left my coat and bag in a locker, and with just a pencil, notebook and my mobile phone, as set out in the house rules, I climbed the stairs to the first-floor reading room.

The records I'd asked to see had been set out on the table ready for my inspection. They were Air Ministry records, specifically those from the Judge Advocate General's office, which dealt with courts-martial of RAF personnel. I took out the first heavy volume, opened it at the page for September 1943, and began scanning the entries. I knew from my dad's RAF service record that his court-martial had been held on 5 October of that year.

Against each date, the handwritten entry gave the name and rank of the prisoner, the place of trial, the nature of the offence and the sentence. A range of misdemeanours were recorded, most concerning theft and absence without leave. In that first register I found no entries for LMF, nor could I find my dad's name. I felt a sense of anti-climax. Was I going to find nothing?

I took the second volume from its box file and turned to September 1943. With diminishing expectation, I again scanned the entries. There were the usual charges for theft and unauthorised absence. Then suddenly there he was. My dad. P. H. Harvey, the name handwritten in neat copperplate. My heart leapt. There was his service number and rank, observer/wireless operator. Plus, the place of trial: Oakington.

My pulse quickened as I looked across the page to the column headed 'Nature of Charge'. That's when the word hit me like a punch in the face – indecency. Indecency! I couldn't believe it. For a moment I was in shock. This was not the story we'd grown up with, not the story my aunt and uncle had sometimes spoken of in hushed tones. That had been about him 'cracking up', losing his nerve, breaking down under fire. It didn't make any sense.

Then as I sat there in that light-filled reading room, things began to unscramble. This would account for so much: his unwavering idolisation of the archetypal macho man, the John Wayne figure, his inability to show tenderness, his homophobia. The staged ferocity with which he'd demonstrated his boxing skills. Somehow, I'd always known these things to be phoney, but he was never able to drop the act.

I thought of his pride in the wonderful naval uniform he'd worn for his job on the Thames Conservancy. Would he have lost all that if the truth had come out? By now I'd made the assumption that 'indecency' meant a gay relationship. The Air Ministry record said the charge covered 'miscellaneous' civil and RAF offences. It would be nearly twenty years until homosexuality was made legal.

Though I searched for details of the court-martial proceedings, I could find none. The file covering court proceedings included a few cases but not my dad's. I found a letter on file referring to his case. It had been sent from the Judge Advocate General's office to the station commander at Oakington. It was to inform him that the papers on the case, having been checked, were being sent to the Huntingdon HQ of Bomber Command's No. 8 Pathfinder group.

Where they were now, I had no idea, but I was determined to find them. I had to know every detail of the incident that was to have such a long-lasting impact on the lives of all our family.

On the train home I was still in a state of shock. While many questions had been answered, there were many more that never would be. Had my mother known the real reason for the court-martial? After Dad had died, I once spoke of making a search of the official records, but she was against it. Was this because she already knew, I wondered, or was she afraid of what I might discover?

As the train sped on towards the West Country, raindrops trickled down the carriage window. I gazed out at the passing fields, feeling overwhelmed by a mass of conflicting emotions. My mind was in turmoil. There were moments I wanted to scream out at the sheer waste of it all. I couldn't think of anything to do but pray, not to Thomas Hardy's cold and fickle fate, but to God, the God of love and mercy. I felt comforted though tears remained close.

As soon as I got home, I began planning my next visit

to Kew. This time I would spend the entire day there and stay over if necessary. I would scrutinise every file, every ledger that might conceivably contain the missing court proceedings. Sadly, this exhaustive search turned up nothing new. In case I'd overlooked some key archive, I passed the details to one of the professional researchers based at Kew. In addition to the sources I'd investigated, he went through the unit's operational records, covering 1409 Met Flight's day-to-day missions. They contained no mention of my dad's court-martial.

The researcher had been thorough, and at the end of it had offered me a crumb of comfort. The sentence, ninety-one days plus a reduction to the ranks, suggested the offence was not considered serious, he said. A serious case (whatever that meant) would have led to an instant discharge from the RAF, while an assault would have been referred to the civilian police.

It was a small comfort but no great surprise. For all his pent-up anger, I could never believe my dad capable of harming anyone. Behind the bluster and arrogance there was, I knew, a gentle, kind and affectionate man. Sadly, these were traits the world he inhabited made it impossible for him to show.

Next, I wrote to the RAF Museum to ask if they held the records of No. 8 Pathfinder group, or, failing that, had any idea where they might be. I didn't hold out a lot of hope, and it was no surprise when they wrote back to assure me that any surviving records would be in the National Archives.

Finally, I wrote to the Air Historical Branch of the Ministry of Defence. Their response was unequivocal. They were sorry to tell me that I'd find no more details of my father's court-martial than I already had. Detailed court records such as proceedings and transcripts from the period were not kept.

So that was it. I would never know the events and circumstances that had led to my dad's public humiliation and shaming. I would have to draw my own conclusions based on what I knew of official attitudes of the time.

In her book *Queen and Country*, historian Emma Vickers investigates same-sex desire in the wartime armed forces. Indecency, she writes, the catch-all term for sexual activity between men, contravened military law. Prosecution could result in a lengthy prison sentence and dismissal. However, prosecutions very rarely took place.

According to one estimate, at least one in five service men and women experienced some form of same-sex intimacy during the Second World War. Yet fewer than 2,000 servicemen were actually tried by courts-martial in all three armed services. In the women's services, same-sex activity was not illegal, though it was discouraged.

The war, Vickers writes, exposed a disjuncture between the law and its application. Ironically, it created the very conditions in which same-sex activity could flourish. Men were thrown together, often in isolated military stations where there were no women. It was not uncommon for intimacy to take place between gay servicemen and men who thought of themselves as heterosexual.

The fact that so few prosecutions took place suggests that commanding officers rarely considered same-sex activity to be a serious matter. When they did, their ways of dealing with it showed huge inconsistency. One man caught for indecency could be sent for court-martial and imprisoned, while another found committing the same offence might be ignored or simply given a verbal warning.

According to Vickers, this 'malleability' in the enforcement of the law implies 'a knowingness and a collusion which goes far beyond the turning of a blind eye'.

Reading this, I found myself becoming angry. Why had my father been picked out for ritual humiliation and disgrace? Was it because he served in a small, elite unit, 1409 Met Flight? This tight-knit group of men were rarely given leave. At a moment's notice, any of them might be sent out on a dangerous mission, sometimes in appalling weather conditions. It was said they'd fly when even the birds wouldn't risk it.

The men doing this work depended on each other for their very lives, so they needed to have absolute trust in each other. In these circumstances I can understand why a commanding officer might view sexual intimacy between members of the group as a threat. Clearly it could harm the social cohesion and efficient running of the group, but why not quietly shift one or both offenders to other units? Why deal them a shaming blow that would haunt them through their future lives?

In researching my dad's wartime career, I came across a number of books by former Mosquito pilots. Among them was *Target for Tonight,* a memoir by Squadron Leader Denys Braithwaite, the first commanding officer of the Oakington Met Flight. The unit was formed in early April 1943, when the meteorological squadron based at Bircham Newton in Norfolk was split in two. Squadron 521 had been under Coastal Command. Now Braithwaite was to take eight 'Mossies', eight pilot and observer crews and associated ground staff, to Oakington, where they'd be part of Bomber Command.

To the aircrew involved it was an exciting move. In the RAF, Coastal Command was seen as the 'workhorse' command, without glamour or extensive press coverage. The exploits of Bomber Command, by contrast, were constantly being publicised, even more so the legendary Pathfinders, which the new flight was to be part of.

For every medal given in Coastal, Braithwaite noted in his memoir, virtually dozens were awarded in Bomber Command. At Oakington the new flight joined one other squadron, No. 7 Pathfinder Squadron, who flew Short Stirling bombers. Braithwaite writes of walking into the mess to find it 'full of mostly youngish men with more medals on them than we'd ever seen'. This was the unit my dad was to join a little over a month later.

In Braithwaite's book there's a group photo of 1409 Flight aircrew in the classic pose in front of a parked aircraft. The picture is undated but I reckon it must have been taken in April 1943, just a week or two before my dad arrived on the station. Some of the names on the caption I remembered seeing in Dad's log book.

Among them was Flying Officer Dennis. The log shows he and my dad flew a number of PAMPA missions across France and Belgium. Before arriving at Oakington, 'Lance' Dennis had broken his back while trying to land a high-altitude Spitfire with a seized engine in poor weather. He broke cloud too far from the aerodrome. His aircraft spun into the ground and exploded. He survived and, when his back had healed, joined 1409 Flight in the Pathfinders.

Then there was Flying Officer A F Pethick. According to the log, he flew a couple of 'ops' with my dad as observer/navigator. Many more of my father's missions were signed off by Pethick, who was officer commanding flying.

I also recognised the name of Flying Officer Hatton.

My father flew two PAMPA missions with him across Holland and Germany. Four months earlier, George Hatton had been returning from a PAMPA flight with Flight Sergeant Bartolotti as navigator when disaster struck. The starboard engine had overheated, and they were having to fly home at reduced speed.

They came under attack from two German Focke-Wulf fighters and were badly shot up before they even realised what was happening. With their plane on fire, Hatton told his navigator to bale out. He then attempted to ram the German fighters with his burning aircraft. Only when his own clothes caught alight did he scramble out and parachute into the sea. His dinghy inflated instantly, and he was soon picked up by the navy. Though Hatton had watched his navigator splash into the sea safely, Sergeant Bartolotti was sadly never seen again.

As I look at that photo from long ago, I see a group of very ordinary young men living extraordinary lives. They had accepted a daily routine fraught with danger as easily as if it were the commute to the office. I get no sense from their expressions that they were unhappy – quite the opposite. There's almost a serenity about them. They were simply doing the job that it had fallen to their generation to accomplish.

Braithwaite later wrote in his book that he'd enjoyed every minute of his time in the RAF. He would never again have memories as poignant, either of the living or the dead.

Forty miles to the north, in Norfolk, my dad was living much the same life. He was then with 105 Squadron, one of two squadrons whose task was to harry the enemy with their fast, twin-engined bombers. They would cross the Channel at little above wave-height so they could not be tracked on enemy radar. They'd then carry out the low-level bombing of targets like railway yards, engine sheds and power stations. The attacks were often carried out at dusk, with the raiders returning home at night.

At the end of May 1943, the daylight bombing policy changed and my dad was transferred to 1409 Met Flight. I imagine he'd have been highly delighted with the new challenge. There'd be more flying, with meteorological flights taking crews deeper into enemy territory. In his first two months on the station, he took part in fifteen such PAMPA operations, mostly over targets in Germany.

I know he'd have had huge admiration and respect for his fellow flyers, his comrades in arms. He'd have been enormously proud to serve with them and share their company, in good times and when things were grim. I can hardly bear to think about how he must have felt following his arrest, detention and public shaming in a court-martial. As he sat in a cell serving his ninety-one-day sentence, he must have been close to despair.

Having been demoted from flight sergeant to aircraftman second class, the lowest rank in the RAF, he was then shipped off to South East Asia Command in India. I've no idea what he was required to do there. No punishment, though, can have hurt so much as his public humiliation in the eyes of his friends and comrades.

In our family we used to have a photo of my dad taken in the early years of the war. He's dressed in his full flying outfit and standing on what appears to be a hotel balcony. On the back someone – probably my mum – has written *Hastings 1940*. I've now learned that the picture was probably taken at Marine Court, a newly completed apartment block on the seafront at St Leonards. During the war it was requisitioned by the RAF to accommodate pilots in training.

The picture is of a tall, handsome young man, proudly wearing his flying kit and ready to answer his country's call. Five years later, following the surrender of Japan, a very different man returned to the family home. That man had been damaged and deeply hurt, not by Hitler's air force nor the Imperial Japanese Army, but by the cruelty of British officialdom.

He carried the shame of his wartime humiliation into a home where his own two sons neither knew him nor wanted him. He had returned to a country that, in peacetime, was even more intolerant of same-sex attractions than the wartime armed services he'd left. There was no support or counselling for men and women who'd suffered these kinds of trauma. To survive and be accepted into civilian society he had to concoct a story to explain his sudden demotion. So, the brave and proud airman let it be known that he'd broken under fire. Somehow this seemed less shameful than the truth.

Knowing this, I have a new respect and admiration for him. Even with his mental anguish, he'd secured and held down a job that gave him some status and satisfaction. Settling into domestic life must have been extraordinarily hard, but somehow, he'd managed it. Despite his demons, he cared and provided for us all, and even if he found it hard to show affection, my brother and I never doubted his love for us.

The Met Flight's first CO described the memories of his RAF days as the most poignant of his life. My dad, I'm sure, looked back with similar feelings. He seldom talked about the war, but I know he never lost his respect and admiration for the men he served with. Until officialdom dealt him such a savage blow, I believe he too would have described his RAF days as the happiest of his life.

Under the 2017 Policing and Crime Act, gay and bisexual men found guilty of sexual offences have now been officially pardoned. This was the so-called 'Alan Turing law', named after the wartime codebreaker who was found guilty of gross indecency. My dad never lived to see this transformation of English society, but to me it was long overdue.

These revelations have brought me great sadness, in part because I don't recall ever telling him how proud he made me feel, but I was and I am. He was, quite simply, an English hero, and I'm immensely thankful to be his son.

11

New Ambridge, New England

IT'S MID-SUMMER AND I'M making a last visit to *Archers* country, the land in the shadow of the two great radio masts beside the M5 motorway. After more than thirty years, I'm soon to be moving from Ambridge. I wanted to leave my village friends with a parting gift, one last story idea. And this one seems perfect.

Phepson Farm lies at the very heart of *Archers* country in a beautiful rural setting close to the village of Himbleton, just a few miles from the Droitwich masts. I'm here to see the farmer, Rob Havard, and take a look at his remarkable, species-rich grasslands. It's why, in the bright July sunshine, the two of us are strolling across a flower-filled pasture that's alive with bees and flickering butterflies.

As well as being a farmer, Rob's an ecologist specialising in conservation grazing, so he's definitely the guy to have around on a spot-the-species plant hunt.

Some of the old agricultural grasses I recognise instantly from their seedheads – crested dog's-tail, a favourite with sheep; timothy grass, said to withstand extremes of heat and cold better than any other species; and cocksfoot, not greatly liked by farmers because of the coarseness of its leaves and its habit of forming dense, uneven clumps.

Though the old grasses are interesting, it's the flowering plants I've come to see. Among the tall grass seedheads I spot red clover, yellow hawkweed, the purple heads of knapweed, and bright yellow meadow vetchling, a wild member of the pea family.

Rob, the expert on his home turf, points out the elegant lilac blooms of field scabious and the frothy yellow flowers of lady's bedstraw, the name derived from its use as a stuffing for mattresses, particularly for women who were about to give birth. Rob also showed me a plant I'd never heard of, Jack-go-to-bed-at-noon, so named because its yellow flowers only last a few hours in the morning.

With its flower-filled pastures, tall hedges and skies filled with the sound of skylarks, this small Worcestershire farm is a real wildlife haven. Though it's seen many changes in recent decades, the way it looks today can't be very different from the way it was back in the early 1950s, when 'Barwick Green', *The Archers*' signature tune, first went out to the world from the Droitwich transmitter.

By now you'll be thinking this small, fifty-acre farm is being run as some kind of wildlife reserve. If so, you're in for a surprise. Bringing back nature has made the farm more profitable than it's been for years. Without chemical fertilisers, the grasslands and the cattle that graze them all year round are building soil fertility year by year, capturing carbon from the atmosphere and helping to combat climate change.

All of which might present the Archers of Brookfield – Pip, David, Ruth, Josh and Ben – with something of a dilemma. Should they call in Adam Macy to replace their grassland with herbal leys like those he once grew at Home Farm? Should they set their dairy cows free from their winter sheds and allow them to graze herb-filled pastures all year round, milking them outdoors if necessary?

And should they finally admit that the much-missed Joe Grundy, with his insistence on traditional, low-input, nature-friendly farming methods, was right all along?

Phepson Farm, Himbleton, remains today what it always has been: a traditional mixed farm with beef cattle, sheep and chickens, plus a few acres of arable crops. When *The Archers* began there were tens of thousands of farms like this across Britain. They were the mainstay of the nation's food system, and with good reason.

One of the leading scientists of the time, Professor Sir George Stapledon, who'd been the architect of the nation's wartime farming policy, described mixed farms as 'ideally suited to Britain'. They were largely self-sufficient, so farmers had no need to import chemicals or animal feed. At the same time, they maintained the fertility of the land year after year, decade after decade, indefinitely. They were genuinely sustainable.

But by the time Rob was growing up at Phepson in the 1980s and 90s, small, mixed farms were struggling to survive. Commodity markets were dominated by large, specialist farms whose reliance on imported animal feeds and chemical fertilisers made them anything but sustainable. Despite this they picked up the lion's share of European farm subsidies, while being subjected to minimal environmental regulation.

In a market dominated by big players, it was difficult for traditional mixed farms to compete. If this weren't enough, the UK livestock industry was hit by two catastrophic disease outbreaks in rapid succession: BSE – mad cow disease – and bovine tuberculosis. Both had a big impact on the markets for beef and lamb, putting yet more pressure on the beleaguered small, mixed farm.

When in 2003 Rob decided to return to Phepson after a spell at university, he knew he'd have to find a new way forward for the farm. Trying to out-compete the big players on production terms alone was clearly not going to work. Instead, he would use science to make the most of the natural advantages of the mixed farm – its ability to produce high-quality, nutrient-dense foods without the need for chemical fertilisers or purchased feeds. The farm would be working with nature.

At university Rob had studied land management. Now he wanted to acquire a new set of knowledge, this time in ecology, particularly grassland ecology. It would enable him to reorder the farm as a balanced ecosystem, with the energy needs of the grazing animals matched to what the farm could grow. In effect, the cattle would become like wild herbivores in a natural habitat, living only on what the local surroundings could provide.

Today the laws of nature are the principal guide to the way things are done at Phepson Farm. The grazing pattern – the way the cattle are moved from field to field through the season – follows closely the grazing behaviour of wild herds like the legendary bison on the American plains.

Packed together as a defence against predators, wild herds are constantly on the move, even as they graze. There's then a long interval of weeks or even months before the animals return to the same area. This means the grasses and herbs of the wild prairie grasslands have a long rest period in which to regrow, flower and set seed before the grazers return to chomp and trample their way through the tangle of vegetation.

As the early American settlers discovered when they first ploughed the prairie grasslands, under this natural grazing regime huge amounts of carbon-rich organic matter are stored in the soil. Under today's arable cropping, most of this carbon has been lost to the atmosphere, exacerbating the climate crisis. The world seems to have forgotten what farmers once knew – that grazing animals are nature's own fertility builders and soil restorers.

At Phepson Farm, Rob Havard has returned to this ancient wisdom and is applying it to good effect in his fields. He runs a herd of pedigree Aberdeen Angus cattle, a traditional British breed that's been exported around the world. He chose the Angus because they were originally bred to thrive on mixed-species pastures like those on his farm.

Rob's a 'Pasture for Life' farmer, which means his beef cattle are fed no cereal grains throughout their entire lives. Their diet consists of grasses, wild herbs and hay alone, all natural foods for ruminant animals.

The switch to nature-friendly methods has paid dividends. Year by year biodiversity has increased, as have fertility levels and the amount of carbon stored in the soil. Profits are on the rise, too. No fertilisers are required, no chemicals, no big machines. Production costs are low. This means that most of the income from the sale of beef cattle stays with the farmer and isn't swallowed up in payments to fertiliser manufacturers and international grain traders.

As we stepped into the farmhouse kitchen, my head was spinning with the thought of what this way of farming might mean for the countryside. Rolled out across Britain, we'd see wildlife returning to the fields and farm animals living healthier, more natural lives. We humans would be healthier, too, as soils became more fertile. For the first time in decades our everyday foods would contain their full complement of nutrients.

Our rivers would be cleaner, our air purer and our communities would be protected from flooding. And the valleys and the hills would leap with joy! Well alright, maybe not the last bit, but you get my drift.

I decided that, in Ambridge, this would have to be a Grundy story. The downtrodden, maligned and often mocked Grundys, trapped as a rural underclass in a village with zero social mobility. This would be their chance to break out of the stereotype. Oliver would surely back Ed and Eddie in bringing holistic grazing, as Rob Havard calls it, to the fifty acres of Grange Farm. As the wildlife flourished, perhaps even to outshine the great Ambridge rewilding project, so the Grundys' status would rise.

Best of all, the new flower-filled meadows at Grange Farm would take it back to the way it would have looked when the much-missed Joe farmed it back in the 1930s and 40s. I loved the idea that after decades of frantic human activity and expenditure, nature would reassert herself and restore the land to the way it properly ought to be.

While I thought about these things, Rob had another surprise for me. 'Did I mention that we've got a family connection with the early Archers?' he said, spooning coffee into a couple of mugs.

It seems that back in the 1940s his grandparents ran a farm called Summerhill, a couple of miles away in

Hanbury. *Archers* creator Godfrey Baseley was Rob's great-uncle and a frequent visitor to the farm. Summerhill was claimed by some local fans to have been the inspiration for Brookfield Farm, though Baseley insisted it was based on an amalgam of several farms in the area.

Certainly, the BBC took some of its early publicity photos at Summerhill. There are shots of farmer Dan Archer and farmworker Simon Cooper inspecting a cow; Dan, his son Phil and farmworker Simon taking a look at some sheep; and Dan rolling a milk churn across the yard.

Another famous *Archers* picture of 1951 showed Dan and Doris Archer, along with their daughter Christine and son Phil, sitting at their fireside. Featured on the front cover of *Radio Times*, the photo was taken at nearby Rush Farm in Stockwood, farmed at the time by Joe Hilman, a good friend of Rob's uncle Tom. It seems Joe had a favourite phrase for people he liked – 'me old pal, me old beauty', later to become Walter Gabriel's catchphrase.

I was thrilled by these disclosures. Not only was the wildflower grazing experiment a perfect story for the Grundys, it had also emerged organically, as it were, from the very culture that had inspired *The Archers*. How amazing was that?

Rob had one more surprise yet. 'Have you ever been to Croome?' he asked as he plonked a mug of coffee in front of me. 'I've got an interesting grazing trial going on over there, too.'

Once the home of the Earls of Coventry, the National Trust-owned Croome, a few miles from Worcester, is a large country estate comprising a grand Palladian mansion of yellow stone, together with its adjoining parkland. When the sixth earl inherited the estate in 1751, he hired architect and landscape designer Lancelot 'Capability' Brown to turn it into an earthly paradise. Croome was Brown's first complete landscape and the project he revisited time and again for thirty years.

Here he was able to develop the style he would become famous for. Its characteristic features were broad sweeps of open grassland running up to the very walls of the house. To create the paradise at Croome, he had to move an entire village and drain a large area of swamp and marshland, constructing miles of underground culverts in the process, and using 1.5 million bricks. In this way a 'deep, dead, fetid morass' was transformed into parkland and farmland.

With the death of the tenth Earl of Coventry in the Second World War, the estate was sold. Much of the land Brown had recovered from swamp was turned over to growing arable crops, with the usual chemical inputs of fertilisers and pesticides. Then in the 1990s, the National Trust took over the estate and set about reinstating his grand landscape vision.

Once more the land was sown to species-rich grassland, bringing new life to the damaged soils. Today, summer visitors gaze over an ocean of waving grass seed-heads, sometimes stirred into a frenzy of ripples, eddies and whirlpools whenever there's a stiff breeze blowing. And in one small area they'll see cattle grazing.

After our coffee, Rob drove me the dozen or so miles to Croome, where he rents land from the National Trust. What started as a grazing experiment is now a fully-fledged farm enterprise. In the park, we walked up a tree-lined track to the Rotunda, a domed summer pavilion designed by Capability Brown as a 'garden room'. From there I could see cattle moving slowly across a grassy, west-facing bank. It appeared from a distance that they had the run of the entire park, grazing and trampling their way through the tall grasses and flowering plants. Then as we got close, it became apparent that the bank was criss-crossed by electric fences, breaking the block of grassland into a collection of small paddocks.

As we stood watching in the bright summer sunshine, it seemed to me that, next to living as a truly wild herd, this was as natural a life for cattle as it was possible to imagine. They spent their days and nights on these open, flower-filled grasslands, selecting their foods from a 'salad bar' of mixed plants, all growing naturally without chemical fertilisers or pesticides.

Out here they were free to express the herd instincts and behaviour patterns evolution had developed over countless centuries. Compare this with the lot of many cattle in Britain, shut up on concrete yards and in sheds, and fed on chemically grown grains and forage crops.

I spotted a kestrel hovering close by. 'That's got to be one of the best-fed kestrels in Worcestershire,' Rob remarked. 'In winter we get a mass of lank, matted grasses, bent over and trampled by the animals' hooves. Underneath there's a real microclimate that keeps the air temperature a couple of degrees higher than outside. So down at ground level, life flourishes, even in the coldest months.

'There's a massive population of small mammals – voles and harvest mice mostly. It's why our kestrels get fat, and why at night, and sometimes in daytime, you see barn owls hunting these grasslands.'

Other birds, too, have moved in to take advantage of the feeding grounds created by the cattle. Large numbers of linnets and pied wagtails follow the animals, foraging among them and sometimes on them. Flocks of starlings feed in the paddocks where the cattle have recently been. Rob has seen a great grey shrike wintering in the park and feeding from the huge vole population.

By recreating the natural grazing behaviour of cattle, he's been able to bring about a massive increase in wildlife – birds, butterflies, flowering plants, small mammals, and a host of other species. He's also shown how, by using the right type of cattle, the system can be made highly profitable for farmers. It's why he has become one of the country's foremost experts on the use of grazing to enhance biodiversity.

Watching his cattle moving across Capability Brown's designer prairie, I couldn't help but think of my own attempts to bring regenerative grazing to Ambridge a few years earlier. Pip and Toby were meant to have spent a summer of love amid the waving seedheads and flowers of Adam's herbal leys. I'd hoped it would lead to one of those special scenes that stays for ever in the memory of listeners, like the day in 1977 when Shula had sex (supposedly) with journalist Simon Parker at the edge of a wheat field.

The other outcome of my not-so-subtle plan was that Pip would be so taken with these beautiful floral forage crops that she'd decide to grow them all over Brookfield, thus putting Ambridge's leading farm on a clear path to sustainability. As so often with soaps, it didn't quite work out that way. Instead, as we've heard, Pip would carelessly leave open a field gate, allowing a few of her cows to infect half the cattle in Ambridge with IBR, a horrific bovine disease.

Perhaps now, matured by motherhood, she might be ready to help create a more sustainable and climate-friendly countryside, for Rosie and her generation if not for herself.

I get the impression that many are now ready for countryside change. In recent years there's been a surge of media interest in life on the land. TV programmes on farming now get scheduled for peak viewing time, while books on shepherding and farm life regularly make the bestseller lists.

Jeremy Clarkson has taken the everyday business of running a farm to a whole new audience. And he's clearly a convert to regenerative farming. At the same time, the interest in nature – rewilding in particular – seems to know no bounds.

With the collapse in biodiversity and the worrying changes to our weather patterns, we're surely going to see a shift in the way we do agriculture. For half a century we've waged chemical warfare against nature on the spurious grounds that this is the only way we'll feed ourselves.

We're beginning to see through this argument. What lies behind our destructive farming systems are not the needs of a hungry world, but the insatiable demand for profit from energy and biotech corporations.

If, as seems likely, the countryside – and farming in particular – is about to go through a change as profound as the one that followed the Second World War, could *The Archers* help the nation make sense of the transition, just as it did in the 1950s? Might we again see half the nation tune into Radio 4 to get the latest bulletin on life in the English countryside? And might the stories they hear be of country people co-operating with nature in order to rescue our planet?

As it happens, the seeds of just such an idea are already taking root. Rob Havard has brought holistic grazing to *Archers* country, but around Britain other farms are pioneering a range of nature-friendly methods known collectively as regenerative agriculture or agroecology. What they have in common is the power to restore the lost fertility of our soils and so unleash the forces of nature to stabilise the climate and revitalise the rural economy.

The centres of this new activity aren't national or global, but local. Food distribution hubs don't need to be giant warehouses spread across the motorway network. There can be 10,000 of them, serving neighbourhoods, small towns and villages around the country, including Ambridge.

Perhaps this feels like yet another utopian dream. But with the experience of Covid and with weather patterns becoming odder, it starts to look not so much likely as inevitable. Too much of our farmland has been used to enrich large corporations. As we come through the Covid crisis, why not put it to the service of us, the people, our animals, and the wild creatures with which we share this island? It's already started to happen in Ambridge, if in a half-hearted sort of way.

Take Adam Macy's herbal leys. For a while, at least, they restored life to the soils of Home Farm after the Great Ambridge Flood and half a century of chemical abuse from Brian Aldridge. With their deep roots enriching the soil, and flowers that held a magnetic attraction for bees, these colour-splashed grasslands helped heal the planet while delivering foods packed with healthy nutrients.

I don't know what's happened to those herbal leys, but if Adam's no longer interested, I'm relying on Ed Grundy to sow them at Grange Farm – with Oliver's backing, of course. Ed's a proper farmer and will get the whole grazing system working well. Who knows, he may even make up his own seed mixture and call it Joe's Herbal Mixture after his granddad.

When Pip, Ruth, David and the rest of them at Brookfield get to see what a great job Ed's making of his beef enterprise, maybe they'll decide to plant herbal leys themselves. Pip may get brave enough to run the dairy cows as an outdoor herd so they get the benefits too.

Then there's the organic farm shop at Bridge Farm and the agroforestry system Tom, Natasha and Helen Archer set up to supply it. The family are planning a whole range of good foods grown sustainably. Bridge Farm is to become a local food hub, a model that could be replicated across Britain to rival the centralised supermarket system, so dependent on road transport.

I see all this as a long-overdue renaissance in real food. There's the prospect of supplying everyone in modern Britain with genuinely fresh, nutrient-dense foods, the kinds of foods earlier generations enjoyed. The supermarkets could be pressurised into dropping their centralised system that fills the roads with trucks. Why not give their managers the freedom to buy locally?

While the Bridge Farm gang are reimagining the food system, Kirsty and Rex are running the Ambridge rewilding project, inspired, no doubt, by Isabella Tree's wonderful book *Wilding*. It has the potential to bring wild populations flooding back to the Ambridge countryside, just as other schemes like it are helping restore our threatened wildlife heritage across Britain.

My rural renaissance would have the rewilded area at its very heart. It would become the biological powerhouse for the region, south Borsetshire. Nature's own local hub. Around it I'd encourage what I like to call 'wilded farms'; farms where the deadly obsession with monoculture has given way to a celebration of diversity. The sterile prairie landscapes we've created in our countryside would be transformed into living mosaics of small-scale features like orchards, pasture fields, hedges, wetlands, small arable fields, copses and horticultural units.

The new Ambridge landscape would provide food, breeding sites and shelter for vast numbers of wild species. They'd quickly move in from the rewilded hub. Counterintuitively, it wouldn't mean less food. Regenerative farming methods like Ed's herbal leys and Bridge Farm's agroforestry quickly improve soil fertility. So the land is able to grow more food, not less. It's nature's form of intensive agriculture and it doesn't need chemicals to make it work.

I've been lucky enough to have stayed a night at Knepp Castle, home of the extraordinary project to bring nature back to England's farmland. I'd been sharing a speaking platform in Chichester with Isabella's husband, Charlie Burrell. He'd invited me to stay at Knepp rather than book into a local hotel as I'd planned.

The following morning, I walked with Charlie and ancient tree expert Ted Green through landscapes nature had created and colonised – wetlands, scrub, open grasslands, woodland and solitary trees. Less than two decades earlier this countryside in West Sussex was being intensively farmed with the full range of chemicals and machinery.

Now, thanks to Charlie and Isabella, it had been given back to nature.

Rare and endangered species are now returning; birds such as turtle doves, nightingales, long-eared owls and ravens, butterflies like the brown hairstreak and the purple emperor. There are dormice and rare bats like the soprano pipistrelle and Bechstein's, along with dozens of rare plant species and fungi. The choking grip of industrial agriculture has been lifted and in this small corner of England the land is beginning to breathe again.

That visit to Knepp was an inspiration to me. For years I'd dreamed of seeing those beautiful, wildlife-rich farms I knew in the 1950s make a return to the English countryside. At the same time, I didn't hold out a great deal of hope. Now I could take fresh heart. Despite the grim state of our fields, little has been lost irrevocably. The Knepp experiment proved that by making space for nature, it would soon return.

As I write this, I can almost hear Brian Aldridge muttering in my ear: 'It's all very well you environmental people expecting us farmers to go green. It's not going to cost you a penny. We're the guys who somehow have to make a living.'

I resist the temptation to tell him that if he doesn't start taking more care of his soil, he's going to go bust anyway. As it happens, there's a perfectly good mechanism for paying farmers to create the new England. The biodiverse landscapes they build will capture and store vast amounts of carbon. It'll be locked up in the trees, hedges, wetlands and, if they use regenerative practices like herbal leys and mob grazing, in their soils.

Carried out across the country, the carbon captured

would come close to, or even exceed, our current emissions. The government has promised there'll be public money for public goods. What more important 'good' can there be than greenhouse gas mitigation and a halt to climate change? Even if the politicians don't have the vision to seize the moment, there'll surely be plenty of commercial organisations willing to fund the change through the sale of carbon credits.

In its early days, *The Archers'* creators backed the government's policy of setting the countryside on an industrial path. They believed, I suppose, that this was in the nation's interest. It's now clear they were wrong.

When I walked round the Knepp Estate, Charlie Burrell told me he'd once hosted a party of local farmers who'd wanted to see the rewilding project. A couple of the older members commented that the emerging wild landscape was not unlike the farmed landscape they remembered from the 1950s, with its hedges, small fields, copses and scrubby areas. What could be more fitting than the Archers rediscovering their lost food and wildlife heritage?

There'll have to be a new committee, of course. Let's call it 'Ambridge Regenerative Food and Farming Committee'. Here are my suggestions for membership. Chair, Jim Lloyd (impartial and knowledgeable); Natasha Archer (drinks marketing and organic food); Ed Grundy (proper farmer); Susan Carter (food retailing); Helen Archer (organic food and catering); Pip Archer (farmer); Lynda Snell (organisational skills); Rex Fairbrother (wilding); Chelsea Horrobin (all-round brilliant).

Had my dad been around to see all this, he'd have loved it. Though you wouldn't have called him an environmentalist, he was a great lover of the countryside and nature. A good part of his working life was spent close to it, as he patrolled up and down the River Thames, sometimes alone but often with an assistant driving the launch.

For much of his time on the Thames Conservancy, he was navigation inspector for what was known as number two district, stretching from Wallingford to Windsor. His daily patrols from the riverside office in Reading took him through some wonderful English countryside. If he headed upstream, the river took him through the chalk escarpment of the Goring Gap, and out along the foothills of the Berkshire Downs.

Downstream, the river meandered through the marshlands beyond Sonning to its junction with the River Loddon. It then passed Wargrave, where my parents had bought their first house, flowing north to Henley and Henley Reach, before turning east along the beautiful Thames Valley towards Marlow. As a boy I used to dream of going out for the day on his launch, though in my heart I knew it would never happen.

I would imagine him on a summer morning, standing on the rear open part of the launch, probably puffing on his pipe, while the mist clung to the bank-side willows and moorhens scuttled in and out of the trailing branches, hanging low over the river. Though he had no special knowledge of wildlife, I know he loved those moments.

I remember him coming home from work one evening almost incandescent with rage. He'd seen a swathe being cut through a wooded hillside above Temple and Bisham Abbey, where the river approaches Marlow. It was the route for a new, fast dual-carriageway linking High Wycombe and the M4 motorway.

'Sheer vandalism,' he raged. 'Bloody road planners. They want locking up, the whole useless lot of them.'

To this day I can't drive along that road, as I sometimes do to visit relatives in High Wycombe, without thinking of his hurt over the loss of his beloved beech wood. From the road I glance down and see a beautiful river valley. How many times must he have looked up from his launch at that wooded hillside and imagined a timeless and enduring England?

Looking back, I can now see how the River Thames would have provided the comfort and healing society couldn't give him. Haunted as he was by wartime events, he could never have gone back to the stultifying atmosphere of a solicitor's office. Out on the river there was little time for brooding. His job was to keep an eye on the river traffic and make sure the river by-laws were being observed.

A good deal of human interaction was involved, requiring tact, diplomacy and sometimes toughness. In summer, huge numbers of people took hire boats on the river. He'd sometimes have to deal with people who were either ignorant of the rules or, if they knew them, didn't care to observe them. He'd often come home exasperated with 'the trippers'.

The river regulars were a different matter. They might be celebrities on expensive cruisers (of which there were many) or sailing enthusiasts in their small dinghies. With all of them he was invariably genial and considerate. His closest working relationships were with the lock-keepers – the 'lockies' – on his district, many of whom he counted among his friends.

The river and its people became my dad's safe haven. The job gave him status, comradeship and a sense of self-worth, those things the RAF had once provided. In quieter moments it also gave him the comfort and healing power of nature, revealed in the life and beauty of the riverbank.

I sometimes wonder if, had he not died so young, he might one day have been able to share the secret he'd guarded for so long. With today's more humane and civilised attitudes to sexuality, might he finally have been able to let it go, robbing it of the power it had exerted over his life? As far as I know, he never spoke of it to anyone. To this day, I'm still unsure whether my mother knew the real reason for his court-martial.

For me there will always be an element of mystery about the man, as there is about the events that led to his wartime trauma. He was carrying a secret that must have given him moments of fear, anxiety and loneliness. Adjusting to civilian life was difficult for all returning servicemen and women, but for my dad it must have been especially hard, knowing that he'd rejoined a society that would be hostile to what he'd done.

I take comfort in remembering the bond that grew between us around our shared interest in the countryside. During my time at university, he took early retirement from the Thames Conservancy and moved with Mum to a thatched cottage in Devon. He started taking an interest in the farming going on around him, particularly the small-scale dairy farming that still survived in east Devon.

Though he didn't live to see me writing for *The Archers*, he was excited when I landed my job on *Farmers Weekly*. When we travelled around Wales and the West Country looking at prospective farms, we were closer than we'd ever been. While we were never destined to discuss the emotional ties that bound us, the world of field and farmyard gave us a language and a shared enterprise, enabling us to enjoy each other's company again.

Decades later I've tried to reimagine that lost English landscape he looked down on from his legendary Mosquito. I think he'd have approved, and I believe, like me, he'd have welcomed the new national mood for returning nature to our countryside, including our farmland. He may not have been an *Archers* fan, but I'm sure he'd have enjoyed my storylines.

I felt sad when the time came to leave Ambridge. It was a wrench saying goodbye to old friends, particularly those I'd known since my early days in the village. However, I'd continue to follow village events, especially those around farming.

If I were a Time Lord, I'd take a trip back to 2004, my twentieth year on the programme. It had been a good year for Elizabeth and Nigel. Their stately-home business at Lower Loxley was thriving. The twins, Freddie and Lily, now toddlers, were the joy of their lives. Everything had worked out well for the couple who'd both had their challenges in the past.

If there was one small shadow in their lives together, it was that they were both so busy they seldom seemed to have any time together. So they hit on the idea of going on a blind date with each other as if they were meeting for the first time. In secret each had taken on a new identity. Nigel had become Rupert Scott-Bennett, a successful local architect. Elizabeth was author Emily Bracken.

The two had met 'by chance' in a café-bar in Borchester. Back in 2004 I'd left them to it to have their fun, but this time I thought I'd hang around. They both seemed to have enjoyed the date, but for Nigel it raised a few old insecurities.

NIGEL You seemed to be quite taken with the chap.

ELIZABETH Only because I knew it was you, really.

NIGEL Do you mean that, Lizzie?

ELIZABETH Why, do you think I make a habit of getting off with men in café-bars?

NIGEL I hope not.

ELIZABETH Well, I don't.

NIGEL I had this horrible moment when we seemed to be getting on so well. I thought, why are we doing this?

ELIZABETH For a bit of fun, that's why.

NIGEL Yes, that's what we tell ourselves. But what if it's really because our marriage is in trouble?

ELIZABETH Oh, Nigel . . .

NIGEL You don't think it is?

ELIZABETH Of course not. Why, do you?

NIGEL I didn't, no. But tonight, I thought, what if she fancies Rupert because she's fed up with boring old Nigel?

ELIZABETH He's not boring.

NIGEL Isn't he?

ELIZABETH He's kind and caring and endlessly fascinating. And I love him to bits.

NIGEL Oh, Lizzie.

ELIZABETH	Just remember why we did this. It was to make more time for ourselves. A little game, that's all.
NIGEL	I know . . .
ELIZABETH	Tonight was for us. And I think we should do it again.
NIGEL	Really?
ELIZABETH	Oh, Nigel, don't look so miserable. I don't mean as Rupert and Emily. As us, a happily married couple.
NIGEL	I'd like that, Lizzie.
ELIZABETH	Good. Now let's have another drink, shall we?
NIGEL	Tell me one thing though. Did you really like him?
ELIZABETH	Rupert? To be honest I found him a tiny bit smug.
NIGEL	(PUT OUT) Lizzie.
ELIZABETH	A bit too full of himself, if you ask me. He didn't know half as much as he thought he did.
ME	(APPROACH) (CLAPPING) Very nice. Well done.
ELIZABETH	(SURPRISED) I'm sorry?
ME	I was watching you both. I thought you played it very well.
NIGEL	Look, do we know you?
ME	Probably not. But I know you. Both of you. I've been following your progress, as a matter of fact.

ELIZABETH	(CROSS) I'm not sure what this is about, but we're having a private meeting, OK?
ME	Of course. Look, I'm sorry . . .
ELIZABETH	If it's Lower Loxley business the contact details are on the website.
ME	(AWKWARD) Yes, I'll, erm, leave you to it. (OFF A BIT) One more thing. I just wanted to say thanks for everything, OK?

That's it, I'm on my way. Or maybe I'll just call in at the Bull first, for a quick one. You never know, Eddie Grundy might be in there.

Acknowledgements

Working on a long-running drama series feels a bit like working on a farm. You're aware it was running perfectly well before you came along, and the chances are it'll go on doing so long after you've gone. All you can do is make it as good as it can be on your watch. In thirty-four years in Ambridge, I've worked with hundreds of talented people who've endeavoured to do just that: actors and writers, producers and directors, technicians and production staff. Working with them on this Great British Institution has been challenging, mostly fun and occasionally highly stressful. Fortunately, I've always felt part of a close, supportive team who I knew would stand by me even when I made daft mistakes. I'd like to thank them all.

It seems invidious to pick out individuals but I'm happy to acknowledge the support, inspiration and friendship of fellow writers, especially Simon Frith, Mary Cutler, Caroline Harrington, Adrian Flynn, Keri Davies and Tim Stimpson. I'm also indebted to three great editors of the show for the opportunities they offered and the confidence they showed in me: William Smethurst, who gave me my first scriptwriting job; Vanessa Whitburn, who first trusted me with the farming storylines; and Sean O'Connor, who encouraged me to 'think epic'. Farming is a world where the epic never seems far away.

The facts and inspiration for my stories came mostly from farmers. I must have interviewed hundreds over the years, going back to my time as a reporter on *Farmers Weekly*. I'm grateful to them all. But a few deserve special mention for their support and encouragement over many years, particularly at times when my views on agriculture weren't going down too well with 'the industry'. My sincere thanks to Duncan and Sally Leaney, Charles and Judy Foot, John Turner, Henry Edmunds, Tim May, Fiona Provan, Will and Pam Best, Rob Havard, Jim Barnard, Stephen Briggs, Martin Howard, Rob Richmond, Tom Chapman, Peter Segger, Patrick Holden, Rosamund and Richard Young, David Lance, Chris Jones, Helen Browning, Tom Malleson and Oliver Surman.

In addition, many scientists and technical specialists have given generously of their time and expertise on my endlessly fascinating journey of discovery into British agriculture. They include Dave Stanley, Christine Jones, Hans Herren, Peter Melchett, Mike Harrington, Andrew Neal, Philip Lymbery, Mike Alcock, Robert Plumb, Neils Corfield, Liz Copas, Luppo Diepenbroek, Zoe Harcombe, Nick Snelgar, John Meadley, Natasha Campbell-McBride, James Crowden, Charlie Burrell, Ted Green, George Gordon and John Reeves.

Over my years on *The Archers*, I've enjoyed the support and inspiration of many good friends, all of whom have contributed in some way to this book. Special thanks to Bob and Joyce Griffin, Pete and Helena Shepherd, David Henry Wilson, Rod Hancox, Richard and June Vincent, Trevor Harrison, Antony Bellekom, Ian Macnab, Martin Hesp, Tim Finney, Gill Powell, Richard Atkinson, Tony Brophy, Malcolm Bole, Andy Woodall and Ken Lindop.

ACKNOWLEDGEMENTS

Huge thanks are due to my agent Ivan Mulcahy at MMB Creative for believing in this book from the start, and to John Mitchinson and the team at Unbound for their unwavering confidence in it. I am especially grateful to my brother, Tony, for his constant support and encouragement, even when I delved into aspects of family history he might have found difficult. I know he believes in the healing power of light. Finally, this book would not have been possible without my wife, Anne. From the very beginning she has been part of my life in Ambridge. It has been a fun and sometimes taxing journey. That she has been willing to share it with me has been my great good fortune. My love and heartfelt thanks to her.

A Note on the Author

After graduating in agriculture, Graham Harvey worked as a journalist, reporting on farming and the countryside for both farming and mainstream media. In 1984 he joined the writing team on *The Archers*, contributing scripts and storylines for more than thirty years. He has written several books on nature-friendly farming, including the award-winning *The Killing of the Countryside*. He has also written for television and the stage, and is co-founder of the Oxford Real Farming Conference, the country's leading conference on ecological agriculture. He lives on Exmoor with his wife Anne and a small flock of Exmoor sheep.

Unbound is the world's first crowdfunding publisher, established in 2011.

We believe that wonderful things can happen when you clear a path for people who share a passion. That's why we've built a platform that brings together readers and authors to crowdfund books they believe in – and give fresh ideas that don't fit the traditional mould the chance they deserve.

This book is in your hands because readers made it possible. Everyone who pledged their support is listed below. Join them by visiting unbound.com and supporting a book today.

Susanne Abetti
Rhona Allin
Lindy Allum XX
Mark Andrews
Kirk Annett
Sabrina Artus
Christine Asbury
Richard Ashcroft
James Aylett
Debby Baker
Johnnie Balfour
William Barnard
Fiona Barnes
Roger Barton
William Barton
Antony Bellekom
Phillip Bennett-Richards
Tim Bentinck
John Beville
Heather Binsch
Steve Bissett
John Blount
Elizabeth Boardman
Charles Boot
Jenna Marie Booth
Stephen Bowden
Kate Bradshaw
Sue Bridges
Amanda Bright
Josie Britt
Danny Brophy
Tony Brophy

Charlie Burrell
Helen M Burrows
Robin Buxton
Wendy Byrne
Sally Cadle
Bernadette Cagnoni
Tatiana Cant
Helen F. Carter
Penny Cartwright
Christine Cawthorne
Esplin Chapman
Jonathan Chapman
Martin Chapman
Nicola Chapman
Jonathan Chenevix-Trench
Heather Close
V Clough
Philippa Coates
Mindy Collins
Melusine Colwell
Kieran Cooper
Sacha Cooper
Christine Coulson
Julie Cox
Alison Crosby
Heather Culpin
Annette Cunningham
Elizabeth Darracott
Pam Davies
Alan Dean
Jan Deane
Jo deBank
Lezli Dickson
Luppo Diepenbroek
Sharon Dinsdale
Pat Dodd Racher
Sarah Drea
Ms Liz Earle MBE
Michael Eavis
Charlotte Eyre
Doug Faunt
Patric ffrench Devitt
Sally Fincher
Tim Finney
Sue Finnis
Richard Fleming
Simon Frith
Mark Gamble
Jessica Gioia
Jane Glover
Boyd Goode
Sue Goodger
Sarah Greenan
Peter Greig
Bob and Joyce Griffin
Jennifer J. Grover
Gruntleigh the Ogron
Corinne Guido
Eileen Hall
Linsay Halladay
Alistair Hammond-Chambers
Rod Hancox
Irene Hannah
Caroline Harrington

Karen Hart
Anne Harvey
Sue Harvey
Tony Harvey
Simon Haslam
Anna Heaton
Sarah Hehir
Dr Colin Hendrie
Joanna Herbert-Stepney
Denise Herschel
Sian Herschel
Tom Hewitt
Roger Higton
Hannah Hiles
Andrew Hingston
Richard Hobbs
Charlotte Hollins
Mark Holmes
Jo Howard
Tim & Shelagh Howson
Caroline Hunt
Eileen Hyde
Ian Hyde
Philippa Illsley
In Memory of Sarah Gledhill
David Jesson
Andrea Johnson
Anne Jones
Christopher Jones
Robin Jones
Judy Jordan
Rosemary Jury
Alan Keech
Jim Kendall
Norah Kennedy
Dan Kieran
Pierre L'Allier
Valerie Langfield
Doug Laver
Ruth Lawrence
Duncan Leaney
Sue Lee
Catherine Legerton
Barrie Levine
Paul Levy
Samantha Lloyd
Sarah Lloyd
David Lowes
Nigel Mackie
Francesca Macnaghten
Philippa Manasseh
Sheila Manning
Emily Maycock
Rebecca Mayhew
Stephen McCarthy
David McEvoy
Beth McHattie
Fran McMahon
Mrs M Mead-Yeo Valley Farms
John Meadley
Bev Milner Simonds eat:Festivals
Sarah Milner Simonds eat:Festivals

Jan Mitchell
John Mitchinson
Sheryl Monk-Pattle
Ellie Monks
David Moore
Roger Morgan-Grenville
Tom Morrison
Hannah Morrisson Atwater
Andrew Morton
Catherine Mycock-Overell
Carlo Navato
Angie Neal
Antony Nelson
Julia Newman
The Nic™
Jo Nicholson
Gary Nicol
Tom Oliver
Marie Osborne
Matthew Parden
Terry Parker
Pennypoopah
Sophie Pierce
Philip Podmore
Justin Pollard
Gill Powell
Sue Pritchard
Mary Quicke
Andy Randle
Nicola Ray
Simon Reap
Elizabeth Reeve
Lilla Rendall Rebellato
Frances Renwick
Electra Rhodes
Sue Richards-Gray
Tom Rigby
Hilary Robarts-Arnold
Anthea Robertson
Kate Robotham
Rachael Rodway
Chris Rose
Alan Ross
Richard Ross
Phil Rothwell
Chris and Deborah Rundle
Déborah Rundle
'Vole' Samuelson
John Sanders
Calvin VJ Saxton
Dick Selwood
Peter Shepherd
Joanna Simmonds
Emily Sleep
Karen Smith
Maureen Smith
Dave Stanley
Natasha 'Nat' Stannard
Jan Stephens
Philip Stewart
Laurie Stuart
Michelle Summers
Phil Sumption
Alison Swan Parente

John and Jane Swanson
Rose Taït
Siobhan Taylor
Richard Thomas
Adam Tinworth
Christina Tran
Roger Trapp
Lucy Traves
Nick Turner
Joyce and Peter Villar
Richard Vincent
Karen & Sjoerd Vogt
Robert Walrond
Hannah Wälzholz
Chris Ward
Tim Waygood
Janet West
Liz West
Fidelity Weston
Katie Weston
Vanessa Whitburn
Christopher Widdows
Mrs P. Wight
Robin Wight CVO CBE
Kim Wilkie
Ian Wilkinson
Maeve Williams
Catherine Williamson
Denise Willis
Karen Wilshere
Howard Wood
Lesley Wood
Andrew Woodall
Rebecca Woods
Tracy Worcester
Richard Young
Roderick Young
Sue Young